Lecture Notes in Computer Science 7744

Commenced Publication in 1973
Founding and Former Series Editors:
Gerhard Goos, Juris Hartmanis, and Jan van Leeuwen

Øystein Haugen   Rick Reed
Reinhard Gotzhein (Eds.)

System Analysis
and Modeling:
Theory and Practice

7th International Workshop, SAM 2012
Innsbruck, Austria, October 1-2, 2012
Revised Selected Papers

 Springer

Volume Editors

Øystein Haugen
SINTEF
P.O. Box 124, Blindern, N-0314 Oslo, Norway
E-mail: oystein.haugen@sintef.no

Rick Reed
Telecommunications Software Engineering
The Laurels, Victoria Road, Windermere, LA23 2DL, UK
E-mail: rickreed@tseng.co.uk

Reinhard Gotzhein
University of Kaiserslautern
67653 Kaiserslautern, Germany
E-mail: gotzhein@informatik.uni-kl.de

ISSN 0302-9743   e-ISSN 1611-3349
ISBN 978-3-642-36756-4   e-ISBN 978-3-642-36757-1
DOI 10.1007/978-3-642-36757-1
Springer Heidelberg Dordrecht London New York

Library of Congress Control Number: 2013931553

CR Subject Classification (1998): D.2.1-2, D.2.5, D.2.11, C.2.4, D.3.2, D.3.4, K.6.3

LNCS Sublibrary: SL 2 – Programming and Software Engineering

Typesetting: Camera-ready by author, data conversion by Scientific Publishing Services, Chennai, India

Printed on acid-free paper

Springer is part of Springer Science+Business Media (www.springer.com)

Preface

These are the proceedings of the seventh SAM, the workshop on System Analysis and Modeling. The workshop brought together practitioners and academics in an environment of open discussion and sharing of ideas.

This year the workshop was co-located with MODELS 2012 and held in Innsbruck, Austria, October 1–2, 2012. The co-location with the MODELS conference was pioneered in 2010 and the experience so far seems to be that this co-location benefits both parties. The SAM workshop was attended by around 30 people at any point in time, but more than 50 people attended at some point or another during the two workshop days. The co-location arrangement allows the participants of the satellite events of MODELS to participate in SAM and the other way around.

This year's workshop included 2 invited keynote addresses and 12 paper presentations and this volume contains updated versions of these contributions. The 12 papers were selected from 27 submitted papers.

Each of the two workshop days was opened by a keynote followed by three sessions of two papers each.

Birger Møller-Pedersen (University of Oslo) opened the first day with his keynote "Models '67 Revisited" where he hinted at both Dylan's Highway 61 Revisited (1965) and the legacy from Simula 67 (1967). He offered challenges and opinions on the merger of modeling and programming.

The keynote was followed by the three sessions, Test and Analysis I, Language Enhancements, and Fuzzy Subjects. The sessions were one and a half hours long and each presenter was given half an hour for his or her presentation. Representatives from the other contributions of the session were then asked to come up with questions and assessments of the presented paper. Since this arrangement had been known in advance, this always provided plenty of enthusiastic discussion.

Joachim Fischer (Humboldt-Universität zu Berlin) opened the second day with the keynote "From Earth-Quake Detection to Traffic Surveillance", where system analysis and modeling were put in the context of advanced distributed systems consisting of many collaborating sensors and actuators for usages in connection with Smart Cities.

The second day consisted of the three sessions Components and Composition, Configuration and Product Lines, and Analysis II. The sessions were conducted in the same way as on the first day and we experienced a similar enthusiasm towards the discussion and sharing of views and technological arguments.

This successful workshop would not have been possible without the dedicated work of the Programme Committee. Some of its members were also session chairs and paper shepherds. The workshop organizers would also like to thank Ruth Breu and the MODELS 2012 organizers for the smooth cooperation in all matters concerning the co-location. We would also like to thank the co-sponsors (ACM, IEEE and SDL Forum Society) for their support. The participants and last (but certainly not least) the authors are thanked for making this a lively and useful workshop.

December 2012   Øystein Haugen
                                                                             Rick Reed
                                                                       Reinhard Gotzhein

SDL Forum Society

The SDL Forum Society is a not for profit organization that, in addition to running the System Analysis and Modelling (SAM) workshop series of events (usually once every 2 years), also:

- runs the System Design Languages (SDL) forums every 2 years between SAM workshop years;
- is a body recognized by ITU-T as co-developing System Design Languages in the Z.100 series (Specification and Description Language), Z.120 series (Message Sequence Chart), Z.150 series (User Requirements Notation) and other language standards;
- promotes the ITU-T System Design Languages.

For more information on the SDL Forum Society, see http://www.sdl-forum.org.

Organization

Organizing Committee

Chair

Øystein Haugen   SINTEF, Norway

SDL Forum Society

Chairman   Rick Reed (TSE) *until 01 Oct 2012, then non-voting board member*;

Secretary   Reinhard Gotzhein (TU Kaiserslautern) *Chairman from 01 Oct 2012*;

Treasurer   Martin von Löwis (Beuth-Hochschule für Technik Berlin)

Programme Committee

Conference Chair

Øystein Haugen   SINTEF, Norway

Members

Daniel Amyot	Ottawa University, Canada
Rolv Bræk	Norges Teknisk-Naturvitenskapelige Universitet, Norway
Reinhard Brocks	HTW Saarland, Germany
Jean-Michel Bruel	Université de Toulouse, France
Laurent Doldi	Aeroconseil, France
Anders Ek	IBM Rational, Sweden
Stein-Erik Ellevseth	ABB, Norway
Martin Euchner	International Telecommunication Union, Switzerland
Joachim Fischer	Humboldt-Universität zu Berlin, Germany
Pau Fonseca i Casas	Universitat Politècnica de Catalunya, Spain
Emmanuel Gaudin	PragmaDev, France
Birgit Geppert	Avaya Labs, USA
Abdelouahed Gherbi	Université du Québec, Canada
Reinhard Gotzhein	Technische Universität Kaiserslautern, Germany
Jens Grabowski	Georg-August-Universität Göttingen, Germany
Peter Graubmann	Siemens, Germany

Øystein Haugen   SINTEF, Norway
Peter Herrmann   Norges Teknisk-Naturvitenskapelige
                                  Universitet, Norway
Dieter Hogrefe   Georg-August-Universität Göttingen, Germany
Michaela Huhn   Technische Universität Clausthal, Germany
Clive Jervis   Nokia Siemens Networks, USA
Ferhat Khendek   Concordia University, Canada
Tae-Hyong Kim   Kumoh National Institute of Technology, South
                                  Korea
Alexander Kraas   T-Systems International, Germany
Frank-Alexander Kraemer   Norges Teknisk-Naturvitenskapelige
                                  Universitet, Norway
Finn Kristoffensen   Cinderella, Denmark
Thomas Kuhn   Fraunhofer IESE, Germany
Anna Medve   Pannon Egyetem, Hungary
Pedro Merino   Universidad de Málaga, Spain
Tommi Mikkonen   Tampereen Yliopisto, Finland
Birger Møller-Pedersen   Universitetet i Oslo, Norway
Os Monkewich   Sympatico, Canada
Gunter Mussbacher   Carleton University, Canada
Ileana Ober   Institut de Recherche en Informatique de
                                  Toulouse, France
Iulian Ober   Institut de Recherche en Informatique de
                                  Toulouse, France
Javier Poncela González   Universidad de Málaga, Spain
Andreas Prinz   Universitetet i Agder, Norway
Rick Reed   Telecommunications Software Engineering, UK
Laurent Rioux   Thales, France
Manuel Rodriguez-Cayetano   Universidad de Valladolid, Spain
Nicolas Rouquette   NASA, USA
Richard Sanders   SINTEF, Norway
Amardeo Sarma   NEC Europe, Germany
Ina Schieferdecker   Fraunhofer Fokus, Germany
Bran Selic   Malina Software, Canada
Edel Sherratt   Aberystwyth University, UK
Martin von Löwis   Beuth-Hochschule für Technik Berlin, Germany
Thomas Weigert   Missouri University, USA
Frank Weil   Uniquesoft, USA

Table of Contents

Components and Composition

Configuring and Product Lines

Analysis II

Models '67 Revisited

Birger Møller-Pedersen

Department of Informatics, University of Oslo, Norway
birger@ifi.uio.no

Abstract. An argument is made why it may be a good idea to go for a combined modelling and programming language instead of using diverging modelling and programming languages, with implied code generation from models to programs and thereby inconsistent artefacts. It may seem as a revolutionary idea, however, the very first object-oriented programming language, SIMULA from 1967, was also a description language. We go back to the future in order to learn what it implies to be a combined language. Modelling has developed since 1967, so we also give some examples from today's modelling languages and how that would be in a combined language as of today. A combined modelling and programming approach to language design is exemplified by mechanisms of BETA, SDL and UML. Finally we revisit the notion of model in the light of this approach[1].

Keywords: Modelling, Programming, Languages.

1 Introduction

Everybody agrees that modelling, as part of system development is important. It raises the abstraction level, leaves out implementation details, makes things independent of implementation platforms, and if models are made precise enough they will allow analysis of properties of systems before they are realized for real on real platforms.

However, very few real system development projects use modelling for real. No modelling language allows you to work solely in this language, we still only have partial code generation, and when time becomes critical, the models are dropped ("All you need is code"). The implication is two sets of artefacts that become inconsistent when implementations are changed due to debugging, maintenance and even further development at code level.

There is also a trend that "real programmers program", i.e. do not even model before or as part of programming! One reason is the above inconsistency; another is the emerging gap between modelling and programming languages.

One may argue that the situation is like this because tools for modelling languages are not good enough. Compared with tools for programming language, tools for modelling languages leave things to wish for, but more important is that

---

[1] This paper is a position paper accompanying a keynote speech and is therefore not a traditional scientific paper.

Ø. Haugen, R. Reed, and R. Gotzhein (Eds.): SAM 2012, LNCS 7744, pp. 1–15, 2013.

programmers are in fact using advanced features of programming languages that are not adequately supported by modelling languages and where they would get no help from a modelling language. An obvious example on this is generics - they have been developed as part of programming languages, and there they are well defined.

There are some attempts to remedy this situation:
- Domain Specific Languages (DSLs);
- Adaptation of modelling languages (e.g. profiling of UML);
- Executable Modelling Languages.

Domain Specific Languages are usually confined to a domain and based upon complete code generation. In-house DSLs, however, also imply complete responsibility for maintenance, of both language and tools. Successful DSLs are DSLs that are not in-house and which have a large user community, however, by their very nature they are not comparable to general purpose modelling and programming languages.

Profiling of UML has the same advantages (and disadvantages) as DSLs: it ties the profile to a specific domain, and code generation will typically be controlled by the stereotypes and generate complete code.

Executable modelling languages (e.g. Executable UML[2], fUML[3]) are steps in the right direction. However, executable modelling languages where model executions are only used for checking properties of model, with a following code generation, will have the same problem as partial code generation, that is inconsistent artefacts. For executable modelling languages that are supposed to take the place of general purpose programming languages, both tools and the support for (executable) language mechanisms will be measured against the tools and mechanisms for general purpose programming languages.

As proposed in the MODELS 2010 keynote [1], the obvious solution to the problem of inconsistent artefacts is to have combined modelling and programming languages. Such languages are not executable modelling languages just for the purpose of executing models (before code generation), and they are not programming languages with support for modelling mechanisms, but rather languages that are designed to be both modelling and a programming languages.

Most new language mechanisms are developed within programming languages, and then carried over to modelling languages. Some of these are well supported in modelling languages, while others are not. An example of the last category is generics: programmers use these extensively, while modelling languages do not support that. By designing combined modelling and programming languages, the development of new language mechanisms will be just done once, and language mechanisms that otherwise would just be designed based upon technical considerations may then also be designed from a modelling point of view. In addition it will only require resources for making one set of tools.

---

[2] http://www.kc.com/XUML/

[3] http://www.omg.org/spec/FUML/1.0/

One may ask why this obvious solution has not been tried before, and the answer is that it has in fact been tried! The very first object-oriented programming language, SIMULA, was in fact designed as a combined modelling and programming language. The following quote is from the introduction to the SIMULA I language definition report from 1965 [2]:

> *The two main objects of the SIMULA language are:*
> - *To provide a language for a precise and standardised description of a wide class of phenomena, belonging to what we may call "discrete event systems".*
> - *To provide a programming language for an easy generation of simulation programs for "discrete event systems".*

Note: At that time the term 'description' was used for what today is called 'model'.

We are not alone in thinking that modelling should not imply inconsistent artefacts. In the famous banquet speech, ECOOP 2010 ('Ten things I hate about object-oriented programming')[4], Oscar Nierstrasz says this about modelling:

> *There similarly appears to be something fundamentally wrong with model-driven development as it is usually understood — instead of generating code from models, the model should be the code.*

2   Combined Modelling/Programming Language Elements

As mentioned above, the MODELS 2010 keynote introduced the idea of combined modelling and programming language, and it gave some general properties of such languages. This paper gives examples from the design of both BETA [3], Specification and Description Language (SDL) [4] represented by the SDL-92 version[5] and UML 2.0 [5] on what it means to have a modelling approach to language design; in addition it reports on some recent efforts.

2.1   SIMULA Lesson: Programming Language Design for Modelling

The most general lesson from SIMULA is that although it primarily was regarded as a programming language, it was also a modelling language: the concepts of the application domain were directly reflected in the programs, by means of classes. Specialized concepts were reflected by subclasses. This was at a time when system analysis and design were made in separate languages/notations for Structured Analysis Design, and then implemented in separate programming languages. SIMULA classes also formed the basis for design, and as a programming language these classes were also parts of the implementation, so there was no need for a separate notation for Structured Design.

---

[4] http://blog.jot.fm/2010/08/26/ten-things-i-hate-about-object-oriented-programming/

[5] http://www.itu.int/rec/T-REC-Z.100/en

In order to be able to make models of systems consisting of concurrently executing entities, in SIMULA it was regarded as obvious that objects had their own behaviour, in addition to behaviour associated with methods. Objects were not just intended for the modelling of data entities, but also for modelling of concurrent processes.

SIMULA was conceived as a simulation language, so concurrency was only supported by mechanisms for quasi-parallelism by means of co-routines: action sequences of objects that would alternate, so that only one at a time is executed.

When BETA was made based upon the ideas of SIMULA, true concurrency was introduced. The modelling rationale for still supporting alternating action sequences of objects was that neither concurrent objects with no common variables, nor partial action sequences represented by method calls might capture all situations. In many situations an object executing concurrently with other objects may have its internal (sequential) behaviour split between different activities, with common data and with only one activity executing at a time. The example used to illustrate this is a flight reservation agent (executing concurrently with other flight reservation agents) will alternate between activities like reservation, tour planning and invoicing, each of these which in turn may consist of partial actions (by methods). The notion of SIMULA alternation was simplified in BETA so that only events outside the concurrent object with alternating objects could trigger a shift from one to another alternating object.

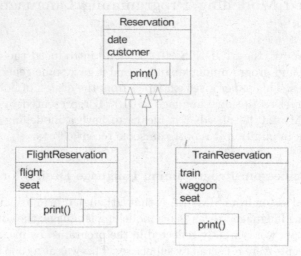

Fig. 1. Specialization of classes, and of methods

Another lesson from SIMULA taken over by BETA was the notion of behaviour specialization. Having classes representing application domain concepts, and subclasses representing special concepts, it was possible to specialise class behaviour. First of all, SIMULA classes could have a body of statements; an object would start executing these when created, and if the object formed a co-routine, this body would be the behaviour of this co-routine, i.e. it was not just constructor or initialize code. An INNER statement in the body of the superclass would imply the execution of the body of the subclass. In BETA this was generalised to work for patterns in general, and thereby also for method patterns. Figure 1 illustrates that the redefined print methods in subclasses of Reservation are specializations of the print method of Reservation.

The history and the design rationale for BETA is described in [6].

2.2 Associations

Association between classes is probably the most well known modelling concept. Even 'real' programmers may be found sketching class diagrams in order to convey the class design of an application or framework, including classes with both associations and specializations between classes. Object-oriented languages have classes and specialization of classes, and these constructs have a direct mapping to that part of class diagrams, so associations is an obvious first candidate for a modelling concept to include in a combined language.

In a masters study experiment, Tormod Vaksvik Hvaldsrud tried to define an executable modelling language by starting with a programming language and adding modelling capabilities, starting out with associations. Being executable it would not do to allow different interpretations of associations, on the other hand one would expect to have most of the features of associations known from modelling languages.

Introducing associations appears innocent, but so far no main programming language supports them. There has been several attempts, e.g. [7,8,9]. Specialization of associations is one of the more advanced features, however, having full coverage of associations imply that even this mechanism should be supported. In a language with class specialization one could take it for granted that specialization of associations can be defined in a similar way as specialization for classes is defined. However, the example in Fig. 2 is in [9] used to argue that specialization of associations is not similar to specialization for classes.

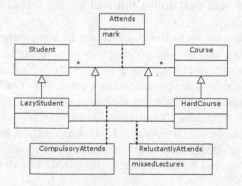

Students attend courses. If a lazy student attends a hard course, he or she may attend both compulsory and reluctantly in addition to just attend. Compulsory and Reluctantly are not disjoint, they are just special ways of attending a course. Compulsory is not the opposite of reluctantly.

Fig. 2. Specialized associations not similar to class specialization

A student that attends a course both compulsory and reluctantly will get three 'mark' attributes, as the CompulsoryAttends and ReluctantlyAttends inherit the 'mark' attribute from Attends. In [9] it is therefore concluded that specialization of associations is not the same as specialization of classes, and that it rather should be done means of delegation, from CompulsoryAttends and ReluctantlyAttends links to an Attends link.

In "Nested and Specialized Associations" [10] there is a counter example showing that in same cases one would expect specialization of associations to be of the same kind as specialization of classes, see Fig. 3.

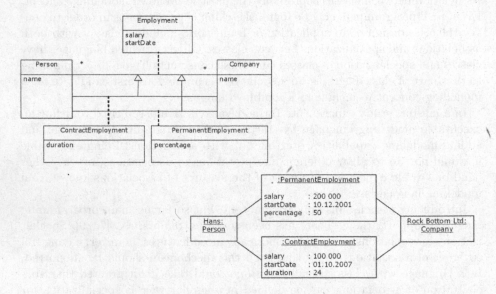

Fig. 3. Specialized associations same as class specialization

The alternative to delegation is to nest associations within an enclosing association [10], thereby not inheriting the mark attribute, but still having access to it from the nested associations, see Fig. 4.

We do not say that nesting of associations is the thing to do in a combined language. This is merely included as an example on applying a programming language mechanism on a modelling concept, in this case applying nesting. Nesting will give the desired properties of association specialization that is not really specialization. The mechanism of nesting is a mechanism that is well known in the world of modelling, while for programming languages this forms the basis for scope rules. Modelling languages, however, support it. UML has method behaviour nested in classes, and users of UML take that for granted. It also has nesting of classes in classes, but compared to users of e.g. Java, this is rarely used.

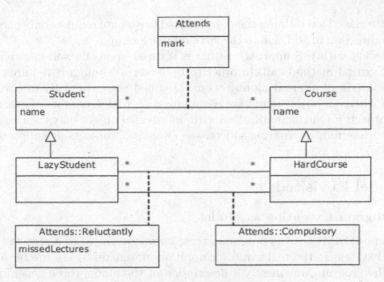

Fig. 4. Nested Associations

2.3 State Machines

The notion of state machine is another modeling language mechanism that is popular in a large number of domains. When considering state machines in a combined modeling and programming language, we are looking for more than design patterns. State machines are often associated with state charts, i.e. a graphical notation; however, SDL has both a graphical and textual syntax for state machines.

In a master study Java (with Morten Olav Hansen) [11] the issue was to explore the inclusion of state machines in a programming language, in this case Java. Granted that this is not the same as making a combined language; this would be too much for a master thesis, but still it gives some insights.

Two extremes were considered: A state machine framework, defining classes for the various elements of state machines, and full inclusion of state machines. UML state machines were taken as the requirement.

The conclusion was that the framework approach is the optimal, and perfect if combined with an embedding of graphical notation (but still abstract syntax covering state machines). Full inclusion of state machines in Java would imply a 24% increase of the number of keywords - a figure that would not be acceptable for Java, and even for a combined language (in size comparable with Java) this number would be high.

The exploration above was based upon events being asynchronous messages communicated by objects with state machine behaviour. A quite different approach, first introduced in [12] and in [13] applied to BETA is that events are method calls as known from object-oriented programming. Events are defined as virtual methods in the state machine class, and overriding of virtual methods are extended so that they can be overridden in different subclasses (representing different states) of the state class. Determining the right method to execute requires only one more level of indirection in addition to the virtual table lookup.

The benefit with this approach is that it is based upon the well-known mechanism of virtual method call. In order to be powerful enough it requires, however, the notion of alternating objects as described above in order to cover the situation where an object may have communication with a number of other concurrent object: Each communication with an external object may then be taken care of an internal, alternating object, see alternating objects as supported by BETA ([3]).

3   Model Revisited

3.1   Program Execution as Model

At the time of SIMULA the program *execution* was regarded as a *model* of some (referent) system in the real world (or application domain to use the term from DSLs); the program was merely a *description* of the model to be generated by the computer.

At some point in time during the development of languages and notations for object-oriented analysis and design (e.g. Booch [14] and OMT [15]), especially when graphics were introduced, the diagrams were considered the model! It is not obvious why this happened, but one explanation may be that the first languages and notations were not comparable to programs; they were simply meant as sketches and for analysis, in order to get to a common understanding. Another explanation could be that diagrams with boxes and lines appear to be objects ('the system consists of these objects').

One may say that the notion of program execution as a model of some referent system only matches the case of simulation programs[6], as then there is obviously some real system that is simulated. However, even without simulation there are examples where it would be more correct (and clarifying) to say that the program execution is a model of some system. The most striking example is a flight simulator.

Even though it is called a flight simulator, the fact is that the users are experiencing the program execution (which they are operating) as a model of the real control system. They do not have anything to do with the program implementing the flight simulator, and the developers will have to know that *the program execution should work as a model of the real system.*

It is true that for other kinds of systems, a program execution may start out as a model and gradually become part of the real world. As an example a ticket reservation system may start out as a model of a combination of the old ticket system and thoughts/ideas for the new system, and when deployed it becomes part of the real world. Still, even then the system in terms of its program execution will have objects that are models of phenomena in the domain of ticket reservation systems, like real persons, real events, and real seats.

---

[6]   SIMULA started out as a simulation language, but became a general-purpose language with predefined mechanism for simulation.

3.2   Executions (Models) versus Descriptions

The notion of program execution as a model may seem just a matter of terminology, but it will also have implications for language design and for the terms used in the definition of a language. A language design should have a distinction between mechanisms for organising/ structuring executions (in terms of instances and links between instances) and mechanisms for organising/ structuring descriptions (or rather prescriptions) of executions.

Mechanisms for organising executions obviously have some implications on the organization of descriptions: class descriptions and associations between classes form the basis for structures of objects and links between objects. Some mechanisms for organising descriptions have no (and should have no) implication on executions: e.g. packages, mechanisms for splitting diagrams into constituent diagrams, relations between description elements.

The following is a number of examples on language designs where this distinction is important.

SDL

SDL has this distinction, and it uses the term 'system specification' for the description. In SDL, a *system* is the result of the interpretation/execution of a *system specification*. A complete specification may contain a number of packages and a system specification:

```
<sdl specification ::=
    <package>* <system specification>
```

A package is just as a collection of description elements. A system specification is in turn just a block specification; a block may contain hierarchies of blocks and concurrent processes, that is, system is just the outermost block.

So, even though SDL may be considered a modelling language in line with UML, it was designed at a time (the first version appeared in 1976) when executions were considered models: Consequently 'model' is coined 'system', and systems are described by system specifications.

When the object-oriented extensions to SDL-84 were designed (in 1987, [16,17]), the modelling approach was used in the sense that concurrent processes were considered the most important objects, so types and subtypes (cf. classes and subclasses in UML) of processes were introduced, including inheritance and specialization of state machine specified behaviour.

From the outset the Specification and Description Language also had blocks containing blocks (and finally processes), so object-oriented SDL-92 also introduced block types. Specialization (subtyping) for block types implied inheritance of the internal block structure of the super block type.

UML

UML is a representative of modelling languages where descriptions are considered models. This is reflected directly in the definition of the language. UML has package as a mechanism for collecting description elements. Model is defined as a special package, and it is defined as one of four auxiliary concepts of UML (UML V2.4.1[7]):

> The Model construct is defined as a Package. It contains a (hierarchical) set of elements that together describe the system being modeled.
> A top-most element representing the system may, however, still just be a package:'
> A model owns or imports all the elements needed to represent a system completely according to the purpose of this particular model. The elements are organized into a containment hierarchy where the top-most **package** or **subsystem** represents the boundary of the system. It is possible to have more than one containment hierarchy within a model (i.e., the model contains a set of top-most packages/subsystems each being the root of a containment hierarchy). In this case there is no single package/subsystem that represents the system boundary.

One might think that the alternative with a top-most 'subsystem' would give a topmost instance representing the whole system (consisting of parts) as in the case with SDL, but UML 1 had a subsystem concept that was a special package. It was also a classifier, but it was mainly a package with a number of different description elements.

When UML 2.0 was designed, structuring of large, complex systems was one of the main requirements. The input to the design was Architecture Description Languages (ADLs), SDL and ROOM [18]. Work on ADLs has produced a number of modelling languages. SDL-92 had block diagrams with the only purpose of specifying the architecture of systems ([19]) in terms of instances. In 1994, ROOM combined state charts and structuring mechanisms like those of SDL-92 (by capsules, ports and connectors).

In contrast to this, UML 1 had class diagrams with classes and relations between classes. Although composition was one of these relations, this could not be used for the structuring of systems, with the implication that UML users had to use packages and subsystems for this purpose, see [20]. There were many problems with the use of subsystem as the means for structuring of systems, e.g. that there were no communication links between subsystems.

SDL-92 supported object orientation by block types and process types, and corresponding subtypes. ROOM also had classes and subclass of capsules. It was therefore an obvious choice in the design of UML2 to do structuring of systems by means of objects (classes) having an internal structure (of instances).

The design choice described above lead to the general notion of composite structures, and these were in turn used to define composite classes and collaborations. A composite structure consists of parts (sets of instances of a given type) connected by connectors. Connectors either connect parts directly or connect ports on parts. The composite structures of collaborations also form the

---

[7] http://www.omg.org/spec/UML/2.4.1/

contexts for Interactions, so these parts are well integrated in UML2. This is illustrated in [21].

In UML 2 Subsystem is a predefined stereotype that applies to components only, so with the above definition of Model (as a package with a topmost package or subsystem) and with components as special composite classes, it *is* possible to specify a top-level instance that represents the system. However, you have to use a component as the top-most, even though it might do with a topmost composite class.

UML1 did not have separate object behaviour, although it had the notion of active objects. Booch and OMT followed the trend in programming languages to do this by means of a special method. UML2 introduced a so-called ClassifierBehavior, so that classes may have a behaviour specification. All kinds of behaviour can be specialized.

Package Templates

The design of the mechanism of Packages Templates ([22]) is yet an example on the distinction between models and descriptions of models. The mechanism was designed in order to support extended reuse of collections of related classes.

Given the fact package is a mechanism for organizing descriptions, then an extended kind of packages, where packages are made more generic than ordinary packages, would not be generic in the sense of generic classes, but templates of descriptions that allow adaption to special situations that involves operations on description elements.

Still, a template package should not be a macro concept a la C++ templates, so the concept was designed so that templates can still be statically type checked.

The package template mechanism is illustrated by a small example. For more in depth description of the mechanism see [22]. The following defines a template package with two related classes defining the concept of a graph:

```
template Graph {
  class Node{
    Edge firstEdge;
    Edge insertEdgeTo(Node to){ ... }
    void display(){ ... }
    ...
  }
  class Edge{
    Node from, to;
    Edge nextEdge;
    void deleteMe(){ ... }
    void display(){ ... }
    ...
  }
}
```

In the following example code this Graph template is used by being instantiated (at compile time) and as part of the instantiation, Node is renamed to City, and Edge to Road. The effect of this instantiation is that the RoadAndCityGraph package has now two classes City and Road, with all occurrences of Node and Edge replaced by City and Road, respectively. In addition the package defines additions to the classes City and Road:

```
package RoadAndCityGraph{
  inst Graph with
  Node => City, Edge => Road;
  class City adds{
    String name;
    ...
  }
  class Road adds{
    int length;
    ...
  }
}
```

In addition to renaming of classes, attributes and methods of class may also be renamed. Instantiation of a package yields a copy of the contents of the templates in the scope with the instantiation, with specified renamings and additions. A template may therefore be instantiated more than once in the same scope; the Graph template may e.g. be used as the basis for defining Pipes between Plants, in addition to Roads and Cities.

When instantiating more than one template in a given scope, classes from different templates may be merged. As an example consider a template GeographyData with data about cities and roads:

```
template GeographyData {
  class CityData{String name; ...;}
  class RoadData{int length; ...;}
}
```

Combined with the Graph templates, merging CityData and Node into City, and RoadData and Edge, will yield a graph of cities and roads with data:

```
package RoadAndCityGraph{
  inst Graph
  with Node => City, Edge => Road;
  inst GeographyData
  with CityData => City, RoadData => Road;
  class City adds{...}
  class Road adds{...}
  ...
}
```

Even though templates may be separately type checked and this checking is also valid after renamings and merges, these operations are still on description elements. Package templates are therefore a language mechanism for organizing descriptions, not for organizing systems structures in terms of objects. One would not expect to have these kinds of possibilities for classes. Classes can be defined as subclasses of another class, but this does not involve merging of class descriptions; it defines a subtype relationship and this is not purely resolved at compile time. An object will have a type in terms of a class, and behavior involving a reference to an object may depend upon the type of the object being referenced.

4 Not All 'Models' Have to Be Executable

There appears to be two major approaches to modelling:

push-the-button approach: This is characterised by executable models and complete code generation;

more-descriptions-are-better-then-just-one approach: More descriptions, often with different purposes and from different viewpoints, of the same system is better than just one - Sketches, analysis models, etc.. Some of these may not be precise and cannot be the basis for execution or code generation.

Although there is no reason that they cannot be used together, they appear to be two very different approaches. One reason for this is that proponents for the first approach consider that proponents of the second approach will have all kinds of descriptions imprecise.

The call for a combined modeling and programming language may seem to address only the push-the-button approach. This is, however, not the case. Obviously such a combined language will only cover modeling mechanisms that can have execution semantics (like class models including associations, state machines, activities), but we believe that these two approaches can work together. Among the descriptions in the second approach there will be some kinds of description that should be tightly integrated with the combined language (e.g. sequence diagrams for expressing executions), while there will be other kinds of description that will not be precise, but still be useful (e.g. use cases).

5 Conclusion

It all started out with a combined modelling and programming language, SIM-ULA. Although one of the main strengths of object-orientation is that it provides a unified approach to modelling and programming, modelling languages developed independently of object-oriented programming languages, and drifted away from execution and became languages in support for analysis and design. Recently we have witnessed the need for executable models, not just for special domain specific languages, but also for modelling in general, and this has called for initiatives like Executable UML. One may say that this is just a return to how it was in the beginning, but the difference is that executable models may still just translate to implementations in existing programming languages, yielding both a model and a program artefact. If development environments for modelling languages for executable models will not be able to match development environments for programming languages, then users still have to cope with both a modelling language and a programming language, and based upon experience the code artefact will be the dominant. Really returning to the original approach would imply going for a combined modelling -and programming language. Class models and state machine models will obviously be part of such a combined language, with e.g. interaction models for the specification of execution semantics, while other parts of modelling languages are obviously just intended as support for analysis methods, like e.g. use cases.

Acknowledgments. The work reported in this paper has been done within the context of the SWAT project (The Research Council of Norway, grant no. 167172/V30). Also thanks to Rick Reed for reviewing.

References

1. Madsen, O.L., Møller-Pedersen, B.: A Unified Approach to Modeling and Programming. In: Petriu, D.C., Rouquette, N., Haugen, Ø. (eds.) MODELS 2010, Part I. LNCS, vol. 6394, pp. 1–15. Springer, Heidelberg (2010)
2. Dahl, O.-J., Nygaard, K.: SIMULA - a Language for Programming and Description of Discrete Event Systems. Norwegian Computing Center, Oslo (1965)
3. Madsen, O.L., Møller-Pedersen, B., Nygaard, K.: Object-Oriented Programming in the BETA Programming Language. Addison Wesley (1993)
4. International Telecommunication Union: Z.100 series, Specification and Description Language, http://www.itu.int/rec/T-REC-Z.100/en
5. Object Management Group: Unified Modeling Language 2.0. OMG. ptc/2004-10-02 (2004)
6. Kristensen, B.B., Madsen, O.L., Møller-Pedersen, B.: The When, Why and Why Not of the BETA Programming Language. In: HOPL III - The Third ACM SIG-PLAN Conference on History of Programming Languages. ACM Press (2007)
7. Rumbaugh, J.: Relations as Semantic Constructs in an Object-Oriented Language. In: OOPSLA 1987 - Conference Proceedings on Object-Oriented Programming, Systems Languages and Applications. ACM Press (1987)
8. ØSterbye, K.: Associations as a Language Construct. In: TOOLS 1999 Proceedings of the Technology of Object-Oriented Languages and Systems. IEEE Computer Society (1999)
9. Bierman, G., Wren, A.: First-Class Relationships in an Object-Oriented Language. In: Gao, X.-X. (ed.) ECOOP 2005. LNCS, vol. 3586, pp. 262–286. Springer, Heidelberg (2005)
10. Haavaldsrud, T., Møller-Pedersen, B.: Nested and Specialized Associations. in Relationships and Associations. In: RAOOL 2009 Proceedings of the Workshop on Relationships and Associations in Object-Oriented Languages. ACM Press (2009)
11. Hansen, M.O.: Exploration of UML state machine implementations in Java. Master Thesis, University of Oslo, Department of Informatics (2011)
12. Taivalsaari, A.: Object-Oriented Programming with Modes. Journal of Object-Oriented Programming 6(3), 25–32 (1993)

13. Madsen, O.L.: Towards Integration of State Machines and Object-Oriented Languages. In: TOOLS 1999: Proceedings of the Technology of Object-Oriented Languages and Systems, p. 261. IEEE Computer Society (1999)
14. Booch, G.: Object-Oriented Analysis and Design with Applications. Benjamin/Cummings Pub. Co. (1991)
15. Rumbaugh, J., et al.: Object-Oriented Modeling and Design. Prentice Hall (1991)
16. Møller-Pedersen, B., Belsnes, D., Dahle, H.P.: Rationale and Tutorial on OSDL - An Object-Oriented Extension of SDL. In: SDL Forum 1987 - State of the Art and future Trends. North-Holland (1987)
17. Møller-Pedersen, B., Belsnes, D., Dahle, H.P.: Rationale and Tutorial on OSDL - An Object-Oriented Extension of SDL. Computer Networks 13(2) (1987)
18. Selic, B., Gullekson, G., Ward, P.T.: Real-Time Object-Oriented Modeling. John Wiley & Sons Inc. (1994)
19. Fischer, J., Holz, E., Møller-Pedersen, B.: Structural and Behavioral Decomposition in Object Oriented Models. In: ISORC 2000: Proceedings of the Third IEEE International Symposium on Object-Oriented Real-Time Distributed Computing. IEEE Computer Society (2000)
20. Weigert, T., Garlan, D., Knapman, J., Møller-Pedersen, B., Selic, B.: Modeling of Architectures with UML Panel. In: Evans, A., Caskurlu, B., Selic, B. (eds.) UML 2000. LNCS, vol. 1939, pp. 556–569. Springer, Heidelberg (2000)
21. Haugen, Ø., Møller-Pedersen, B., Weigert, T.: Structural Modeling with UML 2.0. In: UML for Real, Kluwer Academic Publishers (2003)
22. Krogdahl, S., Møller-Pedersen, B., Sørensen, F.: Exploring the use of Package Templates for flexible reuse of Collections of related Classes. Journal of Object Technology 8(7), 59–85 (2009)

Identification and Selection of Interaction Test Scenarios for Integration Testing

Mohamed Mussa and Ferhat Khendek

Electrical and Computer Engineering, Concordia University, Montreal, Canada
{mm_abdal,khendek}@ece.concordia.ca

Abstract. Integration testing checks for compatibility and interoperability between the components in the system. Integration test models are, typically, generated independently from the other testing level models. In our research, we aim at a model-based framework across unit, integration, and acceptance level testing. This paper contributes to this framework and for the generation of integration test models from unit test models. More precisely, we focus on component interaction test scenarios identification and selection. Following our approach, at each integration step, unit test cases with interaction scenarios involving the component and the context are identified, selected and merged to build the integration test model for the next step. Unit test stubs and drivers are reused in the integration test model. Redundant test cases are eliminated from the generated test models.

Keywords: Testing, Integration, Components, Interactions, Model Based Testing.

1 Introduction

Software testing aims at improving the quality of software products. The main levels of testing are unit-level, integration-level, system-level and acceptance-level. Unit-level testing is applied to individual components and targets frequent developers' bugs. Integration-level testing aims at checking the compatibility, interoperability and consistency among the integrated components. System-level testing is performed to evaluate the system's conformance to the design. Acceptance-level testing is for the validation of the system against user requirements. Several approaches have been developed independently for each testing level. This results in lack of reuse and optimization, and waste of resources.

To master and overcome the increasing complexity of software systems, new development and testing techniques have emerged. The Model-Driven Engineering (MDE) paradigm [1] aims at increasing the level of abstraction in the early stages of the development process and eliminating barriers between modeling (documentation) and implementation (code). On the other hand, Model-Based Testing (MBT) [2] was introduced to cope with model development techniques, involve and enforce test planning in the early stages of the software lifecycle. Test models can be shared among stakeholders and enable common understanding.

Ø. Haugen, R. Reed, and R. Gotzhein (Eds.): SAM 2012, LNCS 7744, pp. 16–33, 2013.

The Unified Modeling Language (UML) [3] is nowadays a widely accepted modeling language. MBT approaches based on UML have been proposed for different testing phases; see for instance [4,5,6]. Moreover, several domains have been targeted including automotive, health, and telecommunications [7,8,9]. UML Testing Profile (UTP) [10] extends UML to support testing activities and artifacts. There have been a number of research investigations based on UTP, see for instance [8,11,12]. However, most of these studies focus on one phase of the testing process, mainly unit-level or system-level testing. We previously presented our MBT framework for integration-level and acceptance-level testing starting from available unit-level test artifacts [13]. The framework aims at enabling reusability between different levels of testing, as well test model optimization. In [13], we discussed the overall integration test generation process. In this paper, we elaborate further and define one of the main steps of this process, interaction test scenario identification and selection.

The rest of this paper is structured as follows. Section 2 introduces our MBT framework. Section 3, presents our approach for identifying interaction test scenarios from unit test cases. Section 4 illustrates the approach with a case study. We discuss related work in Section 5 and conclude in Section 6.

2   MBT Framework

During software development lifecycle, there is a separation between the development and the test processes. Different tools and languages are used in each process. Even within the test process, different expertise is required for every testing level [14]. All these diversities make collaboration among stakeholders more difficult. There is on-going research to tackle such issues, for instance [15]. We proposed a MBT framework that links the main test levels, and enable collaboration among stakeholders. Our targets are the unit-level, the integration-level, and the acceptance-level testing. Reusability and optimization is enabled among these levels to improve the test process and optimize it. The framework uses UML notation to enhance the collaboration among stakeholders. The system-level testing is left out of scope of this work; however, we believe that our framework can handle the system-level testing in the same manner as the acceptance-level when this is required.

Test models, in general, are composed of two parts: structural and behavioral. Structural parts of different test models are identical for the same system under test (SUT); or share sections of the SUT's structure. The behavioral part of a component, which is an element of the SUT, is a portion of the behavior of the SUT. Therefore, test scenarios, which are captured in the test cases, may overlap. Using early test models to build the next level test models and avoid redundancies between the levels will improve the test process. To our knowledge, there is no comprehensive test generation framework in the literature that covers and connects the three testing levels. This section briefly reviews our model-based testing framework proposed in [13] to improve the transitions among the aforementioned testing levels, enable reuse of test models and optimize the overall

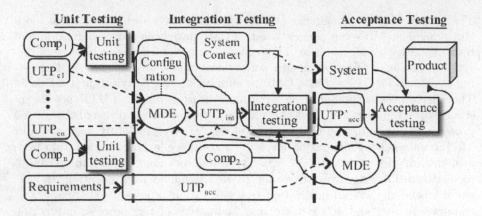

Fig. 1. The overall framework [13]

test process. We make use of the Atlas Transformation Language (ATL) [16] within the Eclipse Framework for implementation.

The proposed MBT framework, shown in Fig. 1, starts from unit-level through integration-level to acceptance-level testing. UTP is used to construct test models. Model transformation is used for the generation of UTP models throughout the process. Unit test models are mapped incrementally to select unit test cases for generating integration test cases. The selected unit test cases must reflect interaction scenarios between the integrated parties. This may lead to merging two test cases to produce an integration test case. The shadowed area in Fig. 1 represents the objectives of our work. In this paper, we focus on the integration-level testing which is illustrated in more details in Fig. 2.

The integration approach takes two UTP models (the context and a new component) as input and produces an integration UTP model. Optionally, a configuration model is submitted to the transformation engine to guide the integration of the two UTP models. The configuration model reveals the necessary internal specification of any complex mediator between the two integrated components, and/or describes design patterns applied in the design of the SUT. The transformation rules identify, select and merge only test cases that are related to the current integration step. The required test drivers and stubs have already been built during unit-level testing. They are reused after eliminating redundancies. Software testers gradually select the next available component and merge it with the context (the integrated components). The integration test model is generated to reflect the interoperability between the context and the new component. The test model will be eventually exercised on the new integrated sub-system. Integration-level testing is an iterative process. It integrates components one by one until reaching the complete system. In this testing phase, we focus on testing the interactions among the system's components, since the acceptance-level testing covers the complete system functionality against user requirements.

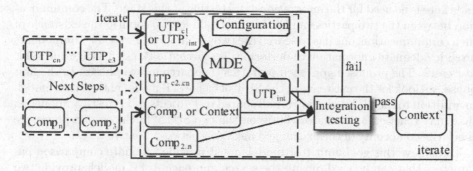

Fig. 2. The integration approach

3 Identification of Interaction Test Scenarios

The main purpose of the integration testing is to check the consistency and interoperability between the integrated components. Integration test models are, typically, generated from the design models, and require a good understanding of the components' interfaces to build integration test models. The unit test models may be partially reused in an ad-hoc manner for generating integration test models. In this research, we are considering a new strategy by generating systematically the integration test models from the unit test models. This enables reusability and strengthens the collaboration between the two testing levels. We consider that unit test cases of integrated components may contain overlapping interaction test scenarios, which can produce integration test cases. A unit test model describes test scenarios that reveal expected, also unexpected, component's behavior through the component's interfaces. The model includes other necessary test drivers and stubs, which represent missing system's and environment's components, to execute the test scenarios. Some of these test drivers and stubs may represent system's components that will eventually be integrated with the component under test. Hence, unit test cases that contain these test drivers and stubs are candidates for the generation of integration test cases. This process can be straightforward when the interaction test scenario is captured in one test case, though it can be more complicated when the interaction test scenario is captured in two test cases, one from each test model of the integrated components. In the first case, the integration test case is generated by replacing the test driver or stub of the unit test case with the integrated component. While in the other case, the integration test case is generated by merging the two unit test cases. The generated test cases have to be compared against each other to remove any redundancy.

To accomplish this, we need to analyze the two test models of the integrated parties. Since integration-level testing emphasize on consistency and interoperability between the integrated parties, the two integrated parties must communicate with each other; otherwise, one can conclude that these parties are independent and there is no need for the integration-level testing at this stage. The communication between the two parties can be direct or indirect. To confirm the existence of such communication, one has to search the two test models. Two UTP components provide adequate information to perform this search: UTP test-package and UTP test cases. The proposed approach performs the search in two phases. In the first phase, we look for the existence of the SUT of each UTP model in the other model. In addition to the SUTs, we look for all shared test objects, UTP test-components, that may function as mediators between the two SUTs. In the second phase, we check the conformity of the exchanged messages between the two SUTs.

To achieve this goal, unit test models must provide adequate comparison parameters that can be used during the search approach. UTP models provide two stereotypes: *SUT* and *Test Component*; *SUT* defines the system under test in the UTP model and *Test Component* defines the test's stubs and drivers. However, a component's *SUT* is stereotyped by *Test Component*, if exists, in the other UTP model since it acts as stub or driver. Hence, the search algorithm cannot rely on the UTP stereotypes alone to analyze the two UTP models. Furthermore, the same applies to the shared UTP test-components. To overcome this issue, we propose two solutions. The first one uses UML stereotypes. Integration testing teams enrich unit test models with UML stereotypes to identify the SUTs, the shared test objects, and test events; e.g.: *SUT1, SUT2, TO1, TO2, TO3*, etc. However, this solution requires some extra effort and knowledge about the unit test models, which it is not always the case. The second solution depends on the naming conventions of the system. The name of an entity within a system must be consistent across all development and test artifacts. We adopt the latter solution. The approach uses the components' names, which must be consistent in all unit UTP models of the system, in addition to the UTP stereotypes.

The framework depends on the quality of the unit test models. Software testing is an important part of the software development life cycle. Nowadays, unit test models are built to check certain component's properties without considering reusability and automation through the whole test process. To align with the MDE paradigm, test models have to enable reusability and automation. Design models are systematically reused and enriched through several development stages to build the final product. To enable reusability and automation through the whole test process, more emphasis should be put on the quality of the unit test models. This is can be achieved by agreeing on a consistent name convention among stakeholders during the test planning phase, and exercising more test cases on the component's interfaces.

The integration approach consists of three stages:

- Identification and Selection: in this stage the approach identifies interactions between the SUTs, and selects unit test cases describe these interactions.
- Merging Test Models: merging two complement unit test cases that together capture an interaction test scenario. The structure of the two test models is merged in this stage to generate the test structure of the integration test model.

– Test Optimization: The approach removes any redundant/overlapping test scenarios that may be exist after generating the integration test model.

This paper focuses on the first stage; while the other two stages are still under investigation. In the following subsections, we discuss further the algorithms used in the first stage of our approach.

3.1 Searching for the SUTs

The first step of the search is to locate, if present, each SUT in the other test model as a test driver/stub. This will reveal the existence of an interaction test scenario, which is captured in one unit test case. These test cases are selected as integration test cases. Algorithm 1 below implements this part of the search. It starts by locating the SUTs in their test models through the UTP stereotype SUT. The result is saved in a variable lists to be used throughout the whole approach. Then, the approach will try to locate each SUT in the other test model among the test objects which are stereotyped with UTP *TestComponent*. The results of this step are also saved in a list to be used throughout the process.

Algorithm 1
Select all entities that are specified with SUT stereotype in the 1st UTP test-package
  Save them in a list **contextSUT**.
Select all entities that are specified with SUT stereotype in the 2nd UTP test-package
  Save them in a list **componentSUT**.
componentCONT: *a null list to hold test stubs that represent the 1st SUT*
  in the 2nd test model.
For each test entity stereotyped by TESTCOMPONENT in the 2nd UTP test-package; **tc**.
  Compare **tc** *against the list* **contextSUT**.
    If there is a match, then add **tc** *to the list* **componentCONT**.
contextCOMP: *a null list to hold test stubs that represent the 2nd SUT*
  in the 1st test model.
For each test entity stereotyped by TESTCOMPONENT in the 1st UTP test-package; **tc**.
  Compare **tc** *against the list* **contextSUT**.
    If there is a match, then add **tc** *to the list* **contextCOMP**.

3.2 Searching for Shared Test Objects

The communication between the two integrated parties may go through intermediate test objects. In this case, if the interaction test scenario is captured in one unit test case, then algorithm 1 will discover this scenario. However, if the interaction test scenario is captured in two unit test cases, then the identification of the intermediate test objects must be revealed first to discover these complement unit test cases. So, to identify the intermediate test objects, we need to compare in algorithm 2 the test objects, stubs/drivers, of the two test models against each other except the ones that had been identified as SUT in the algorithm 1.

Algorithm 2

SharedCOMP: *a null list to hold shared test objects stereotyped by TESTCOMPONENT.*
For each test entity stereotyped by TESTCOMPONENT
       in the 1ˢᵗ UTP test-package; tc1.
   If tc1 is not listed in either **componentCONT** *or* **SharedCOMP**.
   For each test entity stereotyped by TESTCOMPONENT
          in the 2ⁿᵈ UTP test-package; tc2.
      If tc2 is not listed in either **contextCOMP** *or* **SharedCOMP**.
         If tc1 = tc2 then
            Add tc1 to the list **SharedCOMP**.

3.3   UTP Test Context Identification

UTP test context can play a simple or a complex role. It can play the role of:

- The test control,
- The test environment,
- Test drivers and/or stubs,
- Mix of the aforementioned roles.

We are interested with the third role, test driver/stub, since the discovery of this role may reveal the identity of the SUT of the other test model or a shared test object. Hence, revealing the identity of the UTP test context of both test models may enrich our knowledge about the two test models. To identify the role of the UTP test context in a test model, we need to analyze its behavior across all the test cases in the other test model. Furthermore, we compare its behavior to the behavior of known test objects in that test model. However, we have three exceptions in this comparison. First, there is no comparison between the two UTP test contexts since both of them are unknown. Second, there is no comparison with test objects which are already specified in the test case of the test context. Third, there is no comparison with test objects which represent the SUT as stubs/drivers in the test case. Algorithm 3 describes the identification process.

Algorithm 3 maps the UTP test context of the test cases in each test model to the test objects of the test cases in the other test model. The events of objects of the UTP test context, which specified in the test cases, are compared to the events of the objects of the test objects in the other test model. This comparison performed through tree graph representation for the two objects that are currently processing. Each object (tree) is composed of a set of events (nodes), to = { e1, e2, ..., en }; and each event (node) holds as a set of features, te = { type, name, attributes }. To identify the test context, there must be at least two matched paths of the two tree graphs. It can be a full match where all the events of one object are found in the other object with the same order and features, or it can be a partial match where subset of contiguous events of one object are recognized on the other object with the same order and features. Furthermore, this match can be identical, complementary, or mixed. Identical match when all of the compared events have the same direction; e.g. both events are output messages. Complementary match when all of the compared events have the opposite direction; e.g. input message and output message. Mixed match when some of the compared events are identical and the others are complementary. Aside of mixed matches, the algorithm detects that the test context is playing a role of test driver/stub, of a test object which is specified in the other test model. Furthermore, the test context may play the role of one or more test objects in the other test model. Algorithm 4 implements the event mapping algorithm.

Algorithm 3
For each UTP Test Model.
  For each test case which contains a test context: **TC1**.
    Create a tree graph to represent behavior of the test context in **TC1***:* **TCG**.
    Select the other UTP Test Model.
    For each test case: **TC2**.
      For each test object in **TC2***:* **TO**.
        If **TO** *is not test context, specified in* **TC1***, already recognized,*
            or identified as SUT, then
          Create a tree graph to represent behavior of the test object **TO***:* **TOG**.
          Perform **Event Mapping** *between the events of* **TCG**
              and the events of **TOG**.
          Full Match*: Same sequence then*
            Identical*: has same event orientation, then*
                identification succeeded.
            Complement*: has opposite event orientation, then*
                identification succeeded.
            Mixed*: identification inconclusive.*
          Partial Match*: There is partial agreement among*
                the sequence of events, then
            Identical*: has same event orientation, then*
                identification succeeded.
            Complement*: has opposite event orientation, then*
                identification succeeded.
            Mixed*: identification inconclusive.*
          Un-Matched*: identification failed, go to the next iteration.*
If **identification succeeded** *for* **TCG***, then perform* **Test Case Mapping** *(subsection 3.4)*

Algorithm 4 takes two test objects, one from each test case, and makes a comparison between their events. Each test object is tracked independently from the other one (*TO1match* and *TO2Match*). The tracker can be evaluated to one of the states shown in Fig. 3. Initially, the algorithm compares the events' types and names. If they are matched, their attributes are compared. For events of type message, the test object on the other end is checked too. The algorithm finishes when it processes all the events of one of the test objects, or when the two trackers hold a partial match flag.

Algorithm 4
EventMapping(*TO1, TO2)*
    { TO1 = (e1, e2, ..., en), TO2 = (e1, e2, ..., em) }
    TO1match *=NONE,* **TO2match** *= NONE*
    et1 = TO1.e1, et2 = TO2.e1
    While (et1!= NIL AND et2 != NIL)
       If (et1.type = et2.type) AND (et1.name = et2.name) then
          Update **TO1match** *and* **TO2Match** *(NONE◊MATCH;MISMATCH◊PARTIAL)*
          Advance et1 & et2
       Else
          et3= et2.next
          While (et3 != NIL)
             If (et1.type = et3.type) AND (et1.name = et3.name) then
                Update **TO1match** *(NONE◊MATCH; MISMATCH◊PARTIAL)*
                Update **TO2Match** *to PARTIAL*
                Advance et1 & et3
                et2 = et3
                ExitWhile
             EndIf
          EndWhile
          If et2 != et3 then
             Update **TO1match** *(NONE◊MISMATCH; MATCH◊PARTIAL)*
             Advance et1
          EndIf
       Endif
       *If (***TO1match** *and* **TO2Match** *= PARTIAL) then*
          ExitWhile
       EndIf
    EndWhile
    *If et1 != NIL and (***TO1match** *and* **TO2Match** *!= PARTIAL) then*
       Update **TO1match** *(NONE◊MISMATCH; MATCH◊PARTIAL)*
    EndIf
    *If et2 != NIL and (***TO1match** *and* **TO2Match** *!= PARTIAL) then*
       Update **TO2match** *(NONE◊MISMATCH; MATCH◊PARTIAL)*
    EndIf
EndEventMapping

Algorithm 5
Select one of the Unit Test Models.
 For each test case: **TC1**.
  If the SUT of the other test model has been identified as test stub,
        and its object is specified in **TC1**
   Then select **TC1** *as* **complete interaction test case**.
  Select the other Unit Test Model.
  For each test case: **TC2**.
  If the SUT of the other test model has been identified as test stub,
        and its object is in **TC2** *Then*
   select **TC2** *as* **complete interaction test case**.
  If any of the shared test objects is
        specified on both test cases: **TC1** *and* **TC2** *Then*
   perform **Event Mapping** *between the events of the shared test objects.*
   (Build tree graph for shared test objects to compare their events)
   Full Match: *Same sequence (values and number of events) then*
    If **identical**: *has same event orientation. Then*
     select test cases, **TC1** *and* **TC2**,
          as **complement test cases** *to be merged.*
    If **complement**: *has opposite event orientation. Then*
     select test cases, **TC1** *and* **TC2**,
          as **complement test cases** *to be merged.*
    If **mixed**: *test cases,* **TC1** *and* **TC2**, *are not complement, then*
     go to the next iteration.
   Partial Match: *There is partial agreement among the events, then*
   If **identical**: *has same event orientation. Then*
    select test cases, **TC1** *and* **TC2**,
         as **complement test cases** *to be merged.*
   If **complement**: *has opposite event orientation. Then*
    select test cases, **TC1** *and* **TC2**,
         as complement test cases to be merged.
   If **mixed**: *test cases,* **TC1** *and* **TC2**, *are not complement, then*
    go to the next iteration.
   Un-Matched: *identification failed, go to the next iteration.*

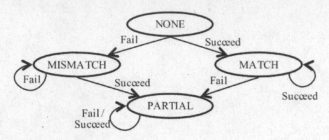

Fig. 3. States of a search tracker

3.4 Mapping Test Cases

To start the mapping, at least one of the algorithms 1, 2 or 3 (mentioned in sub-sections 3.1, 3.2, and 3.3) must succeed. Otherwise, the approach concludes that there are no interactions between the integrated parties according to their unit test specifications and the generation step is skipped. The mapping algorithm, Algorithm 5 selects interaction test scenarios from the test cases specified in the two unit test models, as described below. This interaction test scenario can be captured in one unit test case or two test cases, one from each test model.

4 Case Study: Library System

The case study represents a portion of a library system. In order to focus more on the proposed approach, some abstractions and simplifications have been made. Fig. 5 shows the structural model of the library system; it is composed of three components:

- Browser (BW), which handles the user requests,
- Library (LIB), which maintained the records of the library resources, and
- Account (ACC), which handles user records and authentication.

Fig. 4. Library system

In this case study, we intend to merge the two components, Browser and Account. Their unit test models are specified using UTP, as shown in Fig. 5. Each test model contains two test cases. The approach checks for the existence of any interaction between the two integrated parties through the following steps.

Step 1: Searching for the SUT. In this step, we look for the existence of each SUT in the other test model as a test driver/stub using the algorithm described in subsection 3.1. The results of the algorithm are presented in Table 1.

Table 1. SUT's identification

contextSUT	componentSUT	componentCONT	contextCOMP
{ BW }	{ ACC }	{ }	{ }

The algorithm treats the input test models one as the context and the other as the component, Browser and Account respectively. The algorithm starts by identifying the SUTs in the two models. The SUT(s) of the context are hold in **contextSUT** list; while the SUT(s) of the component are hold in **componentSUT** list. In the second step, the algorithm searches for the existence of context's SUT in the component's test package as scaffold. The results of this step are kept in **componentCONT** list. The algorithm fails to recognize the context's SUT, *BW*, as a test object in the component's test model which leads to an empty list. In the third step, the algorithm searches for the existence of component's SUT in the context's test package as scaffold. The results of this step are kept in **contextCOMP** list. The algorithm fails to recognize the component's SUT, *BW*,, as a test object in the context's test model which leads to an empty list. Hence, we conclude that both SUTs do not play the role of test driver/stub in the other test model.

Step 2: Searching for Shared Test Objects. In this step, we look for a shared test object(s) that may work as a mediator between the two integrated components as described in subsection 3.2. The algorithm starts by initializing a list, **SharedCOMP**, to hold the discovered shared test objects. Then, it scans each test object donated by *TestComponent* stereotype in the context's test package. The test objects have to be neither identified as a component's SUT, from the previous algorithm, nor selected in a previous stage of this algorithm. The context's test objects are compared to test objects donated by *TestComponent* stereotype in the component's test package. The component's test objects have to be also neither identified as a component's SUT nor selected in a previous stage of this algorithm. If the name of context's test object matches the name of the component's test object, then the test object is added to the list, **SharedCOMP**, of the discovered shared test objects. The algorithm completes with a filled-list, **SharedCOMP**, which indicates the existence of a shared test object, *LIB*, between the two integrated components.

Step 3: UTP Test Context Identification. We now analyze the behavior of the test context in both test models since it may behave as a test driver/stub of the SUT in the other test model or a shared test object. The algorithm described in subsection 3.3 is applied, as summarized in Table 2.

Table 2. Identifying the role of the test contexts

#	UTP Test Context to be Analyzed			Test Objects Used in The Comparison			Algorithm Actions & Results
	Test Model	Test Case (TC1)	Test Context (TCG)	Test Model	Test Case (TC2)	Test Object (TO)	
1	Browser	TC11	Test_BW				1.Selects one of the test models, and selects the test context in the first test case. 2.Builds tree *TCG*, as shown in Fig. 6.a.1.
2				Account	TC21	Test_ACC	Ignored, because *Test_ACC* is a Test Context.
3						ACC	1.Builds tree *TOG*, as shown in Fig. 6.c.2. 2.Performs **Event Mapping** on *TCG* and *TOG* which leads to *MISMATCH* result.
4					TC22	Test_ACC	Ignored, because *Test_ACC* is a Test Context.
5						LIB	Ignored, because *LIB* is specified in *TC11*, the current active test case.
6						ACC	1.Builds tree *TOG*, as shown in Fig. 6.d.3. 2.Performs **Event Mapping** on *TCG* and *TOG* which leads to *MISMATCH* result.
7		TC12	Test_BW				1.Selects the test context in the next test case. 2.Builds tree *TCG*, as shown in Fig. 6.b.1.
8					TC21	Test_ACC	Ignored, because *Test_ACC* is a Test Context.
9						ACC	1.Builds tree *TOG*, as shown in Fig. 6.c.2. 2.Performs **Event Mapping** on *TCG* and *TOG* which leads to *MISMATCH* result.
10					TC22	Test_ACC	Ignored, because Test_ACC is a Test Context.
11						LIB	Ignored, because *LIB* is specified in *TC12*, the current active test case.
12						ACC	1.Builds tree *TOG*, as shown in Fig. 6.d.3. 2.Performs **Event Mapping** on *TCG* and *TOG* which leads to *MISMATCH* result.
13	Account	TC21	Test_ACC				1.Since there are no more test cases in Browser's test model, the algorithm selects the other test model, Account. 2.It selects the test context in the first test case . 3.Builds tree *TCG*, as shown in Fig. 6.c.1.
14				Browser	TC11	Test_BW	Ignored, because *Test_BW* is a Test Context.
15						BW	1.Builds tree *TOG*, as shown in Fig. 6.a.3. 2.Performs **Event Mapping** on *TCG* and *TOG* which leads to *MISMATCH* result.
16						LIB	1.Builds tree *TOG*, as shown in Fig. 6.a.2. 2.Performs **Event Mapping** on *TCG* and *TOG* which leads to *MISMATCH* result.
17					TC12	Test_BW	Ignored, because *Test_BW* is a Test Context.
18						BW	1.Builds tree *TOG*, as shown in Fig. 6.b.3. 2.Performs **Event Mapping** on *TCG* and *TOG* which leads to *MISMATCH* result.
19						LIB	1.Builds tree *TOG*, as shown in Fig. 6.b.2. 2.Performs **Event Mapping** on *TCG* and *TOG* which leads to *MISMATCH* result.
20		TC22	Test_ACC				1.Selects the test context in the next test case. 2.Builds tree *TCG*, as shown in Fig. 6.d.1.
21					TC11	Test_BW	Ignored, because *Test_BW* is a Test Context.
22						BW	1.Builds tree *TOG*, as shown in Fig. 6.a.3. 2.Performs **Event Mapping** on *TCG* and *TOG* which leads to *MISMATCH* result.
23						LIB	Ignored, because *LIB* is specified in *TC22*, the current active test case.
24					TC12	Test_BW	Ignored, because Test_BW is a Test Context.
25						BW	1.Builds tree *TOG*, as shown in Fig. 6.b.3. 2.Performs **Event Mapping** on *TCG* and *TOG* which leads to *PARTIAL* result.
26						LIB	Ignored, because *LIB* is specified in *TC22*, the current active test case.

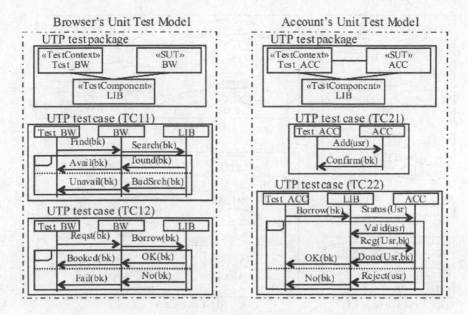

Fig. 5. Unit test models

The algorithm picks one of the test models, the context, and tries to identify the role of its UTP Test Context, *Test_BW*. It compares the behavior of the Test Context, which is specified in the test cases, to the known test objects in the other test model, the component. The algorithm excludes two types of test objects: test objects which represent the UTP Test Context of the other test model (*Test_ACC*), and test objects which are specified within the test cases (*LIB, BW*). A tree graph is used to perform the comparison. Each test object is represented by a tree. Each event is represented by a tree's node, and the event information - e.g.: type, name, etc - is attached to that node. The algorithm applies a depth first search routine, **Event Mapping**, to compare the two trees. The identification of test context *Test_BW* is ended in step 12 with no match; while test context *Test_ACC* is identified in step 25 with the SUT *BW*. Hence, we can conclude that the UTP Test Context *Test_ACC* is playing the role of the other SUT *BW* in the test case *TC22*.

Step 4: Mapping Test Cases. As a result from the previous three algorithms, the test object *LIB* is a shared test object, and the test context *Test_ACC* is playing partially the role of the Browser's SUT, *BW*. With this information in hand, we can analyze the unit test cases in order to select candidates for generating integration test cases. The approach uses the shared test object, *LIB*, to detect complement test cases, one from each test model. There must be synchronization among the events of all shared objects in both test cases to be complementary. These test cases are merged to generate an integration test case. The approach

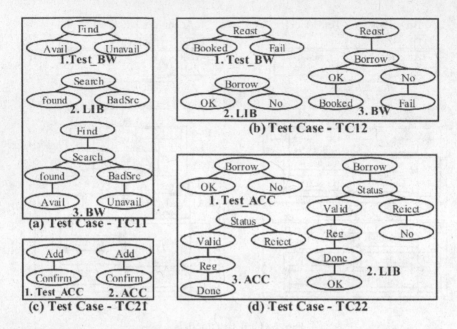

Fig. 6. Graph representation of test objects

uses the identification of the test context, *Test_ACC*, to candidate unit test cases to the integration test model by substituting the test context with the object of the SUT, *BW*. This step can be performed directly during the last stage after the discovery of a match; e.g.: after step 25. The algorithm, which is described in subsection 3.4, is applied to perform this stage.

The algorithm maps the test cases (*TC11*, *TC12*) in the context's test model to the test cases (*TC21*, *TC22*) in the component's test model. On each iteration, first each test case is examined whether the other SUT is specified as stub/driver using information gathered in step 1 & 3. If it is true, then that test case is selected as a complete interaction test case. Second, the two test cases are examined whether they both contain the specification of one of the shared test objects, in our case *LIB*, using the information gathered in step 2 & 3. If a shared test object is specified on both test cases, then the event of these shared objects are compared using the mapping algorithm specified in subsection 3.3. If the result of this comparison is *PARTIAL* or *MATCH*, then these two test cases are selected as a complement interaction test cases. As a result, the approach selects three test cases: *TC22*, *TC12*, and *TC22*. Test case *TC22* is a complete integration test case by substituting *Test_ACC* with *BW*. However, the tester has to introduce a test control to enable the scenario to be executed. The other two test cases, *TC12* and *TC22*, are complementing each other and are merged to generate an integration test case. Hence, *TC22* is part of a larger interaction scenario in the second case, the approach ignores the first case in order to minimize the test cases and optimize the test execution.

5   Related Work

This work aims at introducing a systematic test-generation approach for integration-level by reusing unit-test models. Approaches, in this level, are of ad-hoc nature [14] without associations between the testing levels. The test models are, for instance, generated from the system design specification which is described with Finite State Machines (FSM) [17], UML [3], or mathematical notations.

Machado et al. [18] present a UML based approach for integration-level testing using Object Constraint Language (OCL) [19]. The authors illustrate a complete test process for integration testing. A component is described with a UML class diagram and sequence diagram including OCL constraints. UML use case diagrams are used to describe the components' services (interfaces). To generate interaction test cases, a set of UML interaction diagrams are created based on use case scenarios. However, the authors did not address the synchronization of the events in the generated communication diagrams. The order can be extracted from the provided interaction diagrams, but an interaction diagram may cover a partial view of the component which requires a merging technique to obtain the global behavior. Furthermore, the approach focuses on generating integration test models without utilization of the unit test models. Efforts for building test stubs and drivers are therefore duplicated.

Le [20] proposes a composition approach based on UML 1.x collaboration diagrams. The test model is built manually, and is composed of two roles/players: the component under test role and the tester role. The tester role controls and performs the test-suite, and simulates all necessary stubs and drivers. The author demonstrated the reusability of the tester role from unit-level testing to integration-level testing through introducing adaptors between the unit test models. In this approach, the tester role become more complex since it is composed of the test control and the required stubs and drivers. Separating the test control from the stubs/drivers improves the reusability and simplifies the test implementation. Some stubs may already exist, where utilizing them provides more accurate testing results. The author did not address the synchronization between events of the test behavior. The test case selection is not clear, since not all the unit test cases are suitable for the integration-level testing

6   Conclusion

In this paper, an approach for identifying and selecting unit test cases to generate integration test cases has been presented. The test models are specified using UTP. Unit test models are reused to build integration test models. Notice that this integration can be done, and repeated, at different levels depending on the level of granularity of the units. Our work is still in progress and a full framework is under investigation. We are currently working on a merging algorithm for the complementary test cases. Merging behaviors is a thorny issue which requires a thorough and formal investigation. After implementation and experimentation, the next step will be to move to acceptance-level testing, consider other UTP constructs such as test configuration diagrams, and other diagrams for modeling test cases.

Acknowledgments. This work has been partially supported by the Natural Sciences and Engineering Research Council of Canada (NSERC), Concordia University and the Libyan - North American Scholarship Program.

References

1. Schmidt, D.C.: Guest Editor's Introduction – Model-Driven Engineering. Computer 39, 25–31 (2006)
2. Utting, M., Legeard, B.: Practical Model-Based Testing – A Tools Approach. Morgan Kaufmann Publishers (2007)
3. Object Management Group (OMG): Unified modeling language,
   http://www.uml.org/
4. Bouquet, F., Grandpierre, C., Legeard, B., Peureux, F., Vacelet, N., Utting, M.: A subset of precise UML for model-based testing. In: A-MOST 2007 Proceedings of the 3rd International Workshop on Advances in Model-Based Testing, pp. 95–104. ACM Press (2007)
5. Javed, A.Z., Strooper, P.A., Watson, G.N.: Automated generation of test cases using model-driven architecture. In: AST 2007: Proceedings of the Second International Workshop on Automation of Software Test, p. 3. IEEE Computer Society (2007)
6. Yuan, Q., Wu, J., Liu, C., Zhang, L.: A model driven approach toward business process test case generation. In: 10th International Symposium on Web Site Evolution WSE 2008, pp. 41–44. IEEE Conference Publications (2008)
7. Cartaxo, E.G., Andrade, W.L., Neto, F.G.O., Machado, P.D.L.: LTS-BT – A tool to generate and select functional test cases for embedded systems. In: SAC 2008: Proceedings of the 2008 ACM Symposium on Applied Computing, pp. 1540–1544. ACM Press (2008)
8. Pietsch, S., Stanca-Kaposta, B.: Model-based testing with UTP and TTCN-3 and its application to HL7. Testing Technologies IST GmbH (2008),
   http://www.testingtech.com/download/publications/
   ModelBasedTesting_Conquest08.pdf
9. Süß, J.G., Pop, A., Fritzson, P., Wildman, L.: Towards integrated model-driven testing of SCADA systems using the eclipse modeling framework and modelica. In: ASWEC 2008: Proceedings of the 19th Australian Conference on Software Engineering, pp. 149–159. IEEE Computer Society (2008)
10. Object Management Group (OMG): UML testing profile (UTP) version 1.0 (formal/05-07-07) (2005), http://www.omg.org/spec/UTP/1.0/
11. Liang, D., Xu, K.: Test-driven component integration with UML 2.0 testing and monitoring profile. In: QSIC 2007: Proceedings of the Seventh International Conference on Quality Software, pp. 32–39. IEEE Computer Society (2007)
12. Lamancha, B.P., Mateo, P.R., de Guzmán, I.R., Usaola, M.P., Velthius, M.P.: Automated model-based testing using the UML testing profile and QVT. In: MoDeVVa 2009 – Proceedings of the 6th International Workshop on Model-Driven Engineering, Verification and Validation, pp. 6:1–6:10. ACM Press (2009)

13. Mussa, M., Khendek, F.: Towards a Model Based Approach for Integration Testing. In: Ober, I., Ober, I. (eds.) SDL 2011. LNCS, vol. 7083, pp. 106–121. Springer, Heidelberg (2011)

14. Bertolino, A.: Software testing research – Achievements, challenges, dreams. In: FOSE 2007: 2007 Future of Software Engineering, pp. 85–103. IEEE Computer Society (2007)

15. Grossmann, J., Fey, I., Krupp, A., Conrad, M., Wewetzer, C., Mueller, W.: TestML - A Test Exchange Language for Model-Based Testing of Embedded Software. In: Broy, M., Krüger, I.H., Meisinger, M. (eds.) ASWSD 2006. LNCS, vol. 4922, pp. 98–117. Springer, Heidelberg (2008)

16. The Eclipse Foundation: ATL - a model transformation technology (2012), http://www.eclipse.org/atl/

17. Bogdanov, K., Holcombe, M.: Refinement in Statechart Testing. Software Testing Verification and Reliability 14, 189–211 (2004)

18. Machado, P.D.L., Figueiredo, J.C.A., Lima, E.F.A., Barbosa, A.E.V., Lima, H.S.: Component-based integration testing from UML interaction diagrams. In: IEEE International Conference on Systems, Man and Cybernetics (ISIC), pp. 2679–2686. IEEE Conference Publications (2007)

19. Object Management Group (OMG): OMG object constraint language (OCL), version 2.2 (formal/2010-02-01) (2010), http://www.omg.org/spec/OCL/2.2

20. Le, H.: A collaboration-based testing model for composite components. In: 2nd International Conference on Software Engineering and Service Science (ICSESS), pp. 610–613. IEEE Conference Publications (2011)

An Approach to Specify and Analyze Goal Model Families

Azalia Shamsaei[1], Daniel Amyot[1], Alireza Pourshahid[1], Edna Braun[1],
Eric Yu[2], Gunter Mussbacher[3], Rasha Tawhid[4], and Nick Cartwright[5]

[1] School of Electrical Eng. and Computer Science, University of Ottawa, Canada
{asham092,apour024}@uottawa.ca,
{damyot,ebraun}@eecs.uottawa.ca
[2] Department of Computer Science, University of Toronto, Canada
eric@cs.toronto.edu
[3] Department of Systems and Computer Engineering, Carleton University, Canada
gunter@sce.carleton.ca
[4] See the *in Memoriam* Section
[5] Independent Consultant, Canada
ncart@sympatico.ca

Abstract. Goal-oriented languages have been used for years to model
and reason about functional, non-functional, and legal requirements. It is
however difficult to develop and maintain these models, especially when
many models overlap with each other. This becomes an even bigger challenge when a single, generic model is used to capture a family of related
goal models but different evaluations are required for each individual
family member. In this work, we use ITU-T's Goal-oriented Requirement Language (GRL) and the jUCMNav tool to illustrate the problem
and to formulate a solution that exploits the flexibility of standard GRL.
In addition, we report on our recent experience on the modeling of aerodrome regulations. We demonstrate the usefulness of specifying families
of goal models to address challenges associated with the maintenance of
models used in the regulatory domain. We finally define and illustrate
a new tool-supported algorithm used to evaluate individual goal models
that are members of the larger family model.

Keywords: Goal Modeling, Goal-oriented Requirement Language, Key
Performance Indicator, Legal Compliance, Tools, URN, Variability.

1 Introduction

Goal-oriented modeling has been used successfully in the past to measure compliance of business processes with regulations, to measure business process performance, as well as to analyze organizational security requirements [1,2]. However,
can it handle the modeling of complex regulations that apply to multiple types
of organizations?

There are many regulations to be modeled, and these models can be used for
compliance assessment by regulators. However, different regulatory requirements

Ø. Haugen, R. Reed, and R. Gotzhein (Eds.): SAM 2012, LNCS 7744, pp. 34–52, 2013.

apply to different types of organizations. To have one goal model per type of organization would require significant maintenance effort when the legal context evolves, with the additional risk of introducing inconsistencies and other types of errors in the model. In this context, we should explore ways to capture a family of goal models, whose individual members can be extracted for compliance analysis. Our hypothesis is that a goal language can be tailored to support the concept of a *model family*, and hence mitigate the risks of inconsistencies while minimizing maintenance effort.

There are many existing goal languages and most have been used in one way or another in a legal compliance context [1]. However, in this paper, we selected the Goal-oriented Requirement Language (GRL) for several reasons:

1. GRL is standardized as part of the User Requirements Notation (URN) [3,4];
2. the extensions to GRL that support the concept of Key Performance Indicator (KPI) [5] are useful to measure compliance in units that people doing inspection/audit activities can actually understand;
3. it is possible to tailor (i.e., *profile*) the language through metadata, URN links and constraints;
4. a tool that supports these concepts is available [6] and enables the creation of evaluation algorithms [7] that exploit these concepts.

In this paper, an example related to aerodrome regulations is described in section 2, followed by requirements for the support of families of goal models. In section 3, we report on a first attempt to model regulation families with GRL and KPIs, and show limitations. In order to solve these limitations, we introduce in section 4 (our core contribution) a GRL profile including OCL well-formedness constraints as well as a new propagation algorithm, which are illustrated on the aerodrome regulations example. Related work, limitations, and future work items are discussed in section 5, while section 6 presents our conclusions.

2 Modeling Issues: Illustrative Example

With this example, we will illustrate why modeling and analyzing of regulations that apply to multiple types of organizations is challenging, and why a family of goal models could be used to address this issue. This example is inspired from realistic aerodrome security regulations, with a focus on perimeter signage and access control.

We model regulations starting with their high-level goals (e.g., perimeter security). We decompose these goals into operational and control rules. Furthermore, we define KPIs for each rule that measures their compliance level. Although this works well for compliance measurement [2], when different versions of the same model are used for various types of organizations, one runs into scalability and maintainability issues.

Perimeter Security: One of the important goals of an aerodrome is to provide effective perimeter security. The regulator issues regulations that establish obligations on aerodrome operators and specify various security elements (e.g., signage, requirements for fencing, access control, etc.) that would comprise an appropriate system of perimeter security [8]. Due to the sensitivity of security regulations, we use a simplified and obfuscated example (Fig. 1) instead of a real one. Its structure however is illustrative and representative of the kind of issues faced while modeling real regulations.

GRL Modeling: We use GRL to model the regulations. GRL models (Fig. 1) consist of *intentional elements*, such as *goals* (⬭ , e.g., Perimeter Security). Intentional elements can be connected to each other using *contribution links* (→) with a quantitative weight ([-100..+100]). AND/OR *decomposition links* (+) can be used to connect elements with sub-elements. *Dependency links* (➤-) are used in our example to show that an intentional element depends on another one to satisfy a goal. We also use *resources* (▭) to capture conditions that goals depend on (e.g., in Fig. 1, Access control system rule1 depends on Condition). Finally, a *GRL strategy* describes a particular configuration of alternatives and initial satisfaction values in the GRL model, while a *GRL evaluation mechanism* propagates these values to the other intentional elements of the model (through their links) and compute their satisfaction values (Fig. 2: the values shown just above intentional elements). Different evaluation algorithms exist for GRL [7].

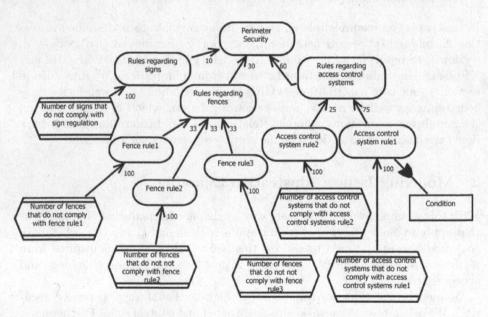

Fig. 1. Goal model of a perimeter security regulation (artificial example)

Key Performance Indicators (KPIs): *Indicators/KPIs* (⬭ , e.g., Number of fences that do not comply with fence rule2) in GRL are goal model elements that convert values from the real world (e.g., $45,000) to a GRL satisfaction level according to a defined conversion method (e.g., target, threshold, and worst-case values). Using GRL strategies, one can initialize the KPI value sets manually or through external data sources (e.g., a Business Intelligence system). KPIs can be used to evaluate the satisfaction of regulation rules and ultimately the overall satisfaction level of the regulation or compliance level of the organization. KPIs can be linked with intentional elements only in the following, limited way. KPIs can be the source of a contribution link or decomposition link and can be used in dependency links. KPIs are included in the second version of the URN standard. GRL models with KPIs can be created, managed, and analyzed with jUCMNav [6], a free, Eclipse-based, open source tool that supports the URN standard and more, including the evaluation of the models with color-coded feedback (Fig. 2: the greener, the better, and the redder, the worse).[1]

Requirement for Families of Goal Models: Aerodromes are divided into various categories (or *types*), based on a set of factors. Some elements of the regulation are only applicable to specific types (e.g., to TYPE1, TYPE2, or TYPE3).

A regulator requires a generic model for each regulation rather than having separate models based on the aerodrome type. The generic model gives a holistic view of the regulation as opposed to a specific model for each type of aerodrome. For instance, out of 15 model elements related to fences, only 3 are specific to TYPE1 aerodromes. Therefore, if a separate model is created for TYPE1 aerodromes, the model will not show the complete picture of the regulation. Furthermore, having separate models for each type increases maintenance costs and the risk of errors in the models as different versions evolve. Hence, a technique is required to create a *family* of goal models, here based on aerodrome types, allowing some of the rules to be ignored or hidden in the generic model when a specific type of aerodrome is being evaluated.

3   Attempt 1: Modeling Families with Standard GRL

To meet the requirements for goal model families, we first tried to use the existing GRL capabilities, including dependency links. In GRL, the satisfaction value of the depender cannot be higher that the satisfaction value of the dependee. We attempted to model the aerodrome categories with GRL *resource* elements and *dependency links* from the rules. Some regulations can apply to more than one type. In Fig. 2, Access control system rule1 is restricted to aerodromes of types TYPE1 or TYPE2. We combine these two by OR-decomposing Condition1.

In addition, some rules are applicable only under certain conditions (independent of the type, and more dynamic by nature). If the conditions are true, then the rule should be imposed. As illustrated in Fig. 2, such a condition also applies to Access control system rule1 for aerodromes of type TYPE1. Yet again, an intermediate node (Condition2) is needed to handle the Condition, this time with an AND-decomposition.

After modeling the regulation, we define GRL strategies, each representing a global situation that indicates the rules that apply to each of the categories

---

[1] Please see the online version of this paper for color diagrams.

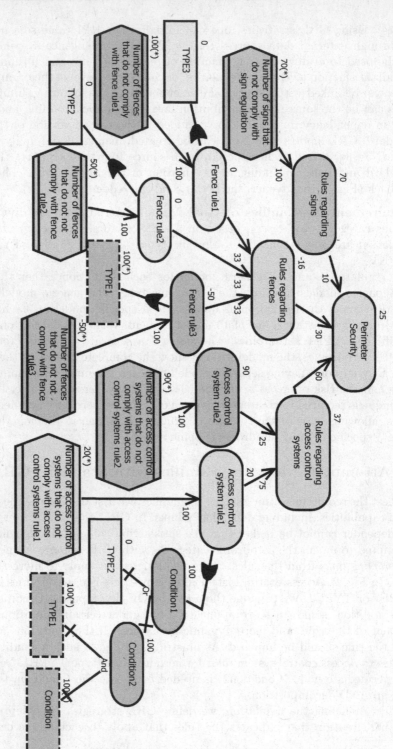

Fig. 2. Generic model evaluated against a TYPE1 strategy (artificial example)

(TYPE1, TYPE2, or TYPE3). Depending on the strategy, either 0 (not selected) or 100 (selected) is used as an initial satisfaction value for the type categories. Fig. 2 illustrates a strategy where the value of the TYPE1 resource element is 100 and the other resource elements (TYPE2 and TYPE3) values are 0. Therefore, all the elements dependent on TYPE2 or TYPE3 will be evaluated to a maximum value of 0 and will not affect the evaluation of the model. Hence, Fence rule1 and Fence rule2 are evaluated to 0, whatever the values of their KPIs, since they are not applied to TYPE1 aerodromes. In addition, Access control system rule1 is used in TYPE1 or TYPE2 aerodromes. Since resource TYPE1 has a satisfaction level of 100, and since the strategy explored here has the value of Condition set to 100, the satisfaction of Condition2 becomes 100 and therefore, Condition1 is also evaluated to 100, which means that Access control system rule1 will not be ignored. The rules that are not dependent on any type represent *all* categories and by default are not ignored in any of the strategies.

Using this method, we managed to create a family of goal models from the generic goal model. Although this approach addresses our requirement to some extent for simple examples, it proved not to be a good solution for more complex real-life examples. We identified four main problems:

1. Noise in the models;
2. Scalability and maintenance;
3. Ambiguity between the two types of conditions;
4. Evaluation and analysis.

First, an additional model element with a dependency link is connected to each rule to specify the category of the rules. In cases where a rule is valid for more than one type, more model elements and links are required. For instance, in the simple case where one rule is applicable to two types of aerodromes, we need three additional intentional elements to show this condition (Fig. 2: Condition 1 goal, TYPE1 condition, and TYPE2 condition). When the number of rules increases, there is much additional *noise* that is not really core to the model but only used to define conditions and categories. This problem can be somewhat mitigated by moving the conditions and categories to separate diagrams of a same model. Hence, although the model still includes the additional elements and links, the diagrams used by the end user for analysis purposes are much cleaner and manageable. However, since some rules may apply to more than one aerodrome type, the rules will be repeated in multiple diagrams, increasing their size as well as maintenance complexity.

Furthermore, there are often conditions other than categories (as illustrated in Fig. 2: Condition) that need to be considered more dynamically when the applicability of the rules is being assessed. If we use resources and dependencies for showing yet another type of conditions, the models with two types of condition nodes become ambiguous and too complex to be used by targeted users of this method (i.e., compliance officers).

Finally, the evaluation of these models using the existing GRL evaluation algorithms is often misleading. For example, if the contribution levels of the eliminated rules and applied rules are kept the same as in the generic model, even with a satisfaction value of 100 for an applicable rule, the target intentional element will have a satisfaction value lower than 100, which in this application is interpreted as non-compliance. For example, if the satisfaction value of Fence rule1 is 100 and TYPE3 organizations are evaluated based on the GRL model in Fig. 2 (i.e., the satisfaction values of Fence rule2 and Fence rule3 are 0 or these model elements are even removed from the model), then the target intentional element Rules regarding fences will evaluate to 33 (and hence non-compliant). However, the satisfaction value of Rules regarding fences should be 100 (and hence compliant), because all rules for TYPE3 organizations are fully satisfied. Existing evaluation algorithms consider all the nodes and contribution links connected to a target intentional element while calculating its satisfaction level. Hence, there is an implicit requirement to redistribute the weight of removed contributions onto the weight of the contributions that remain.

4   Attempt 2: GRL with a Goal Model Family Profile

The URN standard, which includes GRL, offers lightweight mechanisms to extend the language. A GRL profile takes advantage of an important URN concept, namely *metadata*, which are name-value pairs used to annotate any model element (e.g., for stereotyping). Note that the metadata facilities in jUCMNav are generic, i.e., the tool allows an arbitrary set of stereotypes to be used for model annotation. Analysis algorithms can also take advantage of profile information. *Constraints*, expressed in OCL, can be used to enforce well-formedness constraints for GRL models with metadata and to query the GRL model. In this section, we introduce stereotypes (metadata) and a propagation algorithm for GRL model families, with a particular focus on compliance. The profile is called *measured compliance* profile.

4.1   Goal Model Family Concepts

In order to solve the noise, maintenance, and ambiguity issues of the models discussed in section 3, a new profile was created to manage goal model families within GRL. Fig. 3 introduces its basic concepts. In essence, a *family* (a GRL model) is composed of *model elements* (we focus on GRL intentional elements here, but obviously actors and links are included as well). Some of these elements can be *tagged* with metadata describing categories. These tagged model elements are part of *family members*, where a member is a subset of the family regrouping the elements for a given category. A model element can be tagged with multiple categories and hence can be part of many family members.

In our aerodrome context, we tag intentional elements with metadata (where the name is 'ST_CLASSTYPE' and the value is «TYPE1», «TYPE2», or «TYPE3») displayed by jUCMNav as stereotypes. An intentional element *without* a tag means the related rule applies to all aerodrome types. Using this approach, we eliminate all the elements and dependency links used to define the categories, which reduces the noise and ambiguities while improving the maintainability of the model. We still use resources and dependency links to model

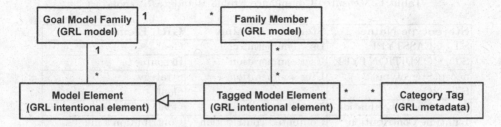

Fig. 3. Conceptual model for our GRL profile for goal model families

conditions that apply to an intentional element. We tag the conditions (metadata named 'ST_CONDITIONTYPE' to differentiate it from the one used for intentional elements, but the values are the same as for 'ST_CLASSTYPE') to specify which aerodrome categories the conditions apply to.

Furthermore, we tag the GRL strategies with metadata (where the name is 'acceptStereotype' and the value is «TYPE1», «TYPE2», or «TYPE3») to specify the model elements that will be evaluated. For instance, when users run a strategy that is stereotyped as «TYPE1» and «TYPE2», all the elements tagged with «TYPE1» and «TYPE2» will be evaluated and tagged elements without those tags will be ignored. The described evaluation method only works with the new proposed algorithm described in the next section.

To ensure traceability with the source legislative documents, two additional stereotypes are used. We tag goals with reference metadata (where the name is 'RegDocRef' and the value is the name of the regulation in the source legislative document) and hyperlink metadata (where the name is 'Hyperlink' and the value is a URL to a section in the source legislative document). The reference metadata enables modelers to query the URN model to spot elements corresponding to a given part of a legislative document, on a name basis, whereas the link metadata establishes clickable traceability links to online legislative documents. Finally, the metadata with name 'ST_Term' is used to provide further information about the structure of the regulation document. The value is a user-defined string that corresponds to one of the many types of sections (e.g., Part, Sub-part, Section, Rule) and hence reflects the structure of a regulation document.

Table 1 gives a complete summary of the stereotypes related to the measured compliance profile and discussed in this section. The stereotypes 'ST_NO', 'IgnoreNodeInEvaluation', and 'Runtime Contribution' are explained in the next section.

In addition, we defined ten well-formedness constraints formalized in UML's Object Constraint Language (OCL) and checked against the model by jUCM-Nav [7]. These constraints, specified in Appendix A, are further discussed in section 4.3.

Table 1. Measured Compliance Profile Metadata/Stereotypes

Stereotype Name	Stereotype Value	GRL Element
ST_CLASSTYPE	User enumeration	Goal
ST_CONDITIONTYPE	User enumeration	Resource
acceptStereotype	User enumeration	Strategy
ST_NO	"No"	Goal
IgnoreNodeInEvaluation	N/A (ignored)	Goal, Resource
Runtime Contribution	Computed contribution value	Contribution Link
ST_Term	User enumeration	Goal
RegDocRef	Reference to source document	Goal
Hyperlink	URL to source document	Goal, Resource

4.2 New Analysis Algorithm

There are three main GRL evaluation algorithms (quantitative, qualitative, and hybrid) that are supported by jUCMNav [7]. More recently, a formula-based quantitative algorithm that supports KPI aggregation has been proposed and prototyped [9]. The quantitative evaluation algorithm also supports KPIs. Hence, we extend the quantitative algorithm to take the defined stereotypes on strategies and intentional elements into consideration during the evaluation process, in order to be able to eliminate the intentional elements that are not of a specific type (i.e., not part of the desired family member), and to distribute the weights of the contribution links of the ignored intentional elements among accepted intentional elements. For instance, assume that goal G gets contributions from X, Y, Z, and W with values 45, 30, 10, and 15 respectively (e.g., see the graph in Fig. 4). The standard quantitative algorithm multiplies the intentional elements' satisfaction values by their contribution weights, sums them up, and then divides the total by 100 to calculate the satisfaction level of the target intentional element. The satisfaction value of goal G is computed from the four other goals through their contribution links:

$$((45 \times 45) + (70 \times 30) + (50 \times 15) + (100 \times 10))/100 = \mathbf{58}$$

Now, assume this is a model family where X is tagged with «TYPE1», Y with «TYPE2», W with «TYPE3», and Z with «TYPE1». If we go with a strategy that restricts the family to members of type TYPE1, then the issue with the conventional algorithm is that the contributions to G sum up to 55 (45 + 10), and hence G's satisfaction value cannot be higher than 55. The actual satisfaction value of goal G with only «TYPE1» elements taken into account is:

$$((45 \times 45) + (0 \times 30) + (0 \times 15) + (100 \times 10))/100 = \mathbf{30}$$

With our modified algorithm however, if the strategy is tagged with «TYPE1», then Y and W will be tagged dynamically (and temporarily) with an

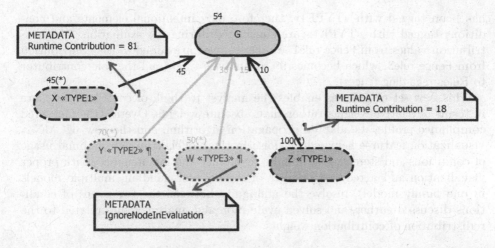

Fig. 4. Example of modified GRL analysis algorithm

'IgnoreNodeInEvaluation' stereotype. The contribution level of ignored elements will be distributed proportionally over the contribution levels of remaining active intentional elements. These elements are tagged with the 'Runtime Contribution' stereotype to show the dynamically calculated contribution values to the modeler. We assume that the sum of contribution levels does not exceed 100; we check this particular style through one of our OCL constraints (see Constraint 1 in Appendix A). In this example, the total contribution value of Y and W computed at analysis time, which is (30+15), is divided proportionally between X and Z as follows:

IgnoredContributionLevel $\quad = 30 + 15 = 45 \quad$ // Not of TYPE1: Y + W
SumConsideredContributionLinks $= 45 + 10 = 55 \qquad$ // TYPE1: X + Z
ContributionLevelX = ContributionLevelX + (ContributionLevelX ×
$\qquad$ IgnoredContributionLevel) / SumConsideredContributionLinks
$\qquad = 45 + (45 \times 45)/55 = 81$
ContributionLevelZ = ContributionLevelZ + (ContributionLevelZ ×
$\qquad$ IgnoredContributionLevel) / SumConsideredContributionLinks
$\qquad = 10 + (10 \times 45)/55 = 18$

This leads to a new satisfaction value of **54** for goal G:

$$((45 \times 81) + (100 \times 18))/100 = \mathbf{54}$$

jUCMNav supports this new analysis algorithm and also greys out intentional elements and links that are not part of the selected family member, as shown in Fig. 4. Furthermore, the 'ST_NO' stereotype can be used for optimization and for dropping a model element from the analysis when it is not measurable.

In our family example for aerodromes, Fig. 5 illustrates a strategy-based analysis of perimeter security using our new GRL algorithm. The strategy used here has been tagged with «TYPE1», therefore only intentional elements and conditions tagged with «TYPE1» are considered during the evaluation. The contribution values from Fence rule1 and Fence rule2 are added to the contribution from Fence rule3, which becomes 99 at analysis time (and the sole contributor to Rules regarding fences).

This new set of features enables the analyst to think of contributions more in terms of relative weights rather than absolute weights. Overall, the measured compliance profile, its adapted propagation algorithm, and the new jUCMNav visualization features help reduce noise in the models (through minimal usage of conditions and stereotypes), handle scalability and maintenance (with proper visualization and a reduced number of symbols for handling multiple models in one family model), resolve the ambiguity between the two types of conditions discussed earlier, and solved evaluation and analysis issues related to the redistribution of contribution weights.

4.3 OCL Well-Formedness Constraints

To ensure the quality of input models before analysts start their analysis, well-formedness constraints must be defined and checked. A set of well-formedness constraints, written in OCL and supported by jUCMNav [6], is presented in Appendix A. These constraints are part of the profile for measured compliance. For example, Constraint 2 will ensure that a GRL resource with metadata 'ST_CONDITIONTYPE' must be a dependee of an intentional element.

Moreover, another OCL constraint (Constraint 9) functions as a query that, on a name basis, finds all goals in the GRL model that represent a specific part of the source legislative document. These constraints take advantage of an OCL library of over 120 pre-defined functions used to query and check URN models, hence simplifying the definition of profile constraints.

Violations to any constraints are reported in jUCMNav's Problems view as a list of problems. By clicking on a problem in the Problems view, the violating element or diagram of the model is highlighted. Figure 6 shows a small example where the ten constraints from the measured compliance profile have been checked and violated. Note that four of these constraints report warnings only as these are either not severe enough to affect the results of the profile's propagation algorithm, or they are simply the result of queries.

5 Related Work and Discussion

There has been much effort devoted to the modeling of variability on goal models. Ali *et al.* [10] present contextual goal models that extend Tropos with variation points where the context may influence the choice among alternatives. They also use tagging with conditions on goals and links (decomposition, dependency, contribution). However, they are more interested in describing runtime adaptation based on a logic-based representation of goals and conditions than in capturing families of related goal models with the automatic adjustment of quantitative contributions. They do not have graphical tool support.

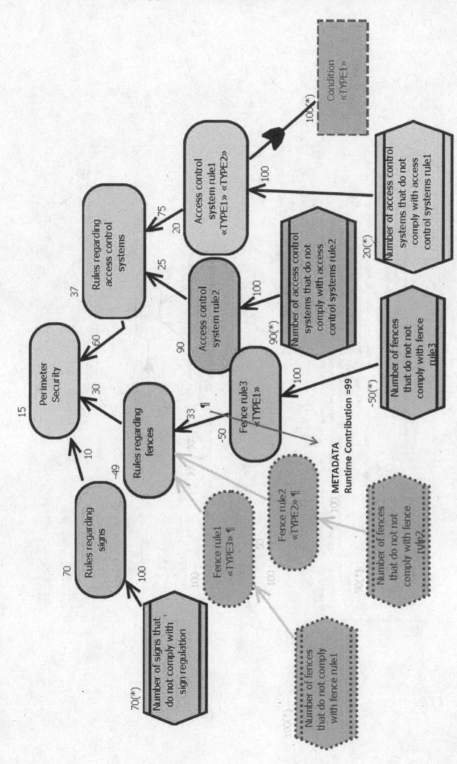

Fig. 5. Example of TYPE1 aerodrome with the modified GRL analysis algorithm

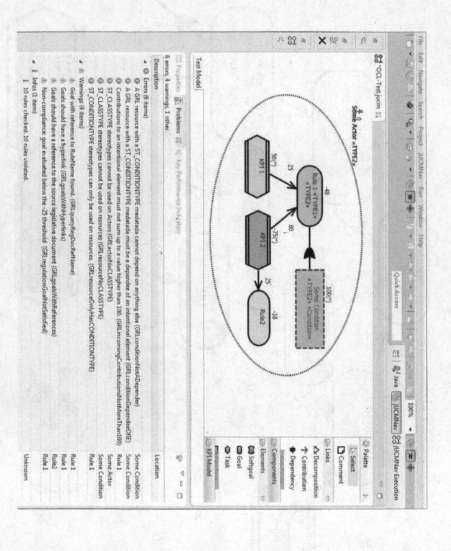

Fig. 6. Example of violations of the profile's OCL constraints in jUCMNav

Lapouchnian *et al.* [11] propose a framework for modeling and analyzing domain variability for goal models. They label model elements that need to be visible with contextual tags. A Boolean variable is assigned to each tag, identifying whether a tag should be active or not. They also propose an algorithm for extracting the parts of the goal model that are dependent on the context variability. Furthermore, they extend the i^* notation to represent and support variations in goal models [12]. Variations of a goal model can be generated from a single context-parameterized i^* model based on the current active contexts. Our approach is similar as we also tag elements with appropriate context information and extract members. However, we take this concept further and use it for quantitative evaluation of the goal models (and not just Boolean evaluation) while automatically adjusting contribution links to produce valid results. In addition in our approach, the tags are visualized with stereotypes, conditions with special intentional elements, and non-member elements with grey shading.

Goal-oriented languages have also been used to support feature models for software product line (SPL). Borba *et al.* [13] provide a comparison between existing goal-oriented techniques for feature modeling in SPL. In particular, Silva *et al.* [14] propose an extension to i^* that enables modeling common and variable features of SPL with cardinalities using tasks and resources of a goal model to capture features. Yu *et al.* [15] propose a tool-based method to create feature models from a goal model. Mussbacher *et al.* [16] review the literature on goal modeling and SPL and propose an SPL framework based on Aspect-oriented URN that allows capturing features and reasoning about stakeholders' needs. Goal models are often used in the literature to express the tradeoffs about non-functional aspects when selecting particular configurations of software products. However, they are not really about families of goal models. To our knowledge, the concept of family of goal models has not been discussed in the literature, and certainly not in a legal compliance context.

A recent systematic literature review revealed that goal-oriented languages have been used to model regulations and compliance [1]. Furthermore, according to another review, some approaches allow organizations to measure their level of compliance [2]. However, none of the existing approaches proposed a technique to analyze individual goal models that are members of a larger family of models.

Although using existing GRL constructs to model conditions addressed our basic needs, this approach can be confusing for current users of GRL models in other application domains. We tried to mitigate this problem by using a different symbol color in the proposed GRL profile (see Condition in Fig. 5), in a way that is compatible with the URN standard. The analysis time contribution information is currently only accessible as metadata in the tool implementation (requiring mouse hovering to be visible), and this might also be confusing to the user.

This profile does not solve the issue of how to choose appropriate contribution levels in goal models. However, this is somewhat mitigated by the availability of recent features in jUCMNav such as *contribution overrides* (with which one can store alternative weights for contributions and use them in combination with GRL strategies during analysis) and *sensitivity analysis* (through which intervals rather than simple values can be attached to contributions and initial satisfaction levels, and then used with jUCMNav's analysis algorithms) [17].

The tool-supported approach from section 4 has been used on real regulations for aviation security, with models containing hundreds of elements. We have not observed any scalability issue at the moment, but there is no guarantee this approach will fit other regulations or other domains outside compliance, and validation experiments are needed to address these issues. The concept of model families could be adapted to other goal-modeling languages, but in general other languages do not provide all the facilities provided for free by the URN language (e.g., strategies and extension mechanisms) and by the jUCMNav tool, hence porting these ideas might prove to be difficult.

6   Conclusions

In this paper, based on the challenges observed through the modeling of aerodrome security regulations with GRL and key performance indicators, the concept of families of goal models was defined. This led to the creation of a GRL profile for measured compliance, comprised of a set of stereotypes and OCL well-formedness constraints exploited by a novel propagation algorithm, with support for modeling, analysis, and visualization provided by the jUCMNav tool.

Although regulators define regulations (e.g., aviation security) that apply to all the organizations they regulate (e.g., aerodromes), not all rules are usually applicable to all types of organizations. This is a common situation that is not limited to aviation security. We used a perimeter security example to illustrate that when regulations apply to various types of organizations, modeling them using existing goal-modeling approaches can lead to various issues including model noise, scalability, and maintenance problems, ambiguity with how conditions are represented, and misleading evaluation and analysis results. We characterized the requirements for potential solutions and proposed a solution that allows modelers to define a generic family goal model for all types of organizations and tag the model elements to specify which ones are applicable to which family member. The solution is formalized as a profile for GRL, with suitable stereotypes, well-formedness constraints, and an analysis algorithm that exploits this new information. After illustrating and discussing the approach, several limitations and items for future work have been identified. Families of goal models fit nicely the problems observed in regulatory compliance, but we suspect they can address a much larger class of problem domains. Generality and scalability will be explored further in future work.

Acknowledgments. This research was supported by NSERC's Business Intelligence Network. We also thank Andrew Miga for his useful contributions to the jUCMNav tool regarding the new compliance profile.

In memoriam Rasha Tawhid. Sadly, Dr. Tawhid (Ph.D., Carleton University, 2012) passed away in October 2012, following her courageous fight against cancer. She is deeply missed by her family, friends and colleagues.

References

1. Ghanavati, S., Amyot, D., Peyton, L.: A Systematic Review of Goal-oriented Requirements Management Frameworks for Business Process Compliance. In: 4th Int. Work. on Requirements Engineering and Law, RELAW, pp. 25–34. IEEE Computer Society (2011)
2. Shamsaei, A., Amyot, D., Pourshahid, A.: A Systematic Review of Compliance Measurement Based on Goals and Indicators. In: Salinesi, C., Pastor, O. (eds.) CAiSE 2011 Workshops. LNBIP, vol. 83, pp. 228–237. Springer, Heidelberg (2011)
3. Amyot, D., Mussbacher, G.: User Requirements Notation – The First Ten Years, The Next Ten Years. Journal of Software, JSW 6(5), 747–768 (2011)
4. International Telecommunication Union: Recommendation Z.151 (10/12), User Requirements Notation (URN) - Language definition, http://www.itu.int/rec/T-REC-Z.151/en
5. Pourshahid, A., Amyot, D., Peyton, L., Ghanavati, S., Chen, P., Weiss, M., Foster, A.: Business process management with the User Requirements Notation. Electronic Commerce Research, ECR 9(4), 269–316 (2009)
6. jUCMNav, Version 5.2.0, University of Ottawa, http://softwareengineering.ca/jucmnav
7. Amyot, D., Ghanavati, S., Horkoff, J., Mussbacher, G., Peyton, L., Yu, E.: Evaluating Goal Models within the Goal-oriented Requirement Language. International Journal of Intelligent Systems 25(8), 841–877 (2010)
8. Canada Gazette - Government Notices, http://canadagazette.gc.ca/rp-pr/p1/2011/2011-12-10/html/notice-avis-eng.html#d101
9. Pourshahid, A., Richards, G., Amyot, D.: Toward a Goal-Oriented, Business Intelligence Decision-Making Framework. In: Babin, G., Stanoevska-Slabeva, K., Kropf, P. (eds.) MCETECH 2011. LNBIP, vol. 78, pp. 100–115. Springer, Heidelberg (2011)
10. Ali, R., Dalpiaz, F., Giorgini, P.: A Goal-based Framework for Contextual Requirements Modeling and Analysis. Requirements Engineering Journal 15, 439–458 (2010)
11. Lapouchnian, A., Mylopoulos, J.: Modeling Domain Variability in Requirements Engineering with Contexts. In: Laender, A.H.F., Castano, S., Dayal, U., Casati, F., de Oliveira, J.P.M. (eds.) ER 2009. LNCS, vol. 5829, pp. 115–130. Springer, Heidelberg (2009)
12. Lapouchnian, A., Mylopoulos, J.: Capturing Contextual Variability in i* Models. In: Proc. iStar 2011, vol. 766, pp. 96–101. CEUR-WS.org (2011), http://ceur-ws.org/Vol-766/paper17.pdf
13. Borba, C., Silva, C.: A Comparison of Goal-Oriented Approaches to Model Software Product Lines Variability. In: Heuser, C.A., Pernul, G. (eds.) ER 2009. LNCS, vol. 5833, pp. 244–253. Springer, Heidelberg (2009)

14. Silva, C., Borba, C., Castro, J.: A goal oriented approach to identify and configure feature models for software product lines. In: 14th Workshop on Requirements Engineering, WER 2011 (2011)

15. Yu, Y., Leite, J.C.S.P., Lapouchnian, A., Mylopoulos, J.: Configuring features with stakeholder goals. In: Symposium on Applied Computing, SAC 2008, pp. 645–649. ACM Press (2008)

16. Mussbacher, G., Araújo, J., Moreira, A., Amyot, D.: AoURN-based Modeling and Analysis of Software Product Lines. Software Quality Journal 20(3-4), 645–687 (2012)

17. Amyot, D., Shamsaei, A., Kealey, J., Tremblay, E., Miga, A., Mussbacher, G., Alhaj, M., Tawhid, R., Braun, E., Cartwright, N.: Towards Advanced Goal Model Analysis with jUCMNav. In: Castano, S., Vassiliadis, P., Lakshmanan, L.V.S., Lee, M.L. (eds.) ER 2012 2012 Workshops. LNCS, vol. 7518, pp. 201–210. Springer, Heidelberg (2012)

Appendix A   Well-Formedness Constraints

This appendix formalizes in OCL the well-formedness constraints of the URN measured compliance profile introduced in section 4. These constraints are available in the jUCMNav tool and make use of jUCMNav's library of predefined OCL functions. Note that Constraint 9 functions as a query and that Constraint 10 is meant to be checked on a model where a GRL strategy is evaluated.

Constraint 1. Contributions to an intentional element must not sum up to a value higher than 100 (Reason: ensures that *all* contributing elements must evaluate to 100 for this intentional element to be fully satisfied).

```
context grl::IntentionalElement
inv GRLincomingContributionsNotMoreThan100:
  self.linksDest
    -> select(link | link.oclIsTypeOf(grl::Contribution))
    -> collect(link | link.oclAsType(grl::Contribution))
    .quantitativeContribution
    -> sum() <= 100
```

Constraint 2. A GRL resource with a ST_CONDITIONTYPE metadata must be a dependee of an intentional element (Reason: ensures that conditions are used as specified by the measured compliance profile). Note: the jUCMNav metamodel uses the term Ressource rather than Resource.

```
context grl::IntentionalElement
inv GRLconditionDependeeOfIE:
  (self.type=IntentionalElementType::Ressource and
    self.hasMetadata('ST_CONDITIONTYPE'))
  implies
  self.linksSrc
    -> select(link | link.oclIsTypeOf(grl::Dependency))
    -> collect(link | link.oclAsType(grl::Dependency)).dest
    -> select(le | le.oclIsTypeOf(grl::IntentionalElement))
    -> size() > 0
```

Constraint 3. ST_CLASSTYPE stereotypes cannot be used on actors (Reason: ensures that this stereotype is used as specified by the measured compliance profile).

```
context grl::Actor
inv GRLactorNoCLASSTYPE:
  not(self.hasMetadata('ST_CLASSTYPE'))
```

Constraint 4. A GRL resource with a ST_CONDITIONTYPE stereotype cannot depend on anything else (Reason: ensures that conditions are used as specified by the measured compliance profile).

```
context grl::IntentionalElement
inv GRLconditionNotADepender:
  (self.type=IntentionalElementType::Ressource and
    self.hasMetadata('ST_CONDITIONTYPE'))
  implies
  self.linksDest
    -> select(link | link.oclIsTypeOf(grl::Dependency))
    -> isEmpty()
```

Constraint 5. ST_CONDITIONTYPE stereotypes can only be used on resources (Reason: ensures that stereotypes are used as specified by the measured compliance profile).

```
context grl::IntentionalElement
inv GRLresourceOnlyHasCONDITIONTYPE:
  not((self.type=IntentionalElementType::Ressource))
  implies
  not(self.hasMetadata('ST_CONDITIONTYPE'))
```

Constraint 6. ST_CLASSTYPE stereotypes cannot be used on resources (Reason: ensures that stereotypes are used as specified by the measured compliance profile).

```
context ggrl::IntentionalElement
inv GRLresourceNoCLASSTYPE:
  (self.type=IntentionalElementType::Ressource)
  implies
  not(self.hasMetadata('ST_CLASSTYPE'))
```

Constraint 7. Goals should have a hyperlink (violations shown as warnings only) (Reason: ensures that the source legislative documents are accessible from the GRL model). Note: this does not ensure that the specified hyperlink is valid.

```
context grl::IntentionalElement
inv GRLgoalsWithHyperlinks:
  self.type=IntentionalElementType::Goal
  implies
  self.hasMetadata('hyperlink')
```

Constraint 8. Goals should have a reference to the source legislative document (violations shown as warnings only) (Reason: ensures that there is a name that can be queried by Constraint 9). Note: this does not ensure that the specified name is valid.

```
context grl::IntentionalElement
inv GRLgoalsWithReferences:
  self.type=IntentionalElementType::Goal
  implies
  self.hasMetadata('RegDocRef')
```

Constraint 9. Functions as a query: finds goals where the reference metadata equals RuleName (shown as warnings only). Note: RuleName is a parameter here and can be substituted with any name. (Reason: ensures that the GRL model can be queried for elements traceable from a specific part of a legislative document as specified by RuleName.)

```
context grl::IntentionalElementRef
inv GRLqueryRegDocRefName:
  not(getDef().getMetadata('RegDocRef') = 'RuleName'
    and
    getDef().type=IntentionalElementType::Goal)
```

Constraint 10. Non-compliance: goal evaluated below the -25 threshold (violations shown as warnings only). Note: the -25 value is a default threshold but could be set to a different value by the analyst. (Reason: this constraint highlights regulation goals against which the organization performs poorly.)

```
context grl::IntentionalElementRef
inv GRLregulationGoalNotSatisfied:
  getDef().type=IntentionalElementType::Goal
  implies
  getDef().getNumEval() > -25
```

Real-Time Tasks in SDL

Dennis Christmann and Reinhard Gotzhein

Networked Systems Group
University of Kaiserslautern, Germany
{christma,gotzhein}@cs.uni-kl.de

Abstract. SDL is a formal design language for distributed systems that is also promoted for real-time systems. To improve its real-time expressiveness, several language extensions have been proposed. In this work, we present an extension of SDL to specify *real-time tasks*, a concept used in real-time systems to structure and schedule execution. We model a real-time task in SDL as a hierarchical order of executions of SDL transitions, which may span different SDL processes. Real-time tasks are selected for execution using time-triggered and priority-based scheduling. We formally define real-time tasks, show their syntactical and semantical incorporation in SDL, present the implementation approach in our SDL tool chain, and provide excerpts of a complex MAC protocol showing the use of real-time tasks in SDL.

1 Introduction

The Specification and Description Language (SDL) [1] is a formal design language for distributed systems. It has matured and been applied in industry for several decades. SDL is also promoted for real-time systems. By its notion of time (**now**) and its timer mechanism, SDL provides significant, yet limited real-time expressiveness. Some real-time extensions have been defined as part of a dialect called SDL-Real-Time (SDL-RT) [2], and there is also tool support for tight integration of code generated from SDL specifications with existing real-time operating systems [3,4]. In this paper, we revisit the design of real-time systems with SDL and propose an extension to specify real-time tasks.

A real-time system is a reactive system in which the correctness of the system behavior depends on the correct ordering of events and their occurrence in time (see, e.g., [5]). Execution of real-time systems is usually decomposed into execution units called *real-time tasks* (or *tasks*[1] for short), which are scheduled according to their urgency. Tasks may be initiated when a significant change of state occurs (event-triggered) or at determined points in time (time-triggered). For predictable timing, it is important to determine worst case execution times (WCETs) of tasks.

Following Kopetz [5], a task is a sequential code unit executed under the control of the local operating system. In SDL, a code unit could be associated with

---

[1] Not to be confused with tasks, i.e., (sequences of) statements, in SDL.

Ø. Haugen, R. Reed, and R. Gotzhein (Eds.): SAM 2012, LNCS 7744, pp. 53–71, 2013.
© Springer-Verlag Berlin Heidelberg 2013

an SDL transition. Correspondingly, an execution unit could be defined as SDL transition that is executed by an SDL engine. However, this is not sufficient for the general concept of real-time tasks in SDL, because system functionalities are often not performed sequentially by a single execution unit but are distributed across several SDL transitions. Hence, we adopt a more general concept of task in this paper: A *real-time task* has one defined starting transition execution and may then fork one to many subsequent and/or concurrent transition executions recursively. Formally, this concept is captured by a hierarchical order of transition executions. SDL transition executions can be associated with one or more SDL processes; hierarchical execution ordering can be achieved by exchanging SDL signals. Note that this allows the same SDL transition to be executed as part of different tasks, a degree of freedom that we consider as crucial. Real-time tasks may be triggered by time or by events, and have a scheduling priority, which determines the local order of execution units if several tasks are active at the same time. Time-triggered execution could be specified with SDL timers.

In our previous work, we have identified ways to augment SDL's real-time capabilities. In particular, we have proposed the following extensions supporting restricted forms of real-time tasks:

- In [6], we have introduced the concept of *SDL real-time signal*, which is an SDL signal for which an arrival time is specified when the signal is sent. The signal is transferred to its destination as usual, and appended to its input queue. However, consumption of the signal is postponed until the specified arrival time. The concept of real-time signals has been adopted in SDL-2010 [1] by adding activation delays to signal outputs. Beside SDL timers, real-time signals state a second way to activate time-triggered tasks in SDL.
- In [7], we have proposed *SDL process priorities* combined with a mechanism to suspend and resume SDL processes, with the objective to achieve short or even predictable reaction delays. In our experiments, we have shown that reaction delays of SDL processes can be substantially shortened. However, this does not reflect the general structure of tasks, which may span several SDL processes and/or share common SDL transitions. Therefore, process-based scheduling of SDL systems is not sufficient for many real-time systems.

In general, real-time tasks enhance SDL specifications by providing information on the dynamics at the system's runtime. Thus, they go beyond existing scheduling approaches that are based on static components like SDL transitions or SDL processes [7,8]: First, by grouping – possibly process-spanning – functionalities, real-time tasks are a structural concept that is orthogonal to SDL systems, and are not limited to a 1:1-correspondence between task and SDL transition. Consider, for instance, an SDL process realizing a communication protocol entity. Obviously, transitions of this process can be executed to transfer messages of different applications, thereby belonging to different tasks. Second, tasks have a scheduling priority, which is not supported in SDL and can also not be emulated by existing scheduling extensions, because they all rely on static system structures without comprehension of dynamic, distributed, and transition-sharing functionalities.

In this paper, we incorporate the general concept of real-time task into SDL. More specifically, we formally define SDL real-time tasks, and outline required syntactical and semantical extensions in Sect. 2. In Sect. 3, we discuss how they can be implemented in our SDL tool chain, consisting of SDL compiler, SDL runtime environment, and environment interfacing routines. In Sect. 4, we show excerpts of a complex MAC protocol to demonstrate the use of SDL real-time tasks. Section 5 surveys related work. Finally, Sect. 6 presents our conclusions.

2   Real-Time Tasks in SDL

In this section, we introduce the concept of real-time tasks in SDL, thereby providing a „language tool" to group functionally related behavior. Particularly, we argue for a transition-spanning notion of real-time task and for the scheduling of these tasks according to their urgency. We formally define real-time tasks (Sect. 2.1), incorporate them in SDL (Sect. 2.2), and present the required extensions of the SDL syntax (Sect. 2.3). Corresponding modifications of the formal SDL semantics can be found in the Appendix.

2.1   Formalization of Real-Time Tasks in SDL

We formalize real-time tasks in SDL by associating a set of transition executions with each task, and by defining a hierarchical order between them. This means in particular that an SDL real-time task has a starting point, which is the first transition execution, and may then spawn further transition executions in an iterative way. Furthermore, transition executions that are not ordered may occur concurrently. A transition may be executed several times as part of the same task. The same transition can also be executed by several tasks (transition sharing). An SDL real-time task terminates as soon as all transition executions have terminated. The set of transition executions is determined at runtime, depending, e.g., on the states of SDL processes.

Definition 1. *A real-time task τ is a tuple $(\tau_{id}, T_e(\tau), f_{prio}, <_{eo})$, where τ_{id} is a unique task id, $T_e(\tau)$ is the set of transition executions, $f_{prio} : T_e(\tau) \to \mathbb{N}$ is a function assigning a priority to each transition execution, and $<_{eo} \subsetneq T_e(\tau) \times T_e(\tau)$ is an execution order, which is a hierarchical order on $T_e(\tau)$:*

- *$<_{eo}$ is irreflexive, transitive, and antisymmetrical*
- *$\exists t_e \in T_e(\tau).\forall t'_e \in T_e(\tau).(t'_e \neq t_e \Rightarrow t_e <_{eo} t'_e)$, i.e. there is a smallest element defining the starting point of the task, which is the first transition execution.*

Note that the definition of real-time tasks allows the execution of particular sub tasks with different priorities. In SDL, transitions can only be executed if all firing conditions (process state, input signal, enabling condition) are satisfied. This means that even if all transition executions preceding an execution t_e have occurred, t_e may still be delayed. Also, the signal triggering t_e may be discarded as result of an implicit transition in a different state. So, to achieve sufficiently

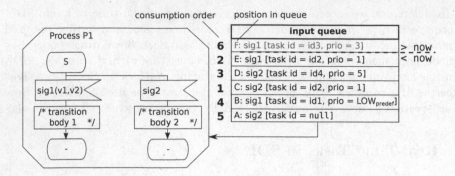

Fig. 1. Implications of real-time tasks to the selection of transitions

predictable execution times of real-time tasks, additional considerations at design time are required.

We furthermore classify real-time tasks regarding their activation paradigm.

Definition 2. *A real-time task is time-triggered, if the first transition is either triggered by a timer instance or by a signal with given activation delay. Otherwise, it is event-triggered.*

Note that an event-triggered SDL task may have time-triggered transition executions by using signals with activation delays or SDL timers.

2.2   Incorporation of Real-Time Tasks in SDL

To incorporate real-time tasks in SDL, we dynamically associate transition executions with task attributes consisting of task ids and task priorities. Thereby, the same SDL transition may be executed in several tasks, and be scheduled with different priorities. Furthermore, we introduce task signals, which extend plain SDL signals and SDL timer signals by task attributes. When consuming a signal, the signal's task attributes are assigned to the execution of the corresponding transition, thereby running the transition in the context of that task. Thus, task signals are used both to trigger task executions and to dynamically associate transitions and tasks at runtime.

Figure 1 shows an example with two transitions of an SDL process P1 and the current state of its input queue. The input queue holds five task signals and one plain SDL signal without associated SDL task. As in standard SDL, the signals have been inserted in FIFO order according to their availability time. This order is illustrated by using the characters from A (lowest availability time) to F (highest availability time). When determining the consumption order of the signals, their task attributes are additionally evaluated. In the absence of task signals, SDL signals are consumed as in standard SDL. Thereby, the extensions are compatible to the standard. If task signals are available, they have preference over plain SDL signals and are consumed according to their task priority. The resulting order of the example is given by numbers 1 to 6 in Fig. 1.

Because task signals are preferential, sig2 at position A is not consumed first. Instead, sig2 at position C with task id id2 is taken to trigger the first transition execution, since it is the first signal in the input queue with highest task priority (lowest integer value). Afterwards, signal sig1 at position E is consumed, which has the highest remaining task priority. According to the task priority, the next signal would be sig1 at position F, which is, however, ignored, because the transition execution is time-triggered and the signal's availability time is larger than the current system time. Instead, sig2 at position D, the first task signal with the next higher task priority, is consumed. The fourth signal is sig1 at position B, which has the lowest possible task priority that is assigned if no task priority is defined explicitly (see also Sect. 2.3). Now, sig2 at position A is consumed, because there is no available task signal left. Finally, sig1 at position F is removed from queue as soon as it becomes available.

With real-time tasks, the language expressiveness of SDL is improved. In particular, we point out that it is not possible to map real-time tasks and task priorities to SDL-2000 [9], or to SDL-2010 [1], which introduces signal priorities and multi-level priority inputs. First, there is no equivalent notion of real-time task in standard SDL, i.e. sets of signals and transition executions can not be grouped and assigned to a specific functionality. Second, there are no mechanisms to let a transition creating signals define the signals' urgencies and to adequately influence their consumption order at the receiver. Signal priorities are not sufficient for this, because they do not take precedence over the signals' availability time. With priority inputs, on the other hand, the state of the receiver and not the urgency of the signal defines the consumption order. Hence, it is, for instance, not possible with standard SDL to achieve the same transition execution order as in Fig. 1, because standard SDL consumes signals of the same type always according to their position in the input queue.

2.3 Syntactical Extensions of SDL

Implications of real-time tasks to the consumption order of signals require several semantical extensions (see Appendix). To create real-time tasks, extensions of the SDL syntax become necessary as well. These modifications are given in List. 1.1 and are based on the syntax in Z.101 (Basic SDL) of SDL-2010 [10].

To control real-time tasks, we introduce task actions with new keywords **new-Task** and **contTask** (line 4 in List. 1.1). Both can be optionally specified when signals are created, i.e. in output and set actions (lines 1 and 2). Specifying **newTask** denotes a *task creation* and using **contTask** causes a *task forking*, which continues an existing task. The created/continued task is associated with the generated signal, which has the role of a task trigger. The task is activated (**newTask**) or continued (**contTask**) as soon as the signal is consumed. If the signal has an activation delay or is a timer instance, the execution of the consuming transition is time-triggered; otherwise, it is event-triggered. Task actions can be specified with attributes task id and task priority (line 5). The task id is a unique value of type **Tid** (line 6), a new type comparable to the SDL type **Pid**, and is only allowed in combination with **contTask**. By forking a task by

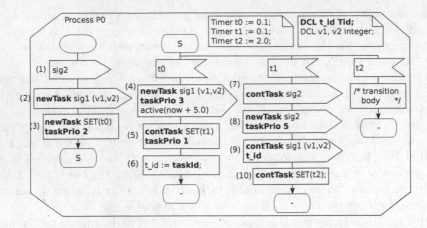

Fig. 2. Example of the usage of tasks in SDL

using **contTask** with a task id, the continuation of the task with the given task id is triggered. If **contTask** is used without task id, the task associated with the executed transition is continued. The specification of a task priority (line 7) is optional. Higher priority values mean lower task priority. If a new task is created without explicit specification of a task priority, the system assigns the predefined lowest priority (denoted as LOW_{predef} in Fig. 1). If **contTask** is used without priority, the task is continued with the same priority. Using **contTask** with priority sets the priority of the corresponding transition execution. Finally, **taskId** is a function returning the task id of the current task, which is **null** if the executed transition is not associated with a task. It can be used in *task assignments* to store the id of an existing task in a variable of type **Tid**.

```
1 <output body item> ::=  [<task action >] <signal identifier>
     [<actual parameters >] [<task parameters >] [<activation
     delay >] [<signal priority >]
2 <set statement> ::=  [<task action >] set <set body> [<task
     parameters >]
3
4 <task action >  ::=  newTask | contTask
5 <task parameters> ::= [<task id >] [<task priority >]
6 <task id> ::= < tid expression0>
7 <task priority > ::= taskPrio < Natural expression>
8
9 <imperative expression> ::= <now expression> | .... | <tid
     expression>
10 <tid expression>  ::=  taskId
```

Listing 1.1. Changes of the concrete SDL syntax (SDL signals and timers).

Figure 2 shows the application of the syntactical extensions in an SDL process P0. The SDL process is specified to generate the input queue of P1 in Fig. 1. Distributed over four transitions, there are four task creations, four task forkings,

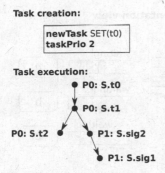

Task creation:

> newTask SET(t0)
> taskPrio 2

Task execution:

- P0: S.t0
- P0: S.t1
- P0: S.t2   P1: S.sig2
- P1: S.sig1

Fig. 3. Example of task creation and execution.

and one regular signal output, showing various ways to apply SDL tasks in a complex synthetic example: At (2), a task is created with the pre-defined lowest priority. The task created with an SDL timer at (3) is defined with priority 2 and is started with the transition consuming t0 in S. This task is continued at (5) by setting another timer t1. At (4), a new task is created by a signal output with activation delay, thereby starting a time-triggered task in P1 remotely. The task assignment at (6) stores the identifier of the task dynamically associated with the execution of the current transition in variable t_id to be used in later transitions. The task executing the transition consuming t1 is continued in (7) and (10) by using **contTask** without task id.

At (9), the same task is continued by using the task identifier explicitly. As an example, Fig. 3 illustrates the resulting hierarchy of transition executions caused by the task creation at (3).

3   Implementation Aspects

Currently, we are in the process of completing the implementation of real-time tasks in our SDL tool chain. This section presents our implementation approach, and addresses implications of real-time tasks on transition scheduling.

3.1   Required Changes of the SDL Tool Chain and Limitations

Our SDL tool chain consists of the code generator *ConTraST* [11], the SDL Virtual Machine (SVM) implementation *SdlRE*, and the *SDL Environment Framework* (SEnF). It is compatible with the model-driven development approach [12] allowing automatic transformations of SDL specifications to platform-specific object files that can be deployed to various hardware platforms. We are currently supporting the Imote2 platform [13], Linux/PC, and various network simulators.

For the specification of SDL, we use the graphical editor of IBM's Rational SDL Suite [4]. To be compatible and to continue using its syntax and semantics analysis tool, we incorporate real-time tasks as annotations. These formal SDL comments are preserved when exporting to SDL/PR files.

By extending ConTraST, the annotations are considered during the transformation of SDL/PR to C++. In particular, actions for task creation and forking have to be attached to the corresponding signals when generating code of output and timer activation statements. Further extensions are required for SdlRE to generate unique task ids and to associate task attributes with SDL signals and transitions. Additionally, the selection of transitions has to be adapted according to the extended SDL semantics. We are furthermore going to change the scheduler of SdlRE to enforce task priorities system-wide (see Sect. 3.2).

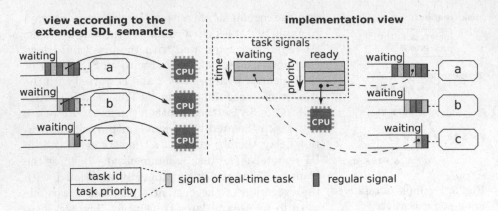

Fig. 4. Comparison of SDL's execution model and the implementation's model

In general, an implementation of real-time tasks has to face the challenge of an unbounded task id domain as introduced by the extended formal semantics. We overcome this problem by taking task ids from a *large* id pool and by reusing them from time to time. Though this is a limitation in theory, we expect that it has no practical relevance.

3.2 Scheduling of Real-Time Tasks

According to the semantics of SDL [14], all agents – SDL agents, SDL agent sets, and link agents – are executed concurrently. However, implementing SDL on real hardware requires serialization of agents. This serialization order is determined by a scheduler, which is in our tool chain part of SdlRE. The only scheduling constraint according to the SDL semantics is that every agent is eventually selected for execution. For real-time systems, this is not sufficient, as urgencies of transitions have to be taken into account.

With priorities of real-time tasks as introduced in Sect. 2, SDL has been extended to privilege important signals of a single agent. However, real-time tasks so far do not affect the global execution order of agents, because they are based on the same concurrent execution model of SDL. Dealing with task priorities system-wide is therefore left to the scheduler of the implementation.

In the left part of Fig. 4, execution according to the extended SDL semantics is illustrated. It is compared to the execution model of our implementation under development. According to the SDL semantics, every agent has its own input queue – separated into available signals and waiting signals – and processing unit. Though all agents consider task signals first and privilege available signals with highest task priority, the selection and execution of transitions of different agents is still independent of each other. In contrast, the implementation view on the right-hand side includes global queues of task signals to privilege the available signal with the highest task priority for execution on a single CPU. There are two queues of task signals: The *waiting queue* contains all signals with an arrival time larger than now, e.g., non-expired timers, and is sorted by the availability time. All available task signals are in the *ready queue*, which is sorted by priority. The scheduler first searches for consumable task signals in the ready queue and selects the signal with the highest priority. If there is no such signal, an arbitrary agent is chosen to process non-task signals according to the standard SDL semantics.

Currently, the SdlRE scheduler only supports non-preemptive strategies. However, this is a design decision of our implementation and no general implication of SDL real-time tasks. Nevertheless, missing preemption may result in large queueing delays of signals with high task priority in the presence of long-running transitions. A way to deal with this problem is the temporary suspension of scheduling entities with low priorities. In [7], we have applied this idea to low-priority agents, thereby decreasing reaction times of single transitions significantly. By borrowing this approach to the scheduling of real-time tasks and by suspending real-time tasks based on task ids and priorities, reaction times of urgent real-time tasks that may consist of several transitions can be reduced.

4   Use of Real-Time Tasks in MacZ

This section illustrates the application of real-time tasks in the MAC layer protocol MacZ [15]. MacZ is a quality-of-service MAC protocol for wireless sensor networks providing tick and time synchronization, medium slotting, contention- and reservation-based medium access, and duty cycling.

Figure 5 presents a simplified excerpt of the architecture of MacZ's service layer. Processes in block ContTxRx are responsible for the contention-based transmission of data frames, i.e. they perform Carrier Sensing Multiple Access with Collision Avoidance (CSMA/CA; process csma) and maintain a Network Allocation Vector (process nav). In the block ResTxRx, reservation-based transmissions are processed. Depending on the synchronization (signal Tick), process ctrl in block Controller activates the transmission components in pre-configured slot regions by sending Enable signals. In addition to the service layer, Fig. 5 contains a single service user in block ServiceUser that is connected to the reservation-based transmission component.

To demonstrate how real-time tasks are used to improve the real-time behavior of MacZ, we specify two tasks. Task 1 is the activation of the contention-based component in the corresponding slot region. Task 2 shows the reservation-based transmission of sensor values.

Figure 6 shows the transitions executed during Task 1. The task consists of four transition executions and spans the processes ctrl, contTxRx, and csma. Its creation is triggered in ctrl when a synchronization tick is consumed. In this transition, there are two signal outputs, both starting a new task with priority 0 by sending Enable signals to resTxRx and contTxRx, respectively[2]. Both signals have two parameters stating the start and end time of the corresponding slot

---

[2] For simplicity, we assume that there is only one contention- and one reservation-based slot region. However, this is no general limitation of MacZ.

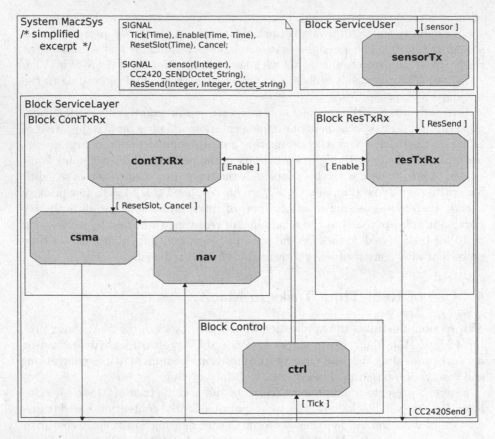

Fig. 5. Simplified excerpt of the SDL specification of MacZ with an example service user

region. In addition, the activation delay as introduced in SDL-2010 [10] is used to delay the signals' consumption to the start time of the slot region. The tasks are specified with highest priority, because slot region borders must be met accurately.

The relevant signal of Task 1 is the Enable signal to contTxRx. When the signal is consumed, task execution is started. In the transition consuming the signal, the associated real-time task is continued by sending a ResetSlot signal to the process csma, and by setting the Disable timer to the end of the slot region. Because no new task priority is given, the task priority remains 0. When csma receives ResetSlot, the start time of the slot region, which is required for slotted CSMA/CA, is set.

The real-time task is continued after expiration of the Disable timer in contTxRx. In the transition consuming the timer signal, it is checked whether there is a pending send job. If this is the case, the task is continued by sending a Cancel signal to csma, thereby stopping the transmission attempt in csma (not

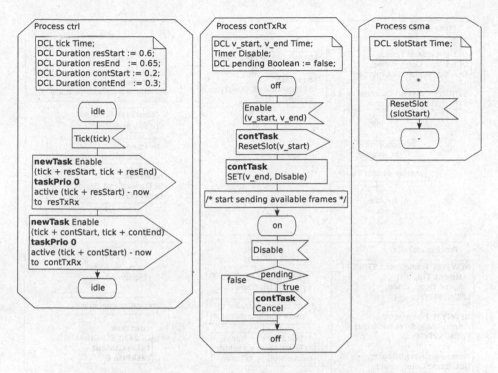

Fig. 6. Task 1: Activation of contention-based slot region

shown in figure). The task terminates as soon as its transition executions are finished, and there are no signals associated with the task.

Task 2 is illustrated in Fig. 7 and involves processes `sensorTx` and `resTxRx`. In process `sensorTx`, the task is created periodically by setting the timer `SendT` with task priority 3. This priority is sufficient, because we assume that the transmission of sensor values is not time-critical in the scenario, and that they are transmitted in the next reservation cycle if they do not arrive at the reservation-based transmission component in time. When consuming the `SendT` signal, the task is started and continued by sending a `ResSend` signal containing the destination's node id, a slot number[3], and the sensor data.

In the example, we assume that process `resTxRx` is not active (state `off`) when receiving `ResSend`, i.e. we are currently not within a reservation-based slot region. Thus, the MAC frame is prepared for transmission and placed in a local queue to be transmitted in the reserved slot. In addition, we keep the id of the task executing the transition by using the `taskId` literal. The task is continued when the reserved transmission slot is reached, which is indicated by the expiry of the `SendNext` timer. In the example, we assume that `SendNext` has been set by another task. In the transition, a `CC2420_SEND` signal continues the task by using the previous task id. In addition, the priority of the task is changed to the highest priority 0 to ensure that the frame transmission hits its slot boundary.

---

[3] In the example, we ignore that this is usually done using a reservation protocol.

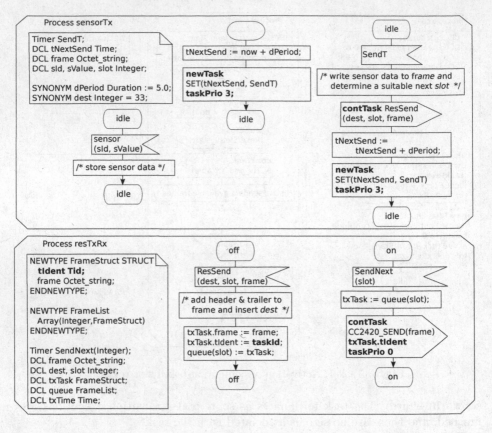

Fig. 7. Task 2: Reservation-based transmission of sensor values

5 Related Work

To the best of our knowledge, the concept of SDL real-time tasks as introduced in Sect. 2 has not been considered in the literature before. However, real-time tasks contain two aspects with existing related work: First, they influence the execution order of SDL transitions. We survey this aspect by looking at the activity thread model and at transition scheduling in SDL systems. Second, real-time tasks identify process-spanning functionalities, which we outline afterwards.

Activity Thread Model. An efficient way to implement node-internal signal transfer is the mapping onto method calls [16,17,18,19]. This approach is different from communication in SDL, since it is synchronous and blocking, and mixes communication and scheduling/execution of transitions [19]. However, in some circumstances, it is a simple, efficient, and standard-compliant way of implementing SDL.

In [16,17], the mapping of SDL onto the activity thread model is discussed. In an activity thread implementation, every input signal is realized by a corresponding procedure, i.e. a series of transitions leads to nested procedure calls. They are also common in manual protocol implementations for up- and downward communication in protocol stacks [20]. Similar to real-time tasks, activity threads state a special paradigm of event-driven implementation, in which not SDL processes but signals are treated as active entities.

Though an activity thread implementation is very efficient, it has several drawbacks. A main shortcoming is their limited applicability to systems with cyclic signal flows [18], which is partially solved in [16,17] by reordering output statements within transitions at compile time. However, several situations remain in which an activity thread implementation would lead to deadlocks or violations of SDL's semantics[4].

Compared to real-time tasks, activity threads do not add language expressiveness to SDL. Their improvements are limited to performance aspects without being capable of preferring urgent SDL transitions at run-time.

Transition Scheduling. According to SDL's semantics, all agents run asynchronously and concurrently that is not realizable on real hardware systems. Here, a scheduler must provide an adequate serialization of system initialization and execution, considering urgencies and priorities where specified.

In [8], Alvarez et al. present a preemptive execution model for SDL. Some details on their implementation are given in [21]. The execution model is based on dynamic process priorities that are derived from fixed transition priorities. One of the authors' objective is a real-time analysis of the system in order to check if the system meets its deadlines. To overcome schedulability problems that may be detected during this process, redesigning heuristics are presented.

The Cmicro integration, which is part of IBM Rational SDL Suite, supports the assignment of signal priorities [4]. By using a global signal queue and sorting signals according to their priority, the Cmicro scheduler selects the transition consuming the signal with highest priority. Thereby, different from SDL-2010 [1], signal priorities in Cmicro take precedence over availability time.

Compared to scheduling based on real-time tasks, process-based scheduling is very limited, because scheduling decisions are based on structural elements and not on functionally related transitions. Though signal priorities seem to be similar to real-time task priorities, they have two disadvantages: First, signal priorities are not sufficient to identify tasks, and therefore are less expressive than real-time tasks. Second, from a scheduling point of view, priorities are not passed on to output signals, i.e. there is no inheritance of priorities, thereby limiting their applicability if transitions are shared by several tasks.

---

[4] To overcome this problem, the authors suggest hybrid implementations, which use the activity thread model as well as the server model, which is a straight-forward implementation of the SDL semantics. By providing a control and specification language called iSDL, the implementor can choose between both models [17].

Design and Analysis Aspects. In [22], Kolloch et al. present a mapping of SDL systems to Real-Time Analysis Models (RTAMs) consisting of several independent analysis task precedence systems, each being triggered by an event. Based on the model, schedulability analysis with the earliest deadline first strategy are performed to the system. The authors' objective is not the improvement of SDL's expressiveness and, hence, they do not introduce the notion of task in SDL. However, the meaning of tasks in an RTAM is similar – yet less generic – to the concept of real-time tasks.

During the requirement phase, identification of system functionalities is often done by means of Message Sequence Charts (MSCs) [23]. Since a real-time task performs a specific system functionality, too, MSCs can be used to visualize them. There is some related work dealing with the automatic transformation of MSCs to SDL. For exmaple, [24] proposes a transformation for early performance predictions. Their approach is very limited – e.g., they do not support states – and the resulting SDL specification is not intended for further reuse. In [25], Khendek and Vincent address the enrichment of an existing SDL specification with new behavior defined by an MSC, e.g., by adding signals and transitions to the system. For this, they present a tool called MSC2SDL, which applies the transformations while preserving the existing behavior. In [26], an algorithm is presented building a complete SDL specification based on (High-level) MSCs and the architecture of the target design.

Though the objective of transformation approaches is completely different (they either want to enable analysis or achieve consistency of MSC and SDL specifications), there is also a similarity with real-time tasks, because in both cases, the SDL system is seen as composition of tasks. In general, such approaches have the disadvantage that they require knowledge of another language and special tool support. Because they are not intended for system implementations, their influence on the run-time behavior is very limited.

6   Conclusions

In this work, we have presented an extension of SDL to formally specify real-time tasks, a concept known from real-time systems. We have defined a real-time task in SDL to be a hierarchical order of executions of SDL transitions, which may span different SDL processes. We have defined syntactical extensions and their semantics, have outlined our implementation approach, and have demonstrated the use of real-time tasks in a complex MAC protocol.

Currently, we are in the process of completing the implementation of real-time tasks in our SDL tool chain. As soon as this is finished, we will run experiments in order to assess the benefits of the extension in terms of shorter and more predictable execution times.

So far, our notion of real-time task is restricted to SDL processes of a single SDL system. For a distributed implementation, an SDL system would typically be split into several interacting SDL systems, which would then be implemented on different nodes and executed under the control of local SVMs. This means that a task may be executed on several nodes, and therefore has to be identified globally. We leave this aspect for our future work.

In our opinion, adding real-time tasks is a significant step towards making SDL a better design language for real-time systems and we are persuaded of SDL tasks being a candidate for inclusion in future SDL standards. Yet, hard real-time systems have further requirements that can still not be met. For instance, the problem of WCETs is an open one, and we feel that it can not be fully addressed in SDL. One reason is that it is not sufficient to consider WCETs of SDL transitions. In addition, the overhead created by running an implementation of the SVM must be considered. This overhead is, for instance, produced by selecting SDL transitions, and difficult to predict. Furthermore, the WCET of a medium priority task can not be predicted without making assumptions on the frequency and WCETs of high priority tasks. Therefore, we believe that another approach is needed, where, for instance, WCETs are measured at runtime to validate real-time requirements. Also, probabilistic WCETs may be an option.

Acknowledgments. This work is supported by the Carl Zeiss Foundation.

References

1. International Telecommunication Union (ITU): Z.100 – Specification and Description Language - Overview of SDL-2010 (2012), http://www.itu.int/rec/T-REC-Z.100-201112-I
2. SDL-RT Consortium: SDL-RT – Specification & Description Language – Real Time V2.2, http://www.sdl-rt.org/standard/V2.2/pdf/SDL-RT.pdf
3. PragmaDev SARL: Real Time Developer Studio, http://www.pragmadev.com/
4. IBM Corp.: Rational SDL Suite, http://www-01.ibm.com/software/awdtools/sdlsuite/
5. Kopetz, H.: Real-Time Systems – Design Principles for Distributed Embedded Applications. Kluwer Academic Publishers (1997)
6. Krämer, M., Braun, T., Christmann, D., Gotzhein, R.: Real-Time Signaling in SDL. In: Ober, I., Ober, I. (eds.) SDL 2011. LNCS, vol. 7083, pp. 186–201. Springer, Heidelberg (2011)
7. Christmann, D., Becker, P., Gotzhein, R.: Priority Scheduling in SDL. In: Ober, I., Ober, I. (eds.) SDL 2011. LNCS, vol. 7083, pp. 202–217. Springer, Heidelberg (2011)
8. Álvarez, J.M., Díaz, M., Llopis, L., Pimentel, E., Troya, J.M.: Integrating Schedulability Analysis and Design Techniques in SDL. Real-Time Systems 24(3), 267–302 (2003)
9. International Telecommunication Union (ITU): Z.100 – Specification and Description Language, SDL (2007), http://www.itu.int/rec/T-REC-Z.100-200711-S
10. International Telecommunication Union (ITU): Z.101 – Specification and Description Language, Basic SDL-2010 (2012), http://www.itu.int/rec/T-REC-Z.101-201112-I
11. Fliege, I., Grammes, R., Weber, C.: ConTraST - A Configurable SDL Transpiler and Runtime Environment. In: Gotzhein, R., Reed, R. (eds.) SAM 2006. LNCS, vol. 4320, pp. 216–228. Springer, Heidelberg (2006)
12. Gotzhein, R.: Model-driven by SDL – Improving the Quality of Networked Systems Development (Invited Paper). In: Proceedings of the 7th International Conference on New Technologies of Distributed Systems (NOTERE 2007), pp. 31–46 (2007), http://vs.cs.uni-kl.de/en/publications/2007/Go07/Go07.pdf

13. MEMSIC Inc.: Data sheet – Imote2 Multimedia, http://www.memsic.com/support/documentation/wireless-sensor-networks/category/7-datasheets.html

14. International Telecommunication Union (ITU): Z.100 Annex F – SDL formal definition (2000), http://www.itu.int/rec/T-REC-Z.100-200011-S!AnnF1, http://www.itu.int/rec/T-REC-Z.100-200011-S!AnnF2, http://www.itu.int/rec/T-REC-Z.100-200011-S!AnnF3

15. Becker, P., Gotzhein, R., Kuhn, T.: MacZ – A Quality-of-Service MAC Layer for Ad-hoc Networks. In: Proceedings of the 7th International Conference on Hybrid Intelligent Systems (HIS 2007), pp. 277–282. IEEE Computer Society (2007)

16. Langendörfer, P., König, H.: Automated Protocol Implementations Based on Activity Threads. In: Proceedings of the Seventh Annual International Conference on Network Protocols (ICNP 1999), pp. 3–10. IEEE Computer Society (1999)

17. König, H., Langendörfer, P., Krumm, H.: Improving the Efficiency of Automated Protocol Implementations Using a Configurable FDT Compiler. Computer Communications 23(12), 1179–1195 (2000)

18. Sanders, R.: Implementing from SDL. Telektronikk 4 (2000), Languages for Telecommunication Applications. Telenor (2000), http://www.telektronikk.com/volumes/pdf/4.2000/Telek4_2000_Page_120-129.pdf

19. Bræk, R., Haugen, Ø.: Engineering Real Time Systems. Prentice Hall (1993)

20. Mitschele-Thiel, A.: Engineering with SDL – Developing Performance-Critical Communication Systems. John Wiley & Sons (2000)

21. Álvarez, J.M., Díaz, M., Llopis, L., Pimentel, E., Troya, J.M.: Deriving Hard Realtime Embedded Systems Implementations Directly from SDL Specifications. In: Proceedings of the Ninth International Symposium on Hardware/Software Codesign (CODES 2001), pp. 128–133. ACM Press (2001)

22. Kolloch, T., Färber, G.: Mapping an Embedded Hard Real-Time Systems SDL Specification to an Analyzable Task Network - A Case Study. In: Müller, F., Bestavros, A. (eds.) LCTES 1998. LNCS, vol. 1474, pp. 156–165. Springer, Heidelberg (1998)

23. International Telecommunication Union (ITU): Z.120 – Message Sequence Chart (MSC) (February 2011), http://www.itu.int/rec/T-REC-Z.120-201102-I/en

24. Dulz, W., Gruhl, S., Lambert, L., Söllner, M.: Early Performance Prediction of SDL/MSC Specified Systems by Automated Synthetic Code Generation. In: SDL 1999: The Next Millennium, pp. 457–472. Elsevier Science (1999)

25. Khendek, F., Vincent, D.: Enriching SDL Specifications with MSCs (2000), http://www.irisa.fr/manifestations/2000/sam2000/PAPERS/P16-Khendek2.ps.gz

26. Khendek, F., Zhang, X.-J.: From MSC to SDL: Overview and an Application to the Autonomous Shuttle Transport System. In: Leue, S., Systä, T.J. (eds.) Scenarios: Models, Transformations and Tools. LNCS, vol. 3466, pp. 228–254. Springer, Heidelberg (2005)

Appendix A.   Semantical Extensions of SDL

To formally incorporate the execution of real-time tasks in SDL, we have modified the dynamic SDL semantics in SDL-2000, Z.100 F3 [14], which is the latest approved version of SDL's formal ASM semantics.

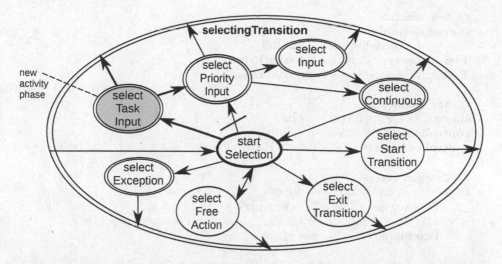

Fig. 8. Extended activity phases of SDL agents when selecting the next transition to be executed [14]: Before searching for transitions of priority inputs, an agent first searches for transitions of task inputs.

Lines 2-5 of List. 1.2 define new ASM domains TID, TASKPRIORITY, and TASKACTION. This is followed by new ASM functions to determine task ids of signal instances and SDL agents, and priorities of tasks. The task id of an agent is initialized with **null** during the initialization of the agent's control block. During a transition, it is set to the task id of the consumed signal. Since this modification is minor, it is not shown in the listing.

Further modifications shown in lines 13-32 apply to output and set actions, which are extended by task action, task id, and task priority. These values are used in the new ASM macro CONFIGTASK (lines 35-50), which sets task id and task priority of signals created in ASM macros SIGNALOUTPUT and EVALTIMER.

An important modification concerns the selection of transitions. Our approach is to give preference to transitions triggered by a signal that is associated with a task. This means that we precede the transition selection phase of Z.100 (sketched in lines 53-68), which considers priority inputs, regular inputs, continuous signals, and spontaneous signals, by *task inputs*. For a given SDL agent, we search the entire input queue of arrived signals in order to determine the first task input with highest task priority, i.e. the active signal with the lowest task priority value. If there is a task input, the selection phase terminates, and the corresponding transition is selected for execution. Otherwise, the selection phase is continued with the priority input selection as described in Z.100 (see also Fig. 8). Thus, transitions associated with real-time tasks always have preference over regular transitions. Also, the extension is compatible with Z.100, as the semantics of SDL systems without real-time tasks remains the same.

```
1   // New domains
2   shared domain TID
3              initially TID = { null }
4   TASKPRIORITY =def NAT ∪ { lowestPriority }
5   TASKACTION =def { newTask, contTask }
6
7   // New functions
8   shared tId : SIGNALINST → TID
9   controlled tId : SDLAGENT → TID
10  controlled taskPriority : TID → TASKPRIORITY
11
12  // Changed tuples
13  OUTPUT =def SIGNAL ×VALUELABEL* ×VALUELABEL ×VIAARG ×
          TASKACTION ×TID ×TASKPRIORITY ×CONTINUELABEL
14  SET =def TIMELABEL ×TIMER ×VALUELABEL* ×TASKACTION ×TID ×
          TASKPRIORITY ×CONTINUELABEL
15
16  // Changed macros regarding ordinary signals
17  SIGNALOUTPUT(s:SIGNAL, vSeq:VALUE*, toArg:TOARG, viaArg:VIAARG,
          taskAction:TASKACTION, taskId:TID, taskPriority:TASKPRIORITY) ≡
18      ...
19          choose g: g ∈ Self.outgates ∧ Applicable(s, TOARG, VIAARG, g,
                 undefined)
20          extend PlainSignalInst with si
21              ...
22              CONFIGTASK(si, taskAction, taskId, taskPriority)
23              INSERT(si, now, g)
24          endextend
25      endchoose
26
27  // Changed macros regarding timers
28  SETTIMER(tm:TIMER, vSeq :VALUE*, t:TIMER, taskAction:TASKACTION, taskId:
          TID, taskPriority:TASKPRIORITY) ≡
29      let tmi = mk–TimerInst(Self.self, tm, vSeq ) in
30          ...
31          CONFIGTASK(tmi, taskAction, taskId, taskPriority)
32      endlet
33
34  // New help macro
35  CONFIGTASK(si:SIGNALINST, taskAction:TASKACTION, taskId:TID, taskPriority:
          TASKPRIORITY) ≡
36      if taskAction = newTask then
37          extend TID with tId
38              si.tId :=tId
39              si.tId.taskPriority :=taskPriority
40          endextend
41      elseif taskAction = contTask then
42          if taskId = null then
43              si.tId :=Self.tId
44          else
```

```
45          si . tId := taskId
46      endif
47      if taskPriority ≠ lowestPriority then
48          si . tId . taskPriority := taskPriority
49      endif
50  endif
51
52 // Sketch of changed macros regarding transition selection
53 AGENTMODE =def { ..., selectTaskInput, ... } // New element added
54
55 SELECTTRANSITIONSTARTPHASE ≡
56      if Self . currentExceptionInst ≠ undefined then
57      ...
58      else
59          Self . inputPortChecked := Self . inport . queue
60          Self . agentMode3 := selectPriorityInput selectTaskInput
61          Self . agentMode4 := startPhase
62      endif
63
64 SELECTTRANSITION ≡
65      ...
66      elseif Self . agentMode3 = selectTaskInput then
67          SELECTTASKINPUT
68      ...
```

Listing 1.2. Changes to the formal semantics of SDL-2000.

Prototyping Domain Specific Languages
as Extensions of a General Purpose Language

Andreas Blunk and Joachim Fischer

Humboldt-Universität zu Berlin
Unter den Linden 6
D-10099 Berlin, Germany
{blunk,fischer}@informatik.hu-berlin.de

Abstract. Domain Specific Languages (DSLs) often consist of general
constructs alongside domain-specific ones. A prominent example is a
state machine consisting of states and transitions as well as expressions
and statements. Adding general concepts to a DSL is a complex and
time-consuming task. We propose an approach to develop such DSLs as
extensions of a General Purpose Language (GPL). We believe that this
approach significantly reduces development times. This is especially important in the first phases of DSL development when language constructs
are evolving and not well conceived. Our development allows trying out
different forms of constructs with an editor to be at hand at all times.
The paper presents first results of the implementation of our approach
on top of Eclipse. The feasibility is shown by applying it to the definition
of state machines as an example DSL.

1   Introduction

General Purpose Languages (GPLs) are designed to be used in many different
application domains. Their language constructs are universally applicable and
not limited to a specific domain. In contrast, Domain Specific Languages (DSLs)
include constructs created for a specific domain.

DSLs are divided into internal and external ones [1]. An internal DSL is
represented within the syntax of a host GPL. Models expressed in the DSL are
valid programs of the host language. They use the host language syntax in a
stylised way for modelling within a given domain. Their advantage is that tools
are already available. However, the representation of models in GPL syntax
hinders their creation and their understanding.

In contrast, external DSLs are represented by a custom syntax. These DSLs
are of special interest to us because models expressed in an external DSL are
easier to create and easier to understand. In addition, DSLs often need to include
general constructs known from GPLs, e.g., expressions and statements. Developing such DSLs is a difficult task today. We propose to tackle this problem by an
approach based on extending a GPL with new domain-specific constructs. These
constructs can be composed of and also used jointly with GPL constructs.

Ø. Haugen, R. Reed, and R. Gotzhein (Eds.): SAM 2012, LNCS 7744, pp. 72–87, 2013.

Our experience shows that the constructs of a DSL are usually not well conceived in the first place. DSLs are created in a number of iterations by talking to domain experts and letting them use the different stages of a DSL. This requires a rapid development process with tools available at all times.

Our approach supports the definition of new syntactic forms for different kinds of GPL constructs. It allows to refer to GPL constructs and to reuse them in DSL constructs. There is instant editor support with syntax checks and content assistance. When an extension definition is written, it is processed at runtime and added to the GPL. The editor instantly supports the syntactic forms of all extensions. We believe that our approach simplifies prototyping DSLs, which make use of general constructs.

In this paper we present the first results of the implementation of our approach. Until now, we have only implemented the possibility of syntactically extending a simple GPL. This GPL we refer to as the Base Language (BL). It includes a reasonably small set of well-known object-oriented language primitives. We plan to describe the semantics of extensions as a mapping to the BL in the future. In this paper, we only describe syntactic extensions of the BL. In this area, we demonstrate a successful application for the definition of a State Machine DSL. This is a neat example because state machines require general constructs like expressions and statements in their definition. A strong point in our approach is that the BL editor is able to provide instant content assistance for extensions. This is an exceptional feature amongst the existing DSL development frameworks. It can result in reduced development times because a DSL can instantly be applied to a problem at hand.

The remainder of the paper is structured as follows. Section 2 presents related approaches and describes their main deficiencies. The BL is introduced in Sect. 3. We summarise its main concepts and describe its definition. These explanations lay the foundation for the extension mechanism presented in Sect. 4. We detail our approach in a general way and give examples for the extension of the BL's syntax. Section 4 concludes with the implementation of an editor capable of instantly supporting extensions. In Sect. 5, we present an example of a definition of a State Machine DSL. The paper concludes in Sect. 6, followed by an outline of future development interests in Sect. 7.

2 Related Work

There are two prevailing groups of approaches to develop external DSLs. One group relies on pre-processor-based extensions to a GPL. These extensions are defined in a separate pre-processor language or in the GPL itself. Their instances are substituted by GPL code before models are executed. Usually, there is insufficient tool support with these approaches. Several representatives are compared with each other in [2].

The other group relies on metamodel-based techniques. Here, the constructs of a GPL are imported into the definition of the abstract or the concrete syntax of a DSL. In a separate step, DSL-aware tools, like an editor, are generated in an automatic way.

In this section we review a selection of each approach's representatives. We describe the general idea of each approach first. After this, we describe each approach's major deficiencies regarding the definition of complex DSLs. These are DSLs whose constructs consist of or refer to other GPL or DSL constructs. An example is a State Machine DSL. It contains a transition construct for defining a transition from one state to another state. Amongst other things, the transition construct consists of action statements (GPL constructs) and a reference to a target state (a DSL construct).

2.1 Pre-processor-Based Approaches

The group of pre-processor based approaches shares a number of deficiencies: (1) there is none or insufficient editor support for extensions, and (2) the syntax extension capabilities are too restrictive for defining more complex DSL constructs. This includes missing description means for defining references between DSL constructs.

The Java Syntactic Extender (JSE) [3] is a pre-processor for the Java programming language. Extensions are limited to a few shapes with partially predefined syntax: function call macros and statement macros. For example, they have to begin with a name and have to end in a predefined way. Extensions can be composed of GPL constructs, but they cannot define references to GPL constructs defined elsewhere. JSE is more powerful compared to the very simplistic macro mechanism in the C language, because the type of GPL construct to be included can be defined, e.g., a for-each statement that is composed of expressions and statements.

Camlp4 [4] is a pre-processor for the multi-paradigm language Ocaml. In contrast to JSE, it performs extensions to GPL transformations by acting on the Ocaml abstract syntax tree (AST). It allows to augment the Ocaml grammar by new rules and to modify or delete existing ones. Because of its AST-based foundation, even extensions of expressions with regard to precedence and associativity are possible. A restriction is imposed by Ocamls type of grammar definition. Extensions have to be parseable by a recursive descent parser.

In the field of simulation modelling, there is a GPL with special simulation constructs called Simulation Language with Extensibility (SLX) [5]. Its extension capabilities are situated on the level of regular expressions. Compared to JSE and Camlp4, SLX is less powerful. The parts of an extension are plain strings, which do not reference GPL constructs. However, there is basic syntax assistance in SLX. The syntax of extensions gets highlighted after each successful compilation step.

2.2 Metamodel-Based Approaches

A prominent representative of the group of metamodel-based approaches is Xtext [6]. In Xtext, DSLs are defined by specifying their constructs in a concrete syntax, which ultimately is an EBNF-like grammar. From this grammar an abstract syntax description in the form of an object-oriented metamodel is derived. The metamodel is used for further processing of DSL instances, e.g., for specifying additional constraints and for defining execution semantics. Another artefact which can be generated from the grammar is a text editor with support for syntax highlighting and content assistance.

Xtext also provides GPL-like constructs in a language called Xbase. Its constructs, e.g. expressions, can be included into a DSL grammar. However, GPL constructs cannot be extended by new ones, e.g. one cannot add a new type of expression useable jointly with all other expressions.

In addition, Xbase is limited to expressions in the form of operators and statements. There are no means for defining functional or structural abstractions. Each DSL which needs to include them has to define them again.

A more powerful approach than Xtext regarding the extension of a GPL is followed by the Meta Programming System (MPS) [7]. In MPS, the definition of a DSL begins with the specification of an abstract syntax in the form of a metamodel. Then for each construct a concrete syntax is defined as a projection to text. In the modelling process one does not write text but instantiates structures defined by the metamodel. These structures are represented in their text form.

As a result, there is no parsing of text necessary. However, the DSL editor is unusual to operate because one cannot enter the single characters forming a certain DSL construct directly. Instead, one has to choose from a set of possible constructs insertable at the current cursor position. After an option is chosen, the fixed textual parts of the construct are expanded and the cursor can be moved from one variable text fragment to the next. For example, when a class is to be added, the first fixed part is the `class` keyword followed by the name of the class as a variable part. Other variable parts are for example super classes and attributes.

In MPS, a GPL called BaseLanguage can be used to extend or to include general constructs into a DSL. Different kinds of GPL constructs can be extended. In addition, defining name-based references to DSL as well as GPL constructs is supported.

Xtext and MPS are able to generate a DSL editor from a DSL description. However, the process of developing a DSL is complex. One has to master an interactive framework in order to define the different aspects of a DSL at the appropriate places. In addition, the editor is not immediately available. Its software has to be generated and compiled first before the editor can be used. The generation step has to be initiated every time the language definition has changed. This manual step hinders rapid prototyping of DSLs.

3   Base Language

The Base Language (BL) is a simplified GPL. It provides a set of object-oriented modelling constructs. The BL allows to solve a problem on a general level first. For similar problems, a library can be developed in the traditional way by using abstractions of the BL. In case other syntactic forms are needed, the BL can be extended. New constructs can be added but existing constructs cannot be changed or deleted. Extensions can add expressiveness but they cannot mutate the BL into something completely different.

We use a subset of the Java programming language as the BL. It has a similar syntax and semantics. The following paragraphs give a short overview of the BL.

3.1 Basic Concepts

The basic modelling concepts are: classes, interfaces, procedures, variables, statements, and expressions. Classes and interfaces are used to define structural and operational parts of objects. Variables of these types have reference semantics. The primitive types are: int, double, boolean, string, and void. Variables of these types have value semantics. There are two collection types: (1) list for ordered and unique collections, and (2) sequence for ordered and non-unique ones. For each of them, a number of list operations is predefined: first-item, last-item, contains-item, index-of-item, item-at-index, before-item, after-item, and size-of-list.

Procedures can be defined in a global way and as methods of classes and interfaces. Variables can be defined global, as attributes of classes, as parameters of procedures, and as local variables inside procedures.

The following kinds of statements exist: local-variable-declaration, assignment, procedure-call, if-then-else, while, for-each, add-to-list, remove-from-list, clear-list, print, and return. There are expressions for logical computation (and, or), number comparisons (greater, less, equals), mathematical computation (e.g. plus, and minus), literals (e.g., 2, true, 3.2, "abc", null), object creation (new), object type related operations (cast, instance-of), element access by punctuation (e.g. xlist.first.getName()), and some predefined element accessors (self and super).

More advanced modelling concepts of Java, e.g., exceptions, threads, packages, and visibility, are not available.

3.2 Syntax Definition

It is important to understand the way the syntax of the BL is defined. This is essential for the definition of extensions, since these are defined by directly referring to constructs defined in the syntax of the BL.

There are two ways to refer to BL constructs. Extensions can add new forms of BL constructs, e.g. they can add a new kind of statement by referring to the BL statement. In addition, extensions can be composed of BL constructs, e.g., a for-statement defined as an extension can be composed of expressions and statements. The next paragraph gives an overview of the techniques used for defining the syntax.

The syntax of the BL consists of an abstract and a concrete syntax. The abstract syntax is defined by an object-oriented metamodel. It consists of classes and attributes. These classes are referred to as metaclasses in order to distinguish them from the classes in a language instance, whose structure they define.

```
extension ExtensionName {
    BaseLanguage_Rule -> Extension_Rule;
    Extension_Rule -> ... ;
    ...
}
```

Listing 1.1. General structure of an extension definition.

As an example, the metaclass `Clazz` defines the possible structure of class definitions in BL models. The metaclass contains attributes like a name and a list of `Variables`. Definitions of BL classes are instances of the metaclass `Clazz`. Each definition assigns specific values to attributes of metaclass instances. For example, the name of a BL class is assigned as a value of the `name` attribute. Attributes defined in a BL class become references to instances of the metaclass `Variable`.

By using metamodels, the structure of language concepts can be defined in an abstract way first. Then, a concrete representation is added by referring to classes and attributes in the metamodel. The metamodel of the BL is defined by using the Eclipse Modeling Framework (EMF) [8]. Its concrete syntax is defined in the Textual Syntax Language (TSL).

TSL is part of the Textual Editing Framework (TEF) [9]. It allows to define a concrete syntax as an attributed EBNF-like grammar. TSL definitions consist of rules, terminals, and non-terminals known from EBNF. In addition, TSL constructs have to be annotated by references to meta-classes and meta-attributes. These annotations define a mapping of the concrete textual representation to an instance of the metamodel.

A LALR parser is generated from a TSL description by using the parser generator RunCC [10] which is able to generate a parser at runtime. Additional code generation (including compilation) is not necessary to invoke the parser on an input stream. The implementation of our approach makes use of this runtime generation feature.

4 Extension Definition

The general structure of an extension definition is shown in Listing 1.1. Extensions can add new constructs, but they cannot redefine or delete existing ones. Hence, the modeller is assured that the basic concepts do not change in their meaning.

4.1 Syntax Definition

The syntax is defined in an attributed BNF-like description language, which is similar to TSL, but has a different syntax. It also provides some semantic additions. This language is named Simple Textual Syntax Language (STSL). It is tightly integrated into the extension concept of the BL.

A syntax definition in STSL consists of a set of rules by which the BL grammar is extended. Since the used parsing technique is LALR, conflicts can arise when adding new rules, e.g., shift/reduce conflicts. These conflicts are reported to the DSL developer, who has to correct them by changing the syntax description.

The first rule in a STSL description is special. It specifies which BL grammar rule (left side) is extended by a new extension rule (right side). The next step is the specification of the parts of this new extension rule and all subsequent rules. Each rule consists of terminals and non-terminals. Terminals can be a fixed sequence of characters or one of the predefined lexical tokens identifier (ID), integer number (INT), and string (STRING). Non-terminals are references to other rules.

In the description of other language aspects, e.g., semantics, the syntactical parts of an extension need to be accessed. Therefore, a mapping of the concrete syntax to an abstract syntax is defined. The mapping is realised in two stages. First, syntax pieces are prefixed by symbolic names, which allows to access their elementary or structured value. Second, a corresponding meta-class is created for each prefixed non-terminal, if one does not already exist. Already existing meta-classes are BL classes like Statement and Expression.

The structure, which is accessible by such a description, is an object tree. The nodes in this tree are the named non-terminals. Each type of non-terminal is an object described by a meta-class. The attribute structure of each such meta-class is defined by all the right-hand sides of rules, which have the same left-hand side. All the named parts on a right-hand side become attributes of the meta-class, which is named by the left-hand side. Attribute values are either references to other object nodes (for non-terminals) or elementary ones (for tokens).

As an example, an excerpt of an extension is shown in Listing 1.2. An A construct begins with the terminal foo (whose value is not accessible). An integer number must follow, which is assigned as value of an attribute named n. After the number, a B construct follows. The structure of B is not accessible. At the end, a C construct must be supplied. The structure of C can be accessed by the name c. From c, one can also navigate to structural parts of C, e.g., c.d refers to another number.

Two new meta-classes are created for the abstract syntax. The meta-class A is created for the rule A. It is defined as a sub-class of the BL rule meta-class BaseRule. A defines the following list of attributes: n of type Integer, s of type String, and c of type C. Note that there is no meta-class created for the non-terminal B because it is not prefixed by an attribute. The other meta-class is C. It defines an attribute d of type Integer.

The class structure derived from such a concrete syntax is an object-oriented description of the abstract syntax. This kind of structure is also known as a metamodel. Usually, a metamodel is the initial artifact in metamodel-based language development. Here, the metamodel is extracted from a concrete syntax description. It is intended to be used as a representation for specifying further processing of extensions, e.g. in the definition of an execution semantics.

```
BaseRule -> A;
A -> "foo" n:INT B c:C ;
B -> s:STRING;
C -> d:INT;
```

Listing 1.2. Excerpt of an example extension.

```
extension For {
    Statement -> ForStm ;
    ForStm -> "for" "(" variable:$Variable "=" value:Expression ";"
        condition:Expression ";" incStm:Assignment ")" "{"
            MultipleStatements
        "}";
    MultipleStatements -> ;
    MultipleStatements -> statements:Statement MultipleStatements;
}
```

Listing 1.3. A for-loop defined as an example extension.

A first realistic example is given in Listing 1.3. The extension defines a for-statement as an additional type of statement. A new same-named meta-class is created for the rule **ForStm**. The **ForStm** meta-class inherits from the meta-class **Statement**. It defines the attributes **variable**, **value**, **condition**, **incStm**, and **statements**. The structure of their values is further described by other meta-classes, e.g., **Variable**, and **Expression**.

The **Variable** non-terminal is notably different. It is prefixed by a dollar sign, which designates the non-terminal as a reference to an already existent object. So in the case of the non-terminal **$Variable**, an identifier referring to the name of an already existent **Variable** object has to be supplied. In case of BL constructs, e.g, variables, and procedures, the identifier can be a single name or a qualified one. Resolution of qualified identifiers is defined for the BL, but it cannot be specified for named extensions. If an extension element needs to be referenced, resolution is done on a global level, i.e., names of extensions have to be globally unique in order to refer to them. Global references are distinguished by using two dollar signs, e.g., **$$Variable** is used to refer to a **Variable** object by a single name only.

4.2   Kinds of Extensions

In this section, we present and discuss the most obvious kinds of extensions that seem to make sense. The discussion is only concerned with syntax here. Limitations of the approach are presented in the subsequent Section.

Statements. A kind of extension which immediately comes to ones mind is the introduction of new statements. For statement extensions, the BL grammar rule **Statement** is extended.

```
extension StateMachine {
   ClassContentExtension -> StateMachine;
   StateMachine -> "stateMachine" name:ID "{" StateListOptional "}";
   ...
}
```

Listing 1.4. Beginning of the definition of a state machine as an extension.

Statement extensions can only be used at certain places where a BL statement is allowed, e.g., in the body of a procedure or in structured statements. They either terminate with a semicolon, e.g., the print statement, or with curly braces, e.g., the while statement. Extensions should follow this style, but they are not forced to. It is possible to define another ending symbol or no ending symbol at all. Nevertheless, conflicts may occur for some combinations.

For example, in an extension with rules `Statement -> S1` and `S1 -> "s1"` `exp:Expression ">"` there is a shift/reduce conflict, because the final symbol > can be a part of an expression as well.

Another characteristic of statements is that they usually start with a keyword. But they can also begin with other kinds of tokens, e.g., with an identifier, an integer number, or an expression. It is also allowed to reuse keywords as long as there is some distinguishable part in the new grammar rule.

For example, the BL includes a for-each statement, which begins with the keyword for. In Listing 1.3, we added a traditional number-based for-loop. This extension is feasible and not in conflict with the for-each statement. Both statements reference a variable after the opening parenthesis of the for keyword. However, the for-each statement is followed by a colon, while the for-loop statement is followed by an equals sign.

Embedded. Extensions with a more declarative nature are those embedded into modules or classes. These are places where classes, variables, and procedures are defined. Extensions embeddable into modules have to extend the rule `Module ContentExtension`. For classes, the rule `ClassContentExtension` has to be extended.

An example for such an extension is the definition of a state machine inside a class, which specifies the behaviour of the objects of that class. The beginning of such an extension is shown in Listing 1.4.

Expressions. Extending expressions is more complicated, because of operator precedence rules. There are 8 priority classes defined in the BL. Table 1 gives an overview of these classes and the grammar rules that they are defined by.

An expression extension begins with a reference to a priority class rule on its left side. The right side is consists of other expression priority classes and terminals.

```
extension PreInc {
    L2Expr -> PreInc;
    PreInc -> "++" left:L1Expr;
}
```

Listing 1.5. Definition of a pre-increment expression.

```
extension Ternary {
    L9Expr -> Ternary;
    Ternary -> cond:L8Expr "?" trueCase:L8Expr ":" falseCase:L9Expr;
}
```

Listing 1.6. Definition of a ternary if-else operator.

As an example, Listing 1.5 shows the definition of the unary operation pre-increment. It has the same priority as an unary plus and an unary minus. Therefore, it extends the rule L2Expr. A same or lower priority expression must be provided on its right side.

Table 1. Operator precedence in BL expressions.

Priority	Operators	Operations	BL rule
1	. ()	member access, procedure call	L1Expr
2	+ - !	unary plus, minus, negation	L2Expr
3	* / %	multiplicative	L3Expr
4	+ -	additive	L4Expr
5	< > <= >= instanceof	relational	L5Expr
6	== !=	equality	L6Expr
7	and	logical and	L7Expr
8	or	logical or	L8Expr

Adding additional priority classes is currently not supported. It would be required to allow the redefinition of existing rules in order to insert a new priority class rule, which is not allowed in this setup. For example, a level 9 priority class is needed for the definition of a ternary if-else operator. It is necessary to redefine the rule Expression -> L8Expr to Expression -> L9Expr and to add the rule L9Expr -> L8Expr. Supporting priority class insertion in future versions should be possible. Then, the ternary if-else operator could be defined as shown in Listing 1.6.

4.3 Limitations

Extensions are limited to certain kinds of BL rules. In the BL grammar there are basically two kinds of rules: (1) *assigned rules*, and (2) *unassigned rules*.

An *assigned rule* is always used in connection with an attribute in some other rule. After an *assigned rule* is successfully parsed, an object of a same-named meta-class is created. This object is assigned to the attribute of another object corresponding to another rule from which the *assigned rule* was called. In contrast, an *unassigned rule* is used without an attribute. It solely defines one or more simple reductions to other rules. Extensions can only be defined for *assigned rules* because the objects created for an extension instance have to be held in an attribute of the abstract syntax graph.

For example in the grammar `A -> b:B C; B -> "b"; C -> "c";`, there is an *assigned rule* named `B` and *unassigned rule* named `C`. An instance of `B` is assigned to the attribute `b` of an `A` object. In contrast, an instance of `C` cannot be assigned to an attribute of an `A` object. So the rule `C` cannot be extended.

Some of the *unassigned rules* are specially prepared for extension. For example, there is the *unassigned rule* `ClassContent`, which is used inside the rule `Clazz`. In order to allow extending the content area of a class, another rule `ClassContentExtension` and a corresponding meta-class are defined. Furthermore, an attribute `extensions` of type `ClassContentExtension` is added to the meta-class `Clazz`.

4.4 Difficulties

A major difficulty results from the use of the Eclipse Modeling Framework (EMF). EMF expects a metamodel to be complete and not changing when instances of its meta-classes are created. The problematic part is the generation of Java code for an EMF metamodel. For each meta-class a corresponding Java class is generated. At runtime, the instances of a metamodel are internally represented as objects of the generated Java classes.

However, in the case of extensions it is complicated to generate and compile these Java classes, and make them useable inside a running Eclipse. As a workaround, the Java class corresponding to an extended BL rule is instantiated instead. For example, in the case of statement extensions, there exists a meta-class as well as a Java class with the name `Statement`. In the workaround, an instance of a statement extension, e.g. the for-loop defined in Listing 1.3, is internally represented as a Java object of type `Statement`. In the next step, the respective meta-class of the Java object is set to the special meta-class of the extension rule. For example, in the case of the for-loop the meta-class is set to `ForStm`. Attributes defined by the extension meta-class are still accessible by using EMF's reflection mechanism. It allows to access an attribute by using generic get and set methods instead of generated ones.

4.5 Editor Implementation

The editor is instantly aware of all defined extensions. An additional software generation step is not needed in order to use the editor. It supports syntax highlighting and content assistance. Its implementation is based on a parser, which is extensible at runtime. Extension definitions are instantly recognised by the BL editor. For each extension, the grammar rules defined by an extension are added to the grammar of the BL. The extended BL editor and its parser continue to work with the extended version of the grammar. When an extension definition is modified, the corresponding rules in the BL grammar are updated as well.

The extensible BL editor is implemented by using the Textual Editing Framework (TEF) and the Eclipse Modeling Framework (EMF) [8]. TEF is used for the definition of the BL concrete syntax and for the BL editor. EMF is used for the definition of a metamodel for the BL, which is required by TEF for describing notations. Implementing an extensible version of TEF is feasible since TEF's implementation is based on a runtime parser generator, called RunCC. It can generate parsers of type LALR at runtime.

5 State Machines as an Example

State machines [11] provide a fair level of abstraction when modelling the behaviour of stateful objects. A DSL for creating state machines provides the necessary modelling constructs in the vocabulary of the domain. In this case, the domain is specifying behaviour in a special way. The major constructs of this domain are states, transitions, and events. In addition, general constructs are necessary for optionally specifying the condition under which an event may take place and for defining actions to be taken when an event occurs. Here, expressions and statements known from GPLs are good abstractions.

State machines are domain-specific in terms of the way they allow to model behaviour. However, they are general-purpose in the sense that they can be used to specify behaviour as a part of modelling in many different domains. For example, they can be used to specify telecommunication protocols as in the Specification and Description Language (SDL) [12]. Another application domain, which we are particularly interested in, is there usage for defining workflows in manufacturing systems.

An example of a simple state machine is depicted in Fig. 1. There are four states: an initial state, the states A and B, and a final state. State transitions take place when events occur. For example, when a Start event occurs in state A, the state machine transitions to state B. For each state transition, actions are specified after the slash symbol /. In addition, a guard condition is defined by placing an expression of type boolean in square brackets [ ] after an event. For example, when a Tick event occurs in state B and the condition i >= 3 is satisified, then the next state will be the final state.

On the one hand, state machines only contain a small set of constructs. On the other hand, they contain general constructs which makes their definition difficult. In SDL, state machines are defined as an external DSL. This way, models can be expressed in a custom syntax which improves understandability. However, handcrafting the necessary tools is very time consuming.

State machines can also be defined as an internal DSL, e.g., as a library or framework in a GPL like Java. The library defines structural and functional

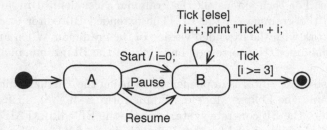

Fig. 1. Example state machine

abstractions which have to be used in a certain way in order to create domain-specific models. The expressiveness of internal DSLs is limited by the abstraction means offered by the underlying GPL. The basic modelling constructs of the GPL cannot be changed. In addition, domain-specific models have to be represented in the syntax of the GPL. This makes understanding the model more difficult as opposed to representations specifically created for a certain domain.

In order to use a state machine framework, one has to know how to apply its structural and functional abstractions in the right way. The state machine itself gets encoded by an unsuitable representation. It is an advantage that an editor is available and that the Java compiler can be used to execute state machines. In addition, Java itself offers necessary general constructs like expressions and statements. However, creating and understanding state machines becomes more complicated.

In our approach, the State Machine DSL is defined as an extension of the BL. In Listing 1.7, the syntax definition of a state machine extension is shown. State machines define the behaviour of stateful objects. Therefore, a good place for their definition is within a class. The definition begins with the keyword `stateMachine` followed by a name, a set of events, and the definition of states. An example for its use is depicted in Fig. 2. The definition of a custom syntax helps creating and understanding state machines. In addition, there is instant editor support.

6   Conclusion

We presented an approach that supports the syntactic extension of a simple GPL by domain-specific constructs. These constructs can be composed of or refer to GPL constructs themselves. Extensions are recognised by the GPL editor, which instantly provides content assistance for them. We believe that such a feature simplifies the development of DSLs and reduces development times in the first phase. In addition, the editor is a usual text editor which can be operated in a familiar way.

```
extension StateMachine {
   ClassContentExtension -> StateMachine;

   StateMachine -> "stateMachine" name:ID "{"
          EventDeclarations initialState:InitialState
             StateListOptional "}";

   EventDeclarations -> "events" ":" EventDeclList ";";
   EventDeclList -> events:EventDecl EventDeclListOptional;
   EventDeclListOptional -> ;
   EventDeclListOptional -> "," EventDeclList;
   EventDecl -> name:ID;

   StateListOptional -> ;
   StateListOptional -> states:Vertex StateListOptional;

   Vertex -> State;
   Vertex -> EndState;

   InitialState -> "initial" "->" target:$$Vertex ";";
   State -> "state" name:ID TransitionsOptional ";";
   EndState -> "end" name:ID ";";

   TransitionsOptional -> ;
   TransitionsOptional -> "(" OutgoingList ")";

   OutgoingList -> outgoing:Transition OutgoingListOptional;
   OutgoingListOptional -> ;
   OutgoingListOptional -> "," OutgoingList;

   Transition -> event:$$EventDecl GuardOptional EffectsOptional
      TargetStateOptional;

   GuardOptional -> ;
   GuardOptional -> "[" condition:Expression "]";

   EffectsOptional -> ;
   EffectsOptional -> "/" effect:Effect;
   Effect -> oneLine:Statement;
   Effect -> multiLine:CodeBlock;
   TargetStateOptional -> ;
   TargetStateOptional -> "->" target:$$Vertex;
}
extension ElseGuardExpr {
   L1Expr -> ElseGuardExpr;
   ElseGuardExpr -> "else";
}
```

Listing 1.7. State Machine DSL defined as BL extension.

```
sml.bl      sml-application.ebl ⊠                                        ▭ ▢
#import "sml"

module sml_application {

    class Counter {
        int i = 0;
        stateMachine CounterBehavior {
            events: Start, Pause, Resume, Tick;

            initial -> A;
            state A (
                Start / i=0; -> B,
                Resume -> B
            );
            state B (
                Tick [i >= 3] -> X,
                Tick [else] / { i=i+1; print "Tick " + i; } -> B,
                Pause -> M
            );                  ↗ X
            end X;              ↗ A
        }                       ↗ B
    }                           </>
                                ⊞ <name>
}
```

Fig. 2. Example state machine.

7   Future Work

Our next step will be to provide a description for the semantics of extensions. We plan to support this by a mapping to the BL. When an extended model is to be executed, extensions are translated to BL constructs first. Then the BL model is translated to an executable target language. Finally, the program in the target language is executed.

Limitations imposed by the semantics have to be investigated as well. We only tested the approach with respect to syntax extensions. This was done for a number of small example extensions including the presented simple State Machine DSL. In future, we plan to conduct a larger case study by applying the approach to a more powerful State Machine DSL. We intend to use this DSL for modelling the behaviour of manufacturing systems. Description means for specifying time passage and state changes based on conditions are necessary modelling constructs to be included.

Another aspect is language composability. It could be possible to combine several DSLs into one. In principle, the extension mechanism supports such modular DSL development. However, further investigation of this aspect is needed.

Beyond that, there is also room for improving the usability of extensions. One such aspect is debugger support. We intend to examine how a DSL-aware debugger can be provided. We already gained experience on automatically deriving DSL debuggers in [13].

An aspect which was not paid much attention to is identifier resolution. When a DSL gets more complex, it may include the concept of a namespace. In this case, DSL constructs cannot be referred to by a globally unique identifier anymore. Instead, identifiers are structured and a context-dependent resolution algorithm has to be described. To our best knowledge, this is always done in a GPL. However, we already identified patterns in these descriptions and we believe that identifier resolution can be described in a more concise way by using an appropriate DSL. We intend to create such a DSL using the extension approach presented in this paper.

References

1. Fowler, M.: Domain-Specific Languages. Addison Wesley (2011)
2. Zingaro, D.: Modern Extensible Languages. Technical report, McMaster University, Hamilton, Ontario, Canada (2007)
3. Bachrach, J., Playford, K.: The Java Syntactic Extender (JSE). In: Proceedings of the 16th ACM SIGPLAN Conference on Object-Oriented Programming, Systems, Languages, and Applications, OOPSLA 2001, pp. 31–42. ACM Press (2001)
4. de Rauglaudre, D.: Camlp4, http://caml.inria.fr/pub/old_caml_site/camlp4
5. Henriksen, J.O.: SLX - The X is for Extensibility. In: Proceedings of the 32nd Conference on Winter Simulation, WSC 2000, vol. 1, pp. 183–190. Society for Computer Simulation International (2000)
6. Xtext: Xtext Documentation, http://www.eclipse.org/Xtext/documentation/
7. JetBrains: Meta Programming System (MPS), http://www.jetbrains.com/mps/
8. EMF: Eclipse Modeling Framework (EMF), http://www.eclipse.org/modeling/emf
9. Scheidgen, M.: Integrating Content Assist into Textual Modelling Editors. In: Modellierung. Lecture Notes in Informatics, vol. 127, pp. 121–131. Gesellschaft fr Informatik E.V. (2008)
10. Ritzberger, F.: RunCC - Java Runtime Compiler Compiler, http://runcc.sourceforge.net/
11. Harel, D.: Statechars - A Visual Formalism for Complex Systems. Science of Computer Programming 8(3), 231–274 (1987)
12. International Telecommunication Union (ITU): Recommendation Z.100, Specification and Description Language - Overview of SDL 2010 (2010), http://www.itu.int/rec/T-REC-Z.100/en
13. Blunk, A., Fischer, J., Sadilek, D.A.: Modelling a Debugger for an Imperative Voice Control Language. In: Reed, R., Bilgic, A., Gotzhein, R. (eds.) SDL 2009. LNCS, vol. 5719, pp. 149–164. Springer, Heidelberg (2009)

Behavioral Fuzzing Operators
for UML Sequence Diagrams

Martin Schneider[1], Jürgen Großmann[1], Nikolay Tcholtchev[1],
Ina Schieferdecker[1], and Andrej Pietschker[2]

[1] Fraunhofer FOKUS, Kaiserin-Augusta-Allee 31, 10589 Berlin, Germany
{martin.schneider,juergen.grossmann,nikolay.tcholtchev,
ina.schieferdecker}@fokus.fraunhofer.de
[2] Giesecke & Devrient GmbH, Prinzregentenstr. 159, 81677 Munich, Germany
andrej.pietschker@gi-de.com

Abstract. Model-based testing is a recognized method for testing the
functionality of a system under test. However, it is not only the functionality of a system that has to be assessed. Also the security aspect has to
be tested, especially for systems that provide interfaces to the Internet.
In order to find vulnerabilities that could be exploited to break into or
to crash a system, fuzzing is an established technique in industry.

Model-based fuzzing complements model-based testing of functionality in order to find vulnerabilities by injecting invalid input data into
the system. While it focuses on invalid input data, we present a complementary approach called behavioral fuzzing. Behavioral fuzzing does not
inject invalid input data but sends an invalid sequence of messages to
the system under test. We start with existing UML sequence diagrams
– e.g. functional test cases – and modify them by applying fuzzing operators in order to generate invalid sequences of messages. We present the
identified fuzzing operators and propose a classification for them. A description of a case study from the ITEA-2 research project DIAMONDS
as well as preliminary results are presented.

Keywords: Model-based Testing, Security Testing, Fuzzing, UML.

1 Introduction

Model-based testing is nowadays a widely used approach for testing the functionality of systems, especially in combination with model-based development.
However, the more parts of our daily lives depend on systems the more important
is that these systems not just only work correctly but also address adequately
various security aspects. The huge number of security incidents shows the great
importance of various security aspects and dimensions such as confidentiality,
integrity and availability of data and systems. In order to find weaknesses that
could be exploited during an attack, fuzzing is an important tool to use. It
is a security testing approach that finds vulnerabilities by injecting invalid input data [1]. It aims at finding deviations in the behavior of the system under

Ø. Haugen, R. Reed, and R. Gotzhein (Eds.): SAM 2012, LNCS 7744, pp. 88–104, 2013.

test (SUT) to its specification which leads to vulnerabilities because invalid input is not rejected but instead processed by the SUT. Such deviations may lead to undefined states of the SUT and can be exploited by an attacker for example to successfully perform a denial-of-service attack because the SUT is crashing or hanging.

The origin of fuzzing dated from Barton Miller, Lars Fredriksen and Bryan So [2]. They injected randomly generated input data into UNIX command line tools and such make them crash. After a first demonstration of this approach for UNIX command line tools in 2000 [2], they showed in 2007 that this approach can be further used for finding vulnerabilities in MacOS [3].

There are different categories of fuzzers:

1. *Random-based fuzzers* generate input data randomly. They know nearly nothing about the protocol of the SUT. Because of the usually huge size of the input space, mostly invalid input data is generated ([4], p. 27).
2. *Template-based fuzzers* use existing, valid traces (e.g. network traces, files) and modify them at some locations to generate invalid input data ([5], p. 49).
3. *Block-based fuzzers* break protocol messages down into static and variable parts and generate fuzzed input data only for the variable parts. They know about field length values and checksums and thus can generate more sophisticated invalid input data ([4], p. 27).
4. *Dynamic generation/evolution-based fuzzers* learn the protocol of the SUT from feeding the SUT with data and interpreting its responses using evolutionary algorithms or active learning [6,7].
5. *Model-based or smart fuzzers* have full knowledge of the protocol used to communicate with the SUT. They use their protocol knowledge to fuzz data only in certain situations that can be reached by simulating the model [8].

Following the traditional approach only input data is fuzzed. Behavioral fuzzing complements this approach by fuzzing not the arguments but the appearance and order of messages. It changes the valid sequence of messages to an invalid sequence by rearranging messages, repeating and dropping them or just changing the type of a message.

Behavior fuzzing differs from mutation testing such that mutation testing in the sense of code fault injection modifies the behavior of the SUT to simulate various situations that are difficult to test ([4], p. 90). Hence mutation testing is a white box approach. In contrast (behavior) fuzzing modifies the use of a SUT such that it is used in an invalid manner. Because the implementation of the SUT does not have to be known behavior fuzzing is a black-box approach.

The motivation for the idea of fuzzing behavior is that vulnerabilities cannot only be revealed when invalid input data is accepted and processed but also when invalid sequences of messages are accepted and processed. A real-world example is given in [9] where a vulnerability in Apache web server was found by repeating the host header in an HTTP request. This vulnerability cannot be found by fuzzing the input data. Data fuzzing would only change the parameter of the host message while behavioral fuzzing would change the number of host messages sent to the web server. Only an invalid number of host messages generated by behavioral fuzzing can reveal this denial of service vulnerability.

2   Related Work

Fuzzing has been a research topic for years. There are several approaches to improve the fuzzing process, in order to generate test data that intrudes deeper in the system under test. The general problem of randomly fuzzed input data is that these data items are largely invalid. Because of that the input data will be rejected by the SUT before getting the chance to get deeper in the SUT [10,11,12]. In that context, model-based fuzzing is a promising approach. Since the protocol is known, model-based fuzzing makes it possible to get deeper in the SUT by fuzzing after passing a certain point in a complex protocol and generating invalid data only for certain message parameters. The model can be created by the system engineer or the tester or it can be inferred by investigating traces or using learning algorithms. There are many possibilities for what can be used as a model. Context-free grammars are widely used as a model for protocol messages [11,13,14]. As a model for the flow of messages, state machines can be employed (as in [10,14,15]) or sequence diagrams as used for the behavioral fuzzing approach presented in this paper.

2.1   Implicit Behavioral Fuzzing

In [11], Viide et al. introduces the idea of inferring a context free grammar from training data that is used for generating fuzzed input data. They used compression algorithms to extract a context free grammar from the training data following the "Minimum Description Length" principle, in order to avoid the expensive task of creating a model of the SUT. The quality of the inferred model directly correlates with the amount and dissimilarity of available traces used for extracting the grammar. Therefore, if the model is not exact, because the available traces have a poor quality, implicit behavioral fuzzing is done when using the inferred model.

Another way of inferring a model of the SUT is by applying evolutionary algorithms. DeMott, Enbody and Punch follow this approach in [6]. They evaluate and evolve pools of sessions, where each session represents a complete transaction with the SUT, using a fitness function that determines the code coverage. The generations are created by crossing pools, selecting, crossing and mutating sessions. After creation of a new generation, the SUT is fed with the sessions of the pools and the fitness of every session and pool is recalculated. This process is stopped after a given number of generations. This is a more advanced but also not explicit way of behavioral fuzzing. Dynamic generation and evolution-based fuzzers try to learn the protocol using different algorithms as mentioned above. At the beginning of the learning process the model is mostly incorrect and so invalid messages and data are sent to the SUT. During the process, the learned model is getting closer to the implemented behavior of the SUT. During this approximation the fuzzing gets less random-based and gets subtler because the difference between the invalid generated behavior and the correct use of the SUT gets smaller. Therefore, implicit behavioral fuzzing performed by dynamic generation and evolution-based is superior to that performed by random-based fuzzers.

But there is a crucial drawback of implicit behavioral fuzzing: While weaknesses like performance degradation and crashes can be found, other kinds of vulnerabilities cannot be detected. That is the case because the revealed behavior of the SUT cannot be compared to a known specification and hence, vulnerabilities, e.g. revealing secret data or enabling code injection, are perceived as intended features.

2.2 Explicit Behavioral Fuzzing

In the PROTOS project on Security Testing of Protocol Implementations [13], Kaksonen, Laakso and Takanen used a Backus-Naur-Form based context-free grammar to describe the message exchange between a client and a server consisting of a request and a response, as well as the syntactical structure of the request and the response messages. The context-free grammar acts as a model of the protocol. In the first step, they replace some rules by explicit valid values. In a second step they insert exceptional elements into the rules of the grammar, e.g. extremely long or invalid field values. In the third step they define test cases by specifying sequences of rules in order to generate test data. Behavioral fuzzing is mentioned in [13] where the application of mutations was not only constrained to the syntax of individual messages but also applied to "the order and the type of messages exchanged" [13]. Understanding behavioral fuzzing in that way, random-based fuzzing implicitly performs behavioral fuzzing. Because the protocol is unknown, randomly generated data can be both messages and data. Hence, in addition to data fuzzing, also behavioral fuzzing is done —- but in a random way.

For testing the IPv6 Neighbor Discovery Protocol, Becker et al. in [15] used a finite state machine as a behavioral model of the protocol and decomposed the messages of the Neighbor Discovery Protocol. They applied several fuzzing strategies, e.g. changing field values or duplicating fields like checksums, which all constitute data fuzzing. The different fuzzing strategies mentioned by the authors are not constrained to fuzzing input data by deleting, inserting or modifying the values of fields but supplemented by the strategies of inserting, repeating and dropping messages which is already to be considered as behavioral fuzzing. Similar strategies are introduced in [7] where the type of individual messages is fuzzed as well as messages are reordered.

Banks et al. describe in [10] a tool called SNOOZE for developing stateful network protocol fuzzers. The tool reads an XML-based protocol specification containing, among other things, the syntax of messages and a state machine representing the flow of messages. A fault injector component allows modifying integer and string fields to generate invalid messages. SNOOZE can be used to develop individual fuzzers and provides several primitives, for instance to fuzz several values depending on their type. Among those primitives, there are functions to get valid messages depending on the state of a session and on the used protocol, but also primitives to get invalid messages. Thus SNOOZE enables fuzzing both, data and behavior.

The most explicit approach of behavioral fuzzing is found in [9]. Kitagawa, Hanaoka and Kono propose to change the order of messages additionally to invalidating the input data to find vulnerabilities. The change of a message depends on a state of a protocol dependent state machine. Unfortunately, they do not describe in which way message order is changed to make it invalid.

3   Fuzzing Operators for UML Sequence Diagrams

The approach of behavioral fuzzing will be presented along UML sequence diagrams. The Unified Modeling Language is a widely used standard to model object-oriented software systems and is currently available in version 2.4.1. It is used to define structural and behavioral aspects of systems. One kind of a behavioral diagram is a sequence diagram. It is a view of an interaction that is used to show sequential processes between two or more objects that use messages to communicate with each other. While in object-oriented programming these messages are method calls, in text oriented protocols such as HTTP they represent specific protocol messages including signaling and payload carrying messages. Messages may have in and outgoing parameters as well as return values. The order of messages represents their appearance in time. Figure 1 (a) shows an example of a sequence diagram.

The goal of behavioral fuzzing of UML sequence diagrams is to generate invalid message sequences. UML sequence diagrams usually show valid message sequences between two or more objects. If we assume that the sequence diagrams define all valid sequences, all other message sequences are invalid. Fuzzing of sequence diagrams generates these invalid message sequences by modifying valid sequence diagrams[1].

We decided on UML sequence diagrams for several reasons: The main reason is that the use of sequence diagrams allows the reuse of functional test cases. While in model-based development often finite state machines are used for describing the behavior of a system, test cases derived from the system's behavior model are generally represented as UML sequence diagrams. By reusing functional test cases generated during model-based testing, non-functional testing of the security aspect could be leveraged. Also existing functional test suites for certain protocols can be reused for non-functional security testing by applying behavioral fuzzing.

---

[1] In general it is not always practical (and may not even be possible) to define every valid sequence with sequence diagrams, therefore a few fuzzed sequences may on inspection turn out to be valid and should be added to the set of valid sequence diagrams.

3.1 Advantages of UML Sequence Diagrams for Behavioral Fuzzing

Combined Fragments. Since UML 2 sequence diagrams may contain control structures, e.g. loops and alternative branches. These control structures are expressed using *combined fragments*. The semantics of a combined fragment is determined by its *interaction operator*. It consists of that interaction operator that denotes the kind of the combined fragment, e.g. *alternatives*, and one or more *interaction operands* that enclose (e.g. alternative) message sub-sequences. Additionally, each interaction operand may be guarded by a Boolean expression called *interaction constraint*. An interaction constraint has to be evaluated to true so that the message sub-sequence of the guarded interaction operand may be executed.

For example a combined fragment with the interaction operator loop contains exactly one interaction operand. The interaction operand contains an interaction constraint that defines at least a value *minint* that defines the number of executions of the interaction operand. Additionally, it can define an upper bound of executions by defining the *maxint* value in order to specify a range of valid loop iterations. A Boolean expression can be specified that exhibits more constraints under which the interaction operand is executed.

These constraints defined explicitly by interaction constraints as guards for interaction operands and implicitly by the interaction operator and its meaning defined by the UML specification, combined fragments are helpful in generating invalid sequences from valid sequences by violating these constraints.

State Invariants. State invariants are associated with a lifeline of a sequence diagram. They exhibit a constraint that is evaluated during runtime. If the constraint evaluates to true, the sequence is valid, otherwise it is invalid. Thus, violating a state invariant is a way to generate an invalid sequence. However, there are some limitations:

- Because fuzzing is a black box approach, the tested SUT cannot be modified. Hence, the only state invariants that can be violated are those associated with a lifeline that is under control of the test component.
- In addition to constraining the object in a direct way, a state invariant may also refer to a state of a statechart diagram. Because we rely solely on sequence diagrams, we cannot use state invariants that reefer to states of a state machine.

Time and Duration Constraints. Similar to state invariants time and duration constraints are evaluated during runtime and distinguish valid and invalid sequences. Sequences are valid if the time or duration constraint is evaluated to true. Like state invariants time and duration constraints can only be violated if they refer to the lifeline of the test component. But in contrast violating them is easier because the constrained element – time – is in direct control of the test component when sending messages, especially in case of a time limit that must not be exceeded.

3.2   General Approach

The aim of our behavioral fuzzing approach is to generate invalid message sequences by breaking the constraints within valid UML sequence diagrams. In order to achieve that goal, we develop behavioral fuzzing operators. A behavioral fuzzing operator modifies one or more elements of a sequence diagram such that an invalid message sequence is generated. By applying a fuzzing operator to a sequence diagram, another sequence diagram is generated. We benefit from this approach by preserving the possibility to use well developed methods for test case generation from UML sequence diagrams. A second benefit of this approach is that several fuzzing operators can be applied to a sequence diagram one after another, in order to create several invalid parts of a message sequence.

In the following, we will discuss the different kinds of elements of UML sequence diagrams and how their constraints can be broken in order to achieve an invalid sequence. We then use this information to propose a set of behavioral fuzzing operators.

3.3   Fuzzing Behavior of UML Sequence Diagram Model Elements

As discussed above, fuzzing of behavior is realized by modifying the different model elements. This could be done in several ways:

- modifying an individual message,
- changing the order of messages,
- changing combined fragments,
- violating time and duration constraints as well as state invariants if possible.

Messages. Generating an invalid message sequence can be achieved by modifying an individual message. To obtain an invalid sequence diagram, a single message

- can be repeated thus it exists twice (see figure 1(b)),
- can be removed from the sequence diagram (see figure 1(c)),
- can be changed by type that is replacing it by another message,
- can be moved to another position,
- can be inserted.

There are two possibilities of fuzzing two and more messages:

- If two messages are selected these messages can be swapped. One invalid sequence can be generated this way.
- If more than two messages are selected, they can be randomly permuted. Because of its randomness, this approach is less powerful than more directed ones [8].
  A less destructive approach could be rotating the selected messages. It tests stepwise omitting messages in the beginning of a sequence and sending it later.

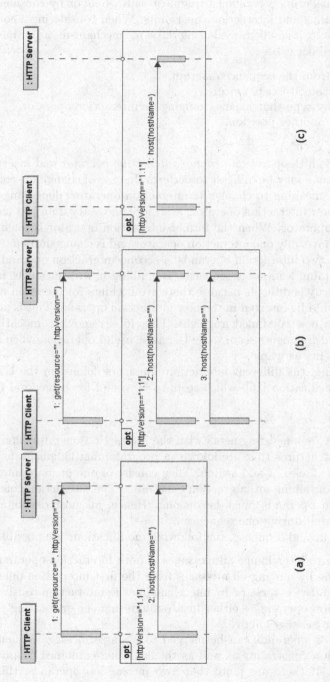

Fig. 1. Modification of an (a) UML sequence diagram (b) after repeating message 2 and (c) after removing message 1

Combined Fragments. Behavioral fuzzing of combined fragments can be done in two ways: considering a combined fragment as a whole or by considering its interaction operands and interaction constraints. When considering a combined fragment as a whole, it can be fuzzed using the same mechanisms as for messages. A combined fragment can

- be removed from the sequence diagram,
- be repeated thus it exists twice,
- be changed by type that means changing its interaction operator,
- be moved to another position,
- be inserted.

The third and the fifth operation - *change interaction operator* and *insert a new combined fragment* - may be difficult to perform. In case of changing a combined fragment's type, meaning to change its interaction operator, depending on the former and the new interaction operator, it is more necessary than just changing the interaction operator. When the former interaction operator is for instance *break* that may have only one interaction operator and is changed to *alternatives* that usually has two interaction operands, a second interaction operand has to be inserted including a message sequence. But filling it with messages in more than a random way is difficult because there are no hints for a certain message sequence that could be inserted in the new interaction operand. This is also true when inserting a new combined fragment. Therefore, removing, repeating and moving combined fragments seem to be the most useful operation when fuzzing combined fragments as whole.

In the following, the different interaction operators defined in the UML Superstructure Specification [16], which seem to be useful for behavioral fuzzing, are discussed.

Alternatives. Combined fragments with the interaction operator *alternatives* realize control structures that are known in programming languages as for instance if ... then ... else ... and switch. They consist of one or more interaction operands each containing an interaction constraint. The interaction constraints of all interaction operands must be disjoint. Hence, at most one interaction operand is executed during one sequence.

To obtain an invalid sequence, the following modifications are possible:

- It is possible to interchange all messages of both interaction operands. This could be done by moving all messages from the first interaction operand to the second and vice versa or by interchanging the interaction constraints of the interaction operands – either in a random manner or rotating them as described for messages above.
- All interaction operands can be merged to a single message sequence and the interaction constraints as well as the enclosing combined fragment can be removed. If there are more than two interaction operands, this could be done by combining stepwise two and more interaction operands until all interaction operands are merged.

Option. An option combined fragment contains an optional message sequence whose execution is guarded by an interaction constraint. It has only one interaction operand. An invalid sequence can be obtained by negating its interaction constraint.

Break. In certain situations, it is necessary to perform some special behavior instead of following the regular sequence diagram. This can be in case of an exceptional situation, for instance if a resource cannot be allocated. To express this in a sequence diagram, the combined fragment with the interaction operator *break* is used. It contains exactly one interaction operand and an interaction constraint. If the interaction constraint is evaluated to true, the interaction operand is executed instead of the remainder of the enclosing interaction fragment.

Invalid sequences can be obtained by the following modifications:

- Negate the interaction constraint. Doing this has the same effect as interchanging the messages of the interaction operand and the remainder of the enclosing interaction fragment.
- Disintegrating the combined fragment results – in contrast to an *option* combined fragment – always to an invalid message sequence because either the interaction operand or the remainder of the enclosing interaction fragment is executed. Disintegrating the combined fragments yields to a sequence where both, the sequence defined by the interaction operand and the remainder of the sequence diagram, is executed.

Weak Sequencing. *Weak* sequencing is the default for how the order of messages must be preserved. If nothing else is specified, weak sequencing is applied to a sequence diagram or an interaction fragment. If weak sequencing is applied, the order of messages regarding each lifeline must be preserved. Moreover, the order of messages that are associated with different lifelines does not need to be preserved. As a consequence, changing the order of messages generates only invalid sequences when they are associated with the same pair of lifelines.

This has an impact on how single or more messages can be modified in order to obtain an invalid message sequence.

Strict Sequencing. In contrast to *weak* sequencing, *strict* sequencing preserves the order of messages independent of the lifelines they are associated with. Thus, invalid sequences can be obtained by changing the order of messages without the necessity to respect the lifelines they are associated with.

Negative. The *negative* combined fragment differs from all other combined fragments in not showing a valid but an invalid message sequence. In order to obtain an invalid sequence, its interaction operator can be changed to *option*.

Consider/Ignore. *Consider* and *ignore* combined fragments are two sides of the same coin. Both are supplemented with a list of messages. In case of an *ignore* combined fragment, it means that these messages are not relevant in order to determine a valid message sequence. Thus, these messages can arbitrarily occur within this combined fragment without affecting the validity of the sequence. In case of a *consider* combined fragment, only the mentioned messages are relevant for a valid sequence. Thus all other messages can arbitrarily occur in the message sequence. Consider and ignore combined fragments cannot behavioral fuzzed itself but has an impact on which of the enclosed messages can be fuzzed.

Loop. A *loop* represents a repetition of a message sequence. It can be set to a certain number of repetitions or limited by a lower and an upper bound. Additionally no limit can be set to tell that all number of repetitions are valid.

Invalid sequences can only be obtained if there is at least one parameter for the loop:

- If there is exactly one parameter, invalid message sequences can be generated by changing it to smaller and greater values to test if there are off-by-one-errors [17].
- If there are two parameters, two different combined fragments can be generated one running from zero to the lower bound −1 and the other by running from the upper bound +1 to a maximum number.

Time and Duration Constraints. Time and duration constraints can be used to specify a relative point in time where a message has to be sent or should be received or the amount of time that may elapse between two messages. Time and duration constraints can be given in different situations but only in a few of them can be violated. There are two conditions that must be met to make a violation of a time or a duration constraint possible:

- The constraint has to be associated with a lifeline of the test component. If this is not the case, the constraint has to be maintained by the SUT that is not under control of the test component.
- The occurrence(s), the constraint is associated with, have to be under control of the test component. This is for the same reason as the first condition.

If these conditions are met, the value of the constraint can be negated to generate invalid sequences. The fuzzed constraints must then be respected at test generation time to ensure the original constraint is violated.

State Invariants. State invariants can specify many different constraints on the participants of an interaction, e.g. values of attributes or internal or external states. As for time and duration constraints state invariants has to be under control of the test component. Because of the black box nature of the presented approach only a few of the many different kinds of constraints that can be expressed by a state invariant can be used for fuzzing. These include the valuation of attributes, but not references to external states.

Another challenge when fuzzing state invariants is that just modifying them does not ensure an invalid sequence. If for example the state invariant refers to an attribute of the test component that should have a specific value, by just changing the specified value does not lead to an invalid sequence in terms of the original state invariant. Actually, the behaviors that happen before the state invariant must be changed, in order to achieve the fuzzed state invariant. Additionally the value of the attribute of the test component may be not under immediate control of the test component because the attribute may get its value by the SUT. Thus it is difficult to use state invariants for behavioral fuzzing.

3.4 Summary of Behavioral Fuzzing Operators

Table 1 illustrates the identified behavioral fuzzing operators are illustrated based on the above discussions on the different elements of UML sequence diagrams.

4 Classification Criteria for Fuzzing Operators

In order to generate fuzzed sequence diagrams, one or more of the identified behavioral fuzzing operators can be applied to a sequence diagram that represents valid message sequences. This sequence diagram can originate from a functional test suite. The transformation of sequence diagrams allows the reuse of a functional test suite for non-functional security testing.

Traditional data fuzzing creates a huge number of test cases because the input space is nearly infinite [4], p. 62. That is the reason for the use of heuristics that reduce the size of the input space. The above discussed fuzzing operators are of heuristic nature. When considering the behavioral fuzzing operators, we can estimate how many modifications can be performed for each of them. For the fuzzing operators *remove message* and *repeat message*, one modification per message is possible. For the fuzzing operator *move message*, a message can be moved to the position of each other message that is not enclosed in a negative combined fragment, because that would change the already negative message sub-sequence, or in a *consider/ignore* combined fragment where it is not mentioned respectively mentioned in the list of considered respectively ignored messages. The number of modifications can be estimated by the number of messages enclosed in a sequence diagram. A message can be inserted at the position of each other message where at each position in turn k different messages can be inserted, where k is the number of operations that the class of the lifeline provides, i.e. $|messages|^k$. A first approximation of the number of test cases when applying n behavioral fuzzing operators is given by:

$$\mathcal{O}(\sum_{i=1}^{n} \frac{o'!}{(o'-i)!}) \tag{1}$$

with

$$o' = o \cdot e^k \tag{2}$$

Table 1. Behavioral fuzzing operators for UML sequence diagrams

Operators for...	
Messages	**Constraints**

Remove Message
Repeat Message
Move Message
Change Type of Message
Insert Message
	- not enclosed in combined fragment *negative*
	- considered respectively not ignored if
	  enclosed in combined fragment
	  consider/ignore

Swap Messages	- not enclosed in combined fragment negative - considered respectively not ignored if enclosed in combined fragment consider/ignore

Permute Messages Regarding
          a Single SUT Lifeline
Rotate Messages Regarding
          a Single SUT Lifeline
	- applicable for messages within a
	  weak combined fragment

Permute Messages Regarding
          several SUT Lifelines
Rotate Messages Regarding
          several SUT Lifelines
	- applicable for messages within a
	  strict combined fragment

Combined Fragments	**Constraints**
Negate Interaction Constraint Interchange Interaction Constraints	- applicable to combined fragments *option, break, negative* - applicable to combined fragment *alternatives*

Disintegrate Combined Fragment
          and Distribute Its Messages
	- applicable to combined fragments with
	  more than one interaction operand

Change Bounds of Loop	- applicable to combined fragment *loop* with at least one parameter
Insert Combined Fragment Remove Combined Fragment Repeat Combined Fragment Move Combined Fragment	- applicable to all combined fragments except *negative*
Change Interaction Operator	- applicable to all combined fragments
Time/Duration Constraint	**Constraints**
Change Time/Duration Constraint	- applicable to constraints that are on the lifeline of the test component

where o is the number of available fuzzing operators, e is the number of elements in the sequence diagram to be fuzzed, n is the number of fuzzing operators to be applied to a sequence diagram and k is a constant representing the number of different modifications that can be applied to an element by a fuzzing operator. This simple approximation shows that a huge number of test cases can be generated by behavioral fuzzing.

This number of test cases can be too big for executing all possible test cases. Hence, a reasonable classification of the fuzzing operators could be helpful for the test case selection. An attempt of a classification of all behavioral fuzzing operators is illustrated in Table 2.

For traditional data fuzzing, the goal is not to generate totally invalid but semi-valid input data meaning that it is invalid only in a few points. Hence, the number of invalid points generated by a heuristic is of interest. We argue that this is also true for behavioral fuzzing and propose a classification of behavioral fuzzing operators by the number of deviations to the original sequence diagram generated by a fuzzing operator when applied to a sequence diagram.

Another classification criterion could be how the behavioral fuzzing operators relate to random-based or smart fuzzing. As discussed above, model-based or smart fuzzing is more effective than random-based fuzzing because the protocol knowledge is used to generate fuzzed input data. From this point of view, the fuzzing operators that modify a single message or a bunch of messages are rather random-based, because they use only minimal information of the protocol (expressed by a sequence diagram), but modify messages in a random way by e.g. inserting or removing random messages. In contrast, fuzzing operators as for instance *interchange interaction constraints* or *change bounds of loop* use information about the protocol from the sequence diagram and thus, are classified rather to smart fuzzing than to random fuzzing. These classification criteria can be employed to select and prioritize behavioral fuzzing operators for test case generation.

Table 2. Classification of behavioral fuzzing operators

	one deviation	a few deviations	many deviations
random	- remove message - repeat message - change type of message - insert message	- move message - swap messages	- permute messages regarding a single SUT lifeline - permute messages regarding several SUT lifelines - insert combined fragment
smart	- negate interaction constraint - change bounds of loop - change time/duration constraint	- interchange interaction constraints - disintegrate combined fragment and distribute its messages - change interaction operator - move combined fragment	- remove combined fragment - repeat combined fragment

5 Case Study from the Banking Domain: Banknote Processing System

We developed a prototype implementing 3 behavioral fuzzing operators and applied them to a functional test case from a case study from the banking domain – a banknote processing system. Basically, the banknote processing machine consists of a sets of sensors for detecting banknotes and a PC that analyzes the sensor data in order to determine the currency and the denomination of a banknote, and whether it is genuine or not. In the context of the DIAMONDS research project, we set up the PC with the software at Fraunhofer FOKUS and simulated sensor data of banknotes. The functional test case consists in general of two phases, the first one is the configuration phase where, for instance, the currency and the denomination is selected. The second phase is counting where the (simulated) sensor data is analyzed by the software. We applied the behavioral fuzzing operators *remove message*, *move message* and *repeat message* to that functional test case, in order to generate behavioral fuzzing test cases.

6 Preliminary Results

Due to long execution time of one test case in our setup, we focused on authentication and selected 30 test cases from those generated where the login was omitted or operations (that need login) are performed without any successful login. In that, we could not find any weakness in the software of the banknote processing system.

7 Conclusions and Future Work

We presented a behavioral fuzzing approach working on UML sequence diagrams that was realized by behavioral fuzzing operators. These operators modify a sequence diagram in order to generate an invalid from a valid one. We provided a classification of these operators for test case selection and prioritization. Finally, we presented a case study from the DIAMONDS research project we applied our approach to. We found with a partial prototype implementation no weaknesses in the banknote processing system, but are hopeful to show the efficacy of this approach when more fuzzing operators are implemented in the prototype. We already improved the performance of our test setup that allows us to execute more test cases in future. Additionally, more studies has to be performed on different SUT in order to evaluate the presented approach. Also combination with other kinds of diagram, e.g. statechart diagrams, may help in improving the approach in order to find vulnerabilities.

While the presented approach is applied to UML sequence diagrams, it may be also applicable to message sequence charts (MSCs). MSCs provide similar concepts as UML sequence diagrams, e.g. inline expressions and guarding conditions that are similar to combined fragments and interaction constraints. Further concepts of MSCs, e.g. high-level-MSCs, may be helpful to this approach.

However, there are some issues that must be solved. On one hand, the goal to generate invalid message sequences by applying behavioral fuzzing operators to valid message sequences does not necessarily lead to invalid sequences. That is, in many cases several sequence diagrams specify the protocol of the system under test while a fuzzing operator respects only one sequence diagram when modifying it. Thus, applying a fuzzing operator to one sequence diagram could lead to a message sequence that is specified as a valid one by another sequence diagram and is therefore not invalid in the sense of the specification. By merging several

UML sequence diagram using combined fragments, this drawback may become an advantage because (a) by applying fuzzing operators to a merged sequence diagram, all different message sequences are respected and (b) commonalities and differences that are expressed using combined fragments can be used by the corresponding fuzzing operators that are considered to be more smart by our classification than message-based fuzzing operators.

Other problems are duplicate test cases generated by applying several combination of fuzzing operators that results in the same message sequence, or useless combinations of fuzzing operators such as *move message A* and *remove message A*. We are currently researching efficient ways to overcome these issues. One idea is to ascribe the presented behavioral fuzzing operators to some basic operators, e.g. *insert* and *remove* and to impose conditions on the combinations of these basic operators. That way, useless combinations of operators may be detected and avoided while test case generation.

Another issue is, as always when performing model-based testing, the quality of the model, especially its completeness. The sequence diagrams, e.g. specified for a functional test suite, do not necessarily contain all valid message sequences. Hence, it cannot be ensured that the message sequence generated by behavioral fuzzing operators is an invalid one. This leads to test cases that do not test the security of a system under test while increasing the number of test cases and thus the total test execution time while not revealing any weaknesses.

It is also of interest how traditional data fuzzing and behavioral fuzzing may complement each other, how they can be combined and if this approach is more powerful than applying only one approach at a time.

Acknowledgments. This work was funded by the ITEA-2 research project DIAMONDS. Please see www.itea2-diamonds.org for more information.

References

1. Bekrar, C., Groz, R., Mounier, L.: Finding Software Vulnerabilities by Smart Fuzzing. In: Fourth IEEE International Conference on Software Testing, Verification and Validation (ICST 2011), pp. 427–430. IEEE Computer Society (2011)
2. Miller, B., Fredriksen, L., So, B.: An Empirical Study of the Reliability of UNIX Utilities. Communications of the ACM 33(12), 32–34 (2000)
3. Miller, B.P., Cooksey, G., Moore, F.: An Empirical Study of the Robustness of MacOS Applications Using Random Testing. SIGOPS Operating Systems Review 41(1), 78–86 (2007)
4. Takanen, A., DeMott, J., Miller, C.: Fuzzing for Software Security Testing and Quality Assurance. Artech House, Boston (2008)
5. Uusitalo, I. (ed.): Review of Security Testing Tools. Project deliverable D1.WP3. DIAMONDS Consortium (2011), http://www.itea2-diamonds.org/_docs/D1_WP3_T1_v11_FINAL_Review_of_Security_Testing_Tools.pdf
6. DeMott, J., Enbody, R., Punch, W.: Revolutionizing the Field of Grey-box Attack Surface Testing with Evolutionary Fuzzing. Black Hat (2007), http://www.blackhat.com/presentations/bh-usa-07/DeMott_Enbody_and_Punch/Presentation/bh-usa-07-demott_enbody_and_punch.pdf

7. Hsu, Y., Shu, G., Lee, D.: A Model-based Approach to Security Flaw Detection of Network Protocol Implementations. In: IEEE International Conference on Network Protocols (ICNP 2008), pp. 114–123. IEEE Conference Publications (2008)

8. Takanen, A.: Fuzzing – the Past, the Present and the Future. In: Actes du 7ème Symposium sur la Séurité des Technologies de l'Information et des Communications (2009), http://actes.sstic.org/SSTIC09/Fuzzing-the_Past-the_Present_and_the_Future/SSTIC09-article-A-Takanen-Fuzzing-the_Past-the_Present_and_the_Future.pdf

9. Kitagawa, T., Hanaoka, M., Kono, K.: AspFuzz: A State-aware Protocol Fuzzer based on Application-layer Protocols. In: IEEE Symposium on Computers and Communications (ISCC 2010), pp. 202–208. IEEE Conference Publications (2010)

10. Banks, G., Cova, M., Felmetsger, V., Almeroth, K.C., Kemmerer, R.A., Vigna, G.: SNOOZE: Toward a Stateful NetwOrk prOtocol fuzZEr. In: Katsikas, S.K., López, J., Backes, M., Gritzalis, S., Preneel, B. (eds.) ISC 2006. LNCS, vol. 4176, pp. 343–358. Springer, Heidelberg (2006)

11. Viide, J., et al.: Experiences with Model Inference Assisted Fuzzing. In: Proceedings of the 2nd Conference on USENIX Workshop on Offensive Technologies (WOOT 2008). USENIX Association (2008)

12. Forrester, J.E., Miller, B.P.: An Empirical Study of the Robustness of Windows NT Applications Using Random Testing. In: Proceedings of the 4th Conference on USENIX Windows Systems Symposium (WSS 2000), p. 6. USENIX Association (2000)

13. Takanen, A., DeMott, J., Miller, C.: Software Security Assessment through Specification Mutations and Fault Injection. In: Communications and Multimedia Security Issues of the New Century, IFIP Advances in Information and Communication Technology, vol. 64, Springer (2001)

14. Abdelnur, H., Festor, O., State, R.: Kif – A Stateful SIP Fuzzer. In: Proceedings of the 1st International Conference on Principles, Systems and Applications of IP Telecommunications (IPTComm 2007), pp. 47–56. ACM Press (2007)

15. Becker, S., Abdelnur, H., State, R., Engel, T.: An Autonomic Testing Framework for IPv6 Configuration Protocols. In: Stiller, B., De Turck, F. (eds.) AIMS 2010. LNCS, vol. 6155, pp. 65–76. Springer, Heidelberg (2010)

16. Object Management Grouo: Unified Modeling Language, Superstructure v2.4.1, formal/2011-08-06 (2011), http://www.omg.org/spec/UML/2.4.1/Superstructure/PDF

17. Denis Howe: off-by-one error. In: Free On-Line Dictionary of Computing, http://foldoc.org/off-by-one+errors

Relativity and Abstract State Machines

Edel Sherratt

Department of Computer Science, Aberystwyth University,
Penglais, Aberystwyth SY23 3DB, Wales
eds@aber.ac.uk

Abstract. The Abstract State Machine (ASM) formalism has proved an effective and durable foundation for the formal semantics of SDL. The distributed ASMs that underpin the SDL semantics are defined in terms of agents that execute ASM programs concurrently, acting on partial views of a global state. The discrete identities of successive global states are ensured by allowing input from the external world only between steps, and by having all agents refer to an external global time. But distributed systems comprising independent agents do not have a natural global time. Nor do they have natural global states. This paper takes well-known concepts from relativity and applies them to ASMs. The spacetime in which an ASM exists and moves is defined, and some properties that must be preserved by transformations of the frame of reference of an ASM are identified. Practical implications of this approach are explored through reservation and web service examples.

Keywords: Abstract state machines, Formal semantics, Distributed system, SDL, spacetime, frame of reference.

1 Introduction

The Abstract State Machine (ASM) model of computation was introduced by Gurevich[1, 2] under the name 'evolving algebras', and was subsequently developed by Blass, Gurevich, Börger and many others [3–11].

The formal semantics of SDL was defined by Glässer, Gotzhein and Prinz in terms of distributed Abstract State Machines [12, 13]. This comprises a number of cooperating agents, each with a partial view of a global state of the ASM.

Throughout the development of Abstract State Machines, the notion of a global state and a global time has formed a recurring theme. While this does not diminish the expressive power of abstract state machines, it leads to awkward formulations of computations involving interaction and persistence.

This paper explores the consequences of abandoning the demand for a global state and global time. Drawing on ideas from relativity, it proposes independent ASMs that can observe projections of each others' states onto commonly accessible locations. This exploration reveals limitations on the kinds of observations that can be made, and therefore on the kinds of interaction that are possible between parallel ASMs.

Ø. Haugen, R. Reed, and R. Gotzhein (Eds.): SAM 2012, LNCS 7744, pp. 105–120, 2013.

A reservation service with client applications is outlined below to illustrate the kind of system that motivates the attempt to develop transformations between the location-value pairs accessible to different abstract state machines. The ideas of state and time in Abstract State Machines are then reviewed. Parallels are drawn with concepts from relativity, leading to an exploration of interaction between ASMs and of observations of ASMs by one another. This analogy facilitates reasoning about the the kinds of interaction that are possible between ASMs, and enables identification of conditions that must be fulfilled by any admissible transformation between the observations made by independent parallel ASMs. Those constraints represent a small but essential first step towards developing transformations that define communication between fully independent ASMs that do not share a global state space and that do not acknowledge a global time.

2   Abstract State Machines' Power and Limitations

Since their original introduction, abstract state machines have repeatedly been shown to be both versatile and powerful. Examples ranging from a simple clock, through Conway's game of life, ambiguous grammars, lift control, Internet telephony, database recovery and more are demonstrated in [4]. That abstract state machines capture every kind of parallel algorithm is shown in [5, 6]. Their application to generalized asynchronous communication is shown in [7], and their capacity to interact and operate in parallel is demonstrated, for example, in [11] and [14] .

Now, all these examples model processes in terms of abstract states and sequences of state transitions. Inherent in this is a notion of global state and global time. But some applications, like database clients and web services, do not directly lend themselves to a model that demands a global state and a global time.

For example, the SDL diagram in Figure 1 illustrates a ticket reservation service that is accessed by an arbitrary number of clients. Each client process progresses through its state transitions, and the reservation process does likewise. The client processes alternate, and the reservation process runs independently of the client processes. However, according to the SDL reference manual [15], all the client processes, and also the reservation process, have access to a global system clock, which supplies an absolute system time by way of the *now expression*, **now**. Furthermore, they all refer to a global state [12].

The model describes asynchronous, parallel processes that capture essential properties of the reservation system, including creation and destruction of clients and update of the state by different processes. However, the existence of global time, external to all the processes of the reservation system, means that something extraneous is being added to the system model.

A better approach would allow the system as a whole to be considered from the perspective of an individual client, or from the perspective of the reservation system, and would also allow a client to see the system state and time as the

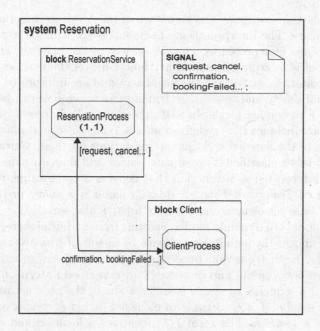

Fig. 1. Reservation system

reservation system sees it, and vice versa. In other words, it would indicate how to transform perspective between different agents.

As a preliminary to enabling such transformations, the following section will explore concepts of state and time in abstract state machines.

3   State and Time in Abstract State Machines

Notions of state and time in various formulations of abstract state machines are explored. These concepts are later compared with concepts from relativity, with a view to identifying constraints on the transformations that would allow a designer to transfer focus between interacting abstract state machines.

3.1   Basic Abstract State Machine

A basic abstract state machine is made up of abstract states with a transition rule that specifies transformations of those abstract states. The rule is often expressed as an ASM *program*.

A *state* in an ASM is defined as the association of values from an under-lying base set with the symbols that form the *signature* of the ASM. This is also expressed by stating that the ASM has a vocabulary, whose symbols are interpreted over a base set, and that interpretation defines a *state*.

Some states are called *initial states*.

The symbols that comprise the signature of an ASM are function symbols, each with an arity. The interpretation of symbols is constrained so that a 0-ary function symbol is interpreted as a single element of the base set, and an n-ary function symbol is interpreted as an n-ary function over the base set. Terms are constructed from the signature in the usual way, and are interpreted recursively. To provide modularity and to enhance legibility, new symbols can be defined as abbreviations for complex terms. In SDL, these are called *derived names* [12].

The signature includes the predefined names *True*, *False* and *undef*, and three distinct values of the base set serve as interpretations for these. Certain function symbols are further classified as predicate names and domain names. A predicate name is interpreted as a function that delivers a truth value, which is the interpretation of *True* or of *False*. A domain name is a unary predicate name that classifies base set elements as being of a particular sort.

The ASM model is a dynamic model. Starting from an initial state, an abstract state machine moves through its state space by means of *transitions*, also called *moves* or *steps*. Each transition produces a new state from an existing state. The differences between old and new states are described in terms of *updates* to *locations*. Such a sequence of states is called a *run* of the abstract machine.

A function symbol f with a tuple of elements $\bar{a}$ that serves as an argument of f identifies a *location*. The term $f(\bar{a})$ identifies a location and evaluates to a value in a state. In a subsequent state, the value of that location may have changed, and $f(\bar{a})$ may evaluate to a new value. In that case, an *update* indicates what the new value will be, and is expressed using the values of terms in the current state. Updates are written as triples $(f, \bar{a}, b)$, to indicate that $f(\bar{a}) = b$ will be true in the new state. In order to limit the cardinality of the update set, [5, 6] also asserts that $f(\bar{a}) = b$ should not be true in the previous state. However trivial updates, where the new and old values of a location are the same are allowed in [11].

Updates are sometimes specified as programming-style assignments, such as: $f(\bar{a}) = b$.

Function names like *True*, *False* and *undef*, whose interpretation is the same in all the states of an abstract state machine, are called *static names*. Names like f above, that identify locations that are subject to updates, are called *dynamic names*.

The set of updates that transformes an ASM state is specified as a rule, expressed as an ASM *program*. Each state transition is realised by interpreting the ASM *program* in a given state. Interpretation of the program delivers a set of updates, which are applied simultaneously to produce the new state. The constructs used to write ASM programs vary (for example, see [3, 7, 12]), and usually allow for non-determinism in the set of updates that is generated.

Two situations can prevent further progress through the state space:

- the update set resulting from interpretation of the program in a given state is empty;
- the update set is inconsistent; that is, it includes two updates $(f, \bar{a}, b)$ and $(f, \bar{a}, c)$ where $b \neq c$.

In either case, the ASM remains in its current state, either by *stuttering* (repeatedly moving back to the current state), or by treating the current state as final and halting. Stuttering allows for external intervention to modify the state so as to enable further progress, or for a non-deterministic ASM program to yield a viable update set on re-evaluation.

That every step in a run of a basic abstract state machine yields an abstract state with a definite interpretation for each element of the ASM signature, is formulated in terms of the Abstract State and Sequential Time postulates of [5, 6]. That the work done at each step is bounded, is formulated as the Bounded Exploration Postulate [5, 6]. Together, these ensure that a basic abstract state machine has at every step a well-defined global state, and that there is a finite amount of work to be done to move from one state to the next.

This, in turn, gives rise to a notion of global time, which increases monotonically with each step.

However, forcing the reservation system and its clients, with its multiple threads of control, into the single process defined by a basic ASM leads to premature sequentialization of moves and ignores alternative scheduling strategies.

3.2 Complex Moves

A state transition can entail activation of one or more sub-machines. If this is done using a 'black-box' approach, in which the moves of the sub-machine are not made visible, the containing ASM is called a turbo-ASM [3]. Alternatively, subcomputations can be interleaved under the control of the containing process – a 'white-box' view of subcomputation[3]. In the first of these cases, moves of the containing ASM preserve the Abstract State and Sequential Time postulates by construction. In the second, a constraint is added by [3] that allows interleaved processes to act in parallel only if they all contribute to a consistent update set. This again means the the computation proceeds through a well defined sequence of abstract states.

Using this kind of approach would allow, for example, client requests to be defined as sub-machines of the reservation system, and those sub-machines could run in parallel. However, it is still not satisfactory because execution of client requests is bounded within steps of the containing ASM that models the reservation system.

3.3 Interaction with the Environment

Interaction between an abstract state machine and its environment is achieved through mutually accessible locations.

Locations that are subject to updates are named by dynamic names. Dynamic names are futher classified as *monitored, controlled* and *shared*. A monitored, dynamic name refers to a location that is updated by the environment and read by the ASM. A controlled, dynamic name refers to a location that is updated by the ASM, and may possibly be read by the environment. A shared, dynamic name refers to a location that is updated by the environment and by the ASM.

In order that each abstract state should form a well defined first order structure, values cannot change within the state. If the statement $f = v$ is satisfied by a given state, then $f = w$ where $w \neq v$ cannot be satisfied by the same state. So the value of a location identified by a monitored name cannot change during a state. That is, updates performed by the environment can only take place between states. This leads to an interpretation in [3] in which each transition is made by applying the updates defined by the rule of an ASM, followed by the updates made by the environment. A similar position is taken in [5, 6] where intervention of an environment only takes effect between steps.

Again, this leads to a model of computation in which the abstract state machine proceeds through a sequence of clearly defined global states.

However, this does facilitate independent modelling of the reservation system and its clients. Using the approach of [14], a client is modelled as an abstract state machine that views the reservation system as part of the environment. Interaction is modelled in terms of queries and replies. This approach is extended by [11] so that queries made at one step can be answered by replies that become available at a later step. Histories, return locations and suitable guards ensure that responses are properly associated with queries and are collected at appropriate times.

The strength of this approach is that it allows the client to view the reservation system as a kind of oracle, that grants or declines requests for reservation in an inscrutable way, and it allows the reservation system to schedule client requests in any way it sees fit. It does not, however, provide any guidance for transforming between client and reservation system views of the interaction.

3.4 Distributed Abstract State Machine

In order to model computations with multiple threads of control, the concept of *ASM agent* is introduced. Agents form part of the distributed ASMs used in the semantic definition of SDL [12, 13], and AsmL [7]. An agent actively interprets an ASM program and so drives the movement of a distributed ASM from state to state.

A distributed Abstract State Machine has a single base set. An agent is distinguished from other agents by having its own unique interpretation of a function *Self* [12] or *me* [5, 6]. In SDL, each agent has its own partial view of a current global state. This view, and, by implication, the locations accessible to the agent, are determined by the agent's program. Agents can be associated with programs using a function *program* as in [12], or a collection of agents can execute a single program, whose branches are selected based on the value of *Self*.

A distributed abstract state machine can be synchronous or asynchronous [3]. A synchronous multi-agent ASM is defined by [3] as a set of agents that execute their own ASMs in parallel, synchronized using an implicit global system clock. The signature of the synchronized multi-agent ASM is formed as the union of the signatures of its component single-agent ASMs. The global clock synchronizes the moves of the multi-agent ASM through a global state, so that all updates that can be performed at a step being performed instantaneously at that step.

Distributed asynchronous multi-agent ASMs [3] are used in the definition of SDL [12, 13] and AsmL [7].

A distributed asynchronous multi-agent ASM consists of a set of (agent, ASM) pairs, each of which executes its own ASM [3]. A run of an asynchronous multi-agent ASM is a partially ordered set of moves $(M, <)$, with the following properties [1, 3, 12]:

- each move has only finitely many predecessors;
- the moves performed by a given agent are linearly ordered by $<$;
- for every finite initial segment X of $(M. <)$, and every maximal element $m \in X$, there is a unique state $\sigma(X)$ that results from performing m in the state $\sigma(X \setminus \{m\})$.

This definition allows a great deal of freedom in constructing a run. Moves can be carried out in parallel, or by interleaving the moves of different agents, or by creating a explicit schedule. However, the last of the three conditions above means that there is a confluence of state transformation, in the sense that every linearization of every initial segment of $(M, <)$ results in the same state. This in turn means that every run of the ASM proceeds through a well defined sequence of abstract states.

This approach also facilitates communication between a reservation system and its clients. Following the approach of [7] a new kind of agent, called a *communicator*, is introduced that transfers messages between communicating applications like a client and the reservation system. This makes a clear separation between the behaviour of the network (as modelled by the communicator), and the behaviour of the reservation system and its client applications.

However, it means that the whole system, comprising the reservation system, its clients and the network are modelled as a single distributed ASM. This in turn means that the end state of every finite prefix of a partially ordered run is pre-determined – a stronger condition than the serializability condition normally required of a database schedule.

3.5   Global Time and Abstract State Machines

Single threaded basic abstract state machines imply a notion of global time, in that moves are said to come before or after each other. In a distributed ASM, moves are partially ordered, but any initial segment of a partially ordered run gives a definite state, and that state can be said to come before the states that result from extending the run. This again gives rise to an implicit notion of global time.

SDL provides an explicit definition of global time in distributed real-time ASMs using a real-valued monitored function *currentTime*, which increases montonically over ASM runs, and is consistent with the notion of moves that come before or after other moves.

A detailed treatment of time in abstract state machines is presented in [17]. Focusing on moves, called events, rather than on states, time is added to event structures in a way that is consistent with the sequences of moves defined by an abstract state machine. All moves are ordered according to some notion of global time, but it is also possible for non-conflicting moves to have an undefined order according to the local time of a single thread.

But global time is not intrinsic to the reservation system and its clients. The reservation system grants or declines client requests according to its own rules, which may include its perception of the relative arrival times of those requests. And even with a single client, the fact that requests are issued in a particular order does not guarantee that the reservation system will perceive them in that order.

3.6 Summary

In summary, different kinds of abstract state machine have been explored, and all include the notion of progress in time through a sequence of well defined global states.

This is achieved by construction for single-agent abstract state machines. For distributed abstract state machines, that every initial segment of every run results in the same state also implies that a sequence of states through which the ASM progresses can be identified.

For independent parallel ASMs, the introduction of an abstract communicator [7] means that the parallel ASMs are brought together into a distributed ASM as before.

Alternatively, focus is given to one of the ASMs, with everything outside that being regarded as an environment that can be queried in [11]. This again means that progress in time is modelled, but it does not say how progress as perceived, for example, by a client, can be transformed to progress as seen by the reservation system.

The following section presents an approach that treats the point of view of every ASM equally, and explores what it means for one ASM to observe the state of another ASM. The requirements that must be met by the transformations that enable such observations are then elucidated.

4 Analogy with Concepts from Relativity

The notion of global state is fundamental to much of the work reviewed above. The term *sequential time* is defined in [5] to describe the progress of an ASM from state to state. That distributed algorithms are not, in general, sequential time algorithms is stated in [14], where intra-step interaction with other agents in the environment of an ASM is explored in depth. The notion of global state of a distributed ASM is defined in [12] by partially ordering the moves of the ASM agents so that contentious moves that would lead to inconsistent update sets are ordered, and by identifying as global the states the result from application of any maximal move in any finite prefix of the partially ordered set of moves. This is similar to the notion of global state defined in terms of cuts through Petri net representations of distributed runs by Glausch and Reisig [8].

A different approach is taken in [14]. There focus is given to a single ASM in a distributed environment. The ASM can query its environment, which has ASM agent-like behaviour. The ASM can also, while executing a step, observe updates that are made by the environment. The ASM operates in sequential time, and the states of the environment are not of concern.

Here, the aim is to enable any ASM agent to see shared locations as other agents see them. No preference is to be given to the perspective of any agent. This is inspired by ideas from relativity concerning permissible transformations between different frames of reference [16]. But for this purpose, it is not necesseary to have a global state, but only to have sufficient overlap between the states that contain the communicating ASM agents.

Towards this end, each ASM has its own state space and its own time. Each ASM progresses through its own well defined states (locally sequential time), but there is no demand for a coherent global state. The challenge is to describe interaction between ASMs and to identify the properties that must be maintained when facts that can be observed by one ASM agent are identified with facts observable by another.

4.1   Space, Time and Abstract State Machines

The space through which an ASM progresses is its state space. The symbols from its signature, excluding the derived names, form a basis for that state space. The paths that an ASM can follow through the state space are constrained by the initial state and by the ASM program.

The passage of time for an ASM is closely tied to a run of the ASM. In SDL, distributed real-time ASMs are defined using a real-valued monitored function *currentTime*, which refers to an external, physical time [12]. Consistency between *currentTime* and a concept of time based on the progress of an ASM through its state space is maintained by requiring that *currentTime* should increase monotonically over ASM runs. The passage of time while an ASM is in a given state is described in [11], where the logical time of an ASM is expressed in terms of interactions with the environment during a single step. But there too the passage of time through a run is described in terms of persistent queries made by an ASM in one state and the delayed responses received in a different, later state.

Here, an ASM has its own local time, which has a value of zero or more in an initial state, and which is incremented by a positive amount at the end of every transition. The increment is demanded so that no two states in a run are identical, even if infinite runs pass and re-pass through otherwise identical states, for example, to model continuous services.

Relativity describes concepts including *spacetime*, *coordinate system* and *frame of reference*. In relativity, events in spacetime are defined by assigning numbers to four spacetime coordinates. These numbers depend on a frame of reference, which is a system used to assign the numbers [16]. The values in one frame of reference can be transformed and used in another frame of reference, so long as the transformation maintains underlying physical laws.

For an ASM, a comparison can be made between spacetime coordinates and the symbols defined by the signature, including a symbol for local time but excluding derived names. The ASM program provides a frame of reference, by which values are assigned to these coordinates.

In general, different ASMs will occupy different state spaces and will have and different local times.

This reveals a point at which the analogy breaks down. In general, different ASMs exist in different state spaces, so translating an observation about the state occupied by one ASM agent to another ASM agent demands not only changes of coordinate values, or even of coordinate systems, but a change of dimensionality. That is, states must be projected onto the shareable dimensions in order to move the information between different state spaces.

A further difference between spacetime as known in relativity and the ASM spacetime outlined here is that the ASM spacetime is not continuous. In place of four real-valued spacetime coordinates, that values that can be assigned to an ASM vocabulary element do not, in general, form a continuous set. On the other hand, a concept not unlike differentiability within a local region is retained for an ASM state space in that the difference between a current state and a next state is contained; this is expressed as the Bounded Exploration Postulate in [5] or, more restrictively, as the small step requirement of [14].

4.2   The History of an ASM

An ASM has a *local history*. A local history of a single-threaded ASM is any sequence of states in a run of the ASM. An event in the ASM's history is a state, including the local time of the ASM. A single threaded ASM has a single ASM agent, and a history of a single threaded ASM is also the history of its agent.

A local history of a distributed ASM is the sequence of states associated the initial segments of a serialization of the partially ordered set of moves of the ASM.

This description of the history of a distributed ASM differs from the notion of history defined in [12]. There, only states that directly contribute to the computation represented by the run are retained, and states that differ from their predecessors only in their values of the external, physical *currentTime* are dropped. It also differs from the histories defined in [11], which record the order in which an ASM receives inputs from its environment during a single step.

The partial ordering of updates in a distributed ASM means that all the agents of the distributed ASM share a common time. Regarding the distributed ASM as a model of a single, multi-threaded computation, that common time, although global to the ASM agents, is local to the ASM. It need not be the same as the time observed by agents of other, parallel, independent ASMs.

4.3   Interaction and Interpretation of Events

In the distributed ASMs described by Glausch and Reisig [8] and in SDL [12], interaction is defined in terms of updates to locations that can be read or updated by more than one ASM. Interaction with the external environment is described in a similar way. In SDL, locations that are updated by the environment and read by the ASM are called *monitored* locations, and locations that are read and written by the environment and by the ASM are called *shared* locations.

Updates performed by the environment are treated as occurring between transitions of the ASM by Blass and Gurevich [5], though it is also possible to model updates made by the environment during a move [11].

Outputs from an ASM to its environment are modelled as updates made by the ASM to locations that can be read by the environment [3, 5]. In this way, the environment is treated as moves by one agent in a distributed ASM that are always in contention with the moves of the original ASM.

Continuing the analogy with concepts from relativity, a state represents an event in the history of an ASM. If an external ASM agent is to observe any part of that event, then there must be an overlap between the state of the external ASM and the opservable part of the state of the original ASM. Also, the external ASM can only observe the event in terms of its own signature and its own local time. Only that part of the event that affects shared locations is visible to the external ASM, and from the perspective of the external ASM agent, the whole event is represented by its projection onto the shared locations.

Moreover, in general the state of an ASM is not stable while the ASM is performing a move [11, 14], though moves can be expressed as having a start, an intermediate point (during which the state is unobservable), and an end [17]. This addresses the fact that an observation of an incomplete state is likely to be unreliable.

4.4   Observation of an Event

Consider two abstract state machines, A and B. A in state S_A associates the value v with a location identified as $f_A(\overline{a})$. B in state S_B identifies the same location as $f_B(\overline{a})$. That is, there is an overlap between state S_B of B and state S_A, a state (event) in the history of A, which in turn means that an agent of B can observe part of a state in the history of A.

To enable this observation, part of S_A is transformed to the corresponding part of B's frame of reference. That is, S_A is projected onto $f_A(\overline{a})$, and $f_A(\overline{a})$ is mapped to $f_B(\overline{b})$, and so B observes the value of the shared location as A sees it.

This example illustrates the first requirements on transformations that map observations made by one ASM to the frame of reference of another ASM.

Common location

> *Suppose A and B are two ASMs. Then a transformation of states from the frame of reference of A to that of B*
> - *is defined for projections of the states of A onto locations that are also accessible to B;*
> - *maps locations of A to locations of B so that $f_A(\overline{a})$ is mapped to $f_B(\overline{b})$ iff the two terms refer to the same location.*

But suppose $f(\overline{a}) = v$ is true in S_A, and $f_B(\overline{b}) = w$ is true in S_B and $v \neq w$. In that case, the two states cannot coincide.

This leads to the following requirements affecting transformation of the time of observations between abstract state machines:

Consistent perspective

Suppose A and B are two abstract state machines.
- *Before the local times of A and B can be synchronized, A and B must be in states that associate the same values to all common locations;*
- *If $f(\overline{a}) = v$ is true in S_A, and $f_B(\overline{b}) = w$ is true in S_B and $v \neq w$, then either S_B is in the past of S_A and S_A is in the future of S_B or vice versa. So if a transformation of the event S_A to the frame of reference of B enables an agent of B to observe that values of one or more commonly accessible locations are different from A's perspective, then that transformation must transform the local time of A to a value that is different from the local time of B. Furthermore, if B's local time is t_B in state S_B, and A's local time is t_A in state S_A, then the transformation must map t_A to a value representing the local time of a state of S_B for which all the commonly accessible locations share the same values from the points of view of both A and B.*

This still allows ASM A in state S_A and B in state S_B to have different values for a given location, provided B does not claim see the value as seen by A as occuring at Bs current local time and vice versa.

It also gives form to the conditions for synchronizing and merging the histories of two ASMs.

Synchronize and merge

In order to synchronize two ASMs and bring their processes together to form a distributed ASM with a shared local time;
- *all commonly accessible locations must be updated so that they have the same values regardless of which ASM agent observes them;*
- *the local time of the two ASMs must be synchronized;*
- *the ASMs must proceed in step.*

While an ASM is mid-transition, its state is not stable. Updates could be rolled back (undone) before the transition is complete. Repeated observations of the value of a location may produce inconsistent results during a transition so only location-value associations on entry to or exit from a transition can be viewed as observations of definite events in the history of an ASM.

The ASMs discussed in [14] allow multiple interactions between an ASM and its environment to occur during a step, with the proviso that an ASM never completes a step before all the queries emanating from that step have been answered, and that the only information about the environment available to the ASM is that obtained in response to queries.

Queries that persist beyond a single step are addressed by [11]. There the ASM that makes the query also supplies a location to receive its response.

These approaches do not rely on direct observation of environmental values by the ASM, but instead allow the environment to control when answers to queries are released, and the ASM to control where those answers are located. Provided the environment only releases stable values, and places those values at the locations stipulated by the ASM, no problems arise.

This leads to the following constraint on observable locations.

Scratch work is private

Locations that can be observed should not be used for changeable 'scratch work' carried out by an ASM during a step. In other words, if an agent of B observes that $f_A(\overline{a}) = v$ is true in state S_A of A, and that $f_A(\overline{a}) = w$ is true in state S'_A, then either $v = w$ or $S_A \neq S'_A$.

A final constraint concerns the immutability of an ASM's history.

History is immutable

If S_A precedes S'_A in the history of A, then any observation of these two states by B must maintain that ordering. That is, the local time of S_A according to A is less than the local time of S'_A, and this ordering must be maintained when these events are represented in B's history.

---

5   Practical Applications

The requirements on interaction outlined above are discussed below with reference to the ticket reservation service and its client applications, and to the reservation service treated as a web service.

5.1   The Reservation Service Revisited

Suppose the ticket reservation service were modelled as an abstract state machine, *Resv*. Now suppose a booking agency created an application, modelled as an abstract state machine *App*, that made use of *Resv*. Merging *Resv* with *App* as a single distributed ASM is impractical, because *Resv* is already deployed, and is likely to have clients other than *App*, with timing requirements likely to be quite different from those of *App*.

How do the requirements outlined above help define non-contentious interaction?

The requirements concerning naming commonly accessible locations, **Common location** is essential to any interaction.

History is immutable means, for example, that if the history of *Resv* records a ticket as available in one state of *Resv*, and as unavailable in a subsequent state of *Resv*, then the states of *App* that correspond to those facts must also occur in the same order.

This leaves two further requirements to consider.

The first concerns consistency between the perspectives of *Resv* and *App*.

The requirement for **Consistent perspective** means that if *App* observes a common location as having a different value from that represented by *Resv*, then that observation must be at a point in time that is different from *App*'s current local time. If the observation refers to a ticket that *Resv* shows as available and *App* wished to book, then the two must be brought into harmony in a future state of *App* and *Resv*. This also applies to all the other applications that might be attempting to book the same ticket, but given an application-specific limit on the number of bookings applicable to each ticket, the two requirements will conspire to show the ticket(s) booked by some application(s) and not booked by others in a future of all the ASMs.

It does not say how the required transaction agency is to be preserved, but only that it should be preserved. For example, a timestamping approach might model the tickets themselves as ASMs, where a ticket maintained its last read and last update timestamps using its own local time, passing that time to applications via *Resv*.

The second concerns visibility of incomplete states; for example, it concerns the possibility that *App* might observe an uncommitted reservation in *Resv*. The requirement **Scratch work is private** prevents observation by other applications of an uncommitted update made, for example, by the application *App*.

5.2   Web Application

Web services provide a good example of distinct agents enacting parallel processes that can be modelled using abstract state machines whose steps proceed without reference to a global state or time.

A web application provides a service that can be accessed using a web browser. Registering a web application with the Universal Description, Discovery and Integration (UDDI) directory service, make it possible to integrate that application into other applications [18]. The original application then becomes a component of the new application. According to the w3schools tutorial on web services description and UDDI, if there were an industry-wide UDDI standard for checking rates and reserving flights, and if airlines registered their services in a UDDI directory, then travel agencies could communicate with the airlines' reservations services using the interface published in the UDDI directory [18].

Suppose the web application for reservations were represented as *Resv*, the UDDI directory service as *Dir* and the client application as *App*. The *Dir* entry for *Resv* defines the locations that are observable by *App*, and helps enable definition of the transformations by which each *App* interacts with *Resv*. But *Dir* is itself an ASM, with a large observable space, whose transformations must comply with the above requirements.

Developing such transformations would mean that different variants of *Resv* and of *App* could be modelled as abstract state machines, and could interact without the need for a global state and time. This would be more in tune with the brokering philosophy of UDDI than would a model that prescribed, for example, an absolute global system time.

6 Summary

Some promising initial steps towards ASM modelling that allows parallel ASMs to interact without demanding that they should refer to a common global state is outlined above. Inspired by concepts from relativity, the observation of states of one ASM by another ASM is described in terms of the requirements that must be fulfilled by an transformation of observations between the different state spaces occupied by the ASMs. Some of the practical implications of these requirements are briefly discussed. A fuller study based on application of these ideas to real systems would be desirable, and would help the development of practical transformations.

References

1. Gurevich, Y.: Evolving Algebras 1993: Lipari Guide. In: Specification and Validation Methods, pp. 9–36. Oxford University Press (1995)
2. G.Y.: Evolving Algebras 1993. Lipari Guide, 2005 version with table of contents and footnote, http://research.microsoft.com/en-us/um/people/gurevich/opera/103.pdf
3. Börger, E., Stärk, R.: Abstract State Machines – a Method for High-Level System Design and Analysis. Springer (2003)
4. Börger, E.: The ASM Refinement Method. Formal Aspects of Computing 15, 237–257 (2003)
5. Blass, A., Gurevich, Y.: Abstract State Machines Capture Parallel Algorithms. ACM Transactions on Computational Logic 4(4), 578–651 (2003)
6. Blass, A., Gurevich, Y.: Abstract State Machines Capture Parallel Algorithms: Correction and Extension. ACM Transactions on Computational Logic 9(3), Article 19 (2008)
7. Glässer, U., Gurevich, Y., Veanes, M.: Abstract Communication Model for Distributed Systems. IEEE Transactions on Software Engineering 30(7) (2004)
8. Glausch, A., Reisig, W.: Distributed Abstract State Machines and Their Expressive Power. Humboldt University Berlin (2006)

9. Glausch, A., Reisig, W.: An ASM-Characterization of a Class of Distributed Algorithms. In: Abrial, J.-R., Glässer, U. (eds.) Rigorous Methods for Software Construction and Analysis. LNCS, vol. 5115, pp. 50–64. Springer, Heidelberg (2009)

10. Börger, Cisternino, A., Gervasi, V.: Ambient Abstract State Machines with applications. Journal of Computer and System Sciences 78(3), 939–959 (2011)

11. Blass, A., Gurevich, Y.: Persistent Queries in the Behavioral Theory of Algorithms. ACM Transactions on Computational Logic 12(2), Article 16 (2011)

12. International Telecommunication Union (ITU): Recommendation Z.100 Annex F1 (11/00) SDL formal definition – General overview. http://www.itu.int/rec/T-REC-Z.100-200011-S!AnnF1/en

13. Glässer, U., Gotzhein, R., Prinz, A.: The formal semantics of SDL-2000: Status and perspectives. Computer Networks 42, 343–358 (2003)

14. Blass, A., Gurevich, Y.: Ordinary Interactive Small-Step Algorithms – I. ACM Transactions on Computational Logic 7(2), 363–419 (2006)

15. International Telecommunication Union (ITU): Recommendation Z.101 (12/11) – Specification and Description Language - Basic SDL-2010 (2010) http://www.itu.int/rec/T-REC-Z.101-201112-I/en

16. Norton, J.D.: General Covariance and the foundations of general relativity– eight decades of dispute. Reports on Progress in Physics 56(7), 791–858 (1993)

17. Graf, S., Prinz, A.: Time in State Machines. Fundamenta Informaticae, 77(1-2), 143–174 (2007)

18. WSDL and UDDI, http://www.w3schools.com/wsdl/wsdl_uddi.asp

From Earthquake Detection to Traffic Surveillance – About Information and Communication Infrastructures for Smart Cities

Joachim Fischer[1], Jens-Peter Redlich[1], Björn Scheuermann[1], Jochen Schiller[2],
Mesut Günes[2], Kai Nagel[3], Peter Wagner[4], Markus Scheidgen[1],
Anatolij Zubow[1], Ingmar Eveslage[1], Robert Sombrutzki[1],
and Felix Juraschek[2]

[1] Humboldt Universität zu Berlin
{fischer,redlich,scheuermann,scheidge,zubow,sombrutz,
eveslage}@informatik.hu-berlin.de
[2] Freie Universität Berlin
{jochen.schiller,mesut.guenes,felix.juraschek}@fu-berlin.de
[3] Technische Universität Berlin
kai.nagel@tu-berlin.de
[4] Deutsches Zentrum für Luft und Raumfahrt
peter.wagner@dlr.de

Abstract. Smart cities use networks of sensors, actuators, and centralized computing clusters to observe physical reality, derive information, and thereby influence citizens and authorities. Smart city applications therefore require three components to work: wireless sensor networks, geo-information systems, and frameworks for distributed analysis of sensor and geo-data. In this paper, we provide an overview on a set of concrete technologies for such information and communication infrastructures for smart cities. These technologies include a combination of WiFi- and PAN-based sensor networks, City GML data, a model-driven approach to collect and manage data, as well as distributed data analysis based on domain specific languages. We show how we use these technologies to research two typical smart city applications: earthquake early warning and traffic surveillance.

1   Introduction

Smart cities use networks of sensors, actuators, and centralized computing clusters to observe physical reality, derive information, and thereby influence citizens and authorities. A series of smart city applications was discussed the last years: *SmartGrids* [1,2] use *SmartMeter* and dynamic energy prices to help consumers use electricity for efficiently. Wireless sensor networks in *earthquake early warning systems* [3] detect earthquakes quickly and automatically shutdown cities energy and traffic infrastructure. Smart parking space control systems use sensors to direct drivers to free parking spots [4]. Many cities already maintain wireless

Ø. Haugen, R. Reed, and R. Gotzhein (Eds.): SAM 2012, LNCS 7744, pp. 121–141, 2013.
© Springer-Verlag Berlin Heidelberg 2013

sensor networks to research such applications. Two examples are *CitySense* in Bosten, USA [5] and *SmartSantander* in Santander, Spain [4,6].

All these applications and services require three fundamental technology components. First, *wireless sensor networks* (WSN) that aquire data about the physical reality and privide the means to transport data. Secondly, *geo information systems* (GIS) provide context data necessary to interpret sensor data. Thirdly, we need *data analysis frameworks* that can process large amounts of heterogeneous data in complex chains of individual computation steps. These components are depicted in Fig. 1.

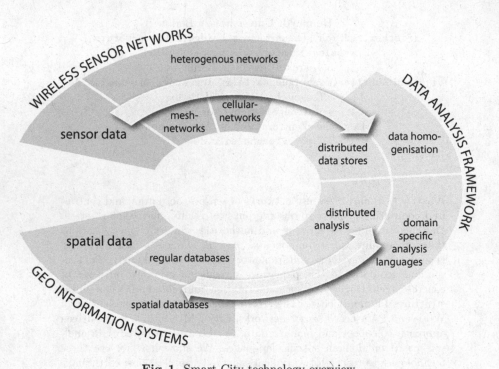

Fig. 1. Smart City technology overview

In this paper, we describe the combined efforts of researchers at Berlin's three major universities to develop an infrastructure that provides these three components and therefore allows researchers to build smart city application and services. The paper is organized as follows. The next three sections present the used sensor networks, the used data standards and geo information systems, and our approach on analysing the vast amount of expected data by modern software engineering means. The next two sections present our efforts in research two smart city applications: earchquake early warning and traffic surveillance. We end the paper with a discussion of possible future developments and implications.

2 Wireless Sensor Networks

Wireless sensor networks (WSNs) [7] are battery powered wireless multi-hop networks, where each node is equipped with multiple sensors. WSNs allow to sense the environment without any existing infrastructure. Typical WSNs use low powered and energy-efficient hardware with short-range radio communication (e.g. tmote sky) typically based on Wireless Personal Area Networks (WPAN), e.g. IEEE 802.15.4. As main characteristic these WSNs use short duty cycles and long periods of inactivity to preserve batteries. Thus, WSNs are tailored for measurements at low sensor sample rates or over short periods of time. Due to high energy consumption of radio communication, WSNs typically record data locally and communicate only aggregated data of small size (Fig. 2, left).

Typically WSNs are used to measure a single physical variable. Applications include measurement of temperature, sensing the presence or absence of objects, monitoring the structural health of buildings via vibrations and natural frequencies (Structural Health Monitoring (SHM) [8]), or sensing the acoustic stress by measuring noise levels [9].

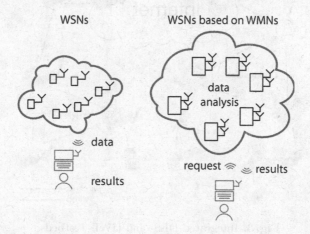

Fig. 2. The HWL-Testbed enables the development and analysis of applications for HP-WSN

WNS applications are limited by computation and networking capabilities of WSNs. Applications such as SHM with higher sample rates at multiple channels, recording of audio (e.g. speech in contrast to just noise levels), measuring patterns such as bitmaps created by video cameras [10], or measuring multiple properties at once (e.g. detecting correlation between temperature and natural frequencies in concrete) require a different kind of WSN. Such applications produce different types of data in large amounts in a short period of time.

WSNs based on Wireless Local Area Network (W-LAN), e.g. IEEE 802.11 with a larger physical size, higher battery weight, or even cable based power supply are a new class of sensor networks based on wireless mesh networks (WMNs). Compared to managed wired networks these ad-hoc WMNs still allow fast and cost effective way to install a communication and sensing infrastructure in a previously unknown and changing environment. Beyond sensing, this WMNs provide enough capabilities to run data analysis within the network (Fig. 2, right).

We use combinated WSN/WMN testbeds that comprise both kinds of sensor nodes. Our two test-beds at the Humboldt and Freie University in Berlin form a interconnected network configuration. A network configuration [11] is an architecture that describes the way how different kinds of networks can be connected and integrated to support particular applications and services for Smart Cities. In the following, we describe existing network configurations for WMNs and WSNs and how those configurations can be recombined into a heterogeneous network configuration for smart cities.

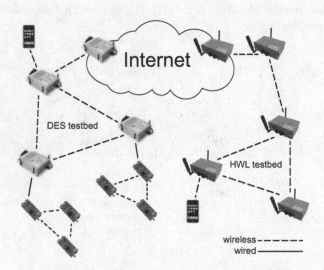

Fig. 3. Integrated DES- and HWL-Testbeds

The basic building blocks of smart city network configurations are *WMNs* and *WSNs*. Both are self-organized mesh networks that provide autonomous configuration, self-healing and basic deployment capabilities. WMNs are traditionally studied as stationary or mobile (mobile ad-hoc networks – MANET) access networks for mobile wireless clients. WMNs are typically based on 802.11x hardware; WMN nodes have larger radio range, higher computational capabilities, run more complex software and require more power than the nodes of a WSN. WSNs on the other hand are only used to monitor the environment with sensors. They are smaller, only wake for short sensing cycles, and only communicate to provide sensor data to clients. Nodes of traditional WMNs can also be equipped with sensors to create *high performance WSNs* [12] in contrast to typical WSNs.

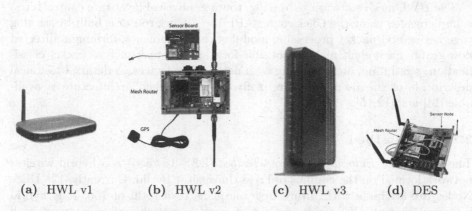

(a) HWL v1   (b) HWL v2   (c) HWL v3   (d) DES

Fig. 4. Three different types of HWL nodes are used: (a) HWL v1 which is an indoor node with a single 802.11b/g radio device, (b) HWL v2 which is an outdoor node with two 802.11a/b/g radio devices and (c) HWL v3 is an indoor node with two 802.11a/b/g/n (MIMO) devices, and the DES node (d) comprising the multi-radio mesh router and the MSB-A2 sensor node

Fig. 3 shows the integrated DES- and HWL-Testbeds as a combination of WMNs and WSNs with WMNs acting as integrator between WSNs and access network for clients; the Internet provides an interconnection between the two networks. In the following, we first describe the HWL-Testbed at HU Berlin and the DES-Testbed at FU Berlin and their features.

2.1   HWL-Testbed

The Humboldt Wireless Lab (HWL) is a large-scale wireless mesh network at the campus of the Humboldt University, Germany. It consists of about 125 mesh nodes based on 802.11a/b/g as well as the new 802.11n standard which are deployed indoor as well as outdoor. The indoor nodes, which are placed in several buildings, form a fully connected wireless network, which can be combined with the outdoor network to improve the connectivity between the buildings. The aim of HWL is to evaluate large-scale mesh networks, since small- and medium-scale mesh networks are already well understood. The upcoming IEEE 802.11n standard promises to significantly increase coverage, reliability, and throughput which comes from the advanced antenna technology based on Multiple Input Multiple Output (MIMO) techniques.

All indoor nodes are connected via a wired VLAN backbone to a central testbed server, which provides services like TFTP, DHCP, DNS and NFS. In contrast the outdoor nodes are connected by a wireless mesh network backbone and a gateway with the testbed server. Therefore the second wireless interface is used and cannot be used for experiments. All experiments are centrally controlled from the testbed server where also the data collected in the experiments is stored, which simplifies the analysis considerably.

The HWL mesh software (adressing, routing, physical layer rate control, etc.) is implemented using the Click router API [13]. A Click router is built by sticking together several packet processing modules, called elements, forming a directed flow graph. Each element is responsible for a specific task such as packet classification, scheduling, or interfacing with networking devices. A detailed technical description of the used hardware, software and testbed architecture is available [14] and [12,15].

2.2   DES-Testbed

The *Distributed Embedded Systems Testbed* (DES-Testbed) is a hybrid wireless network located on the campus of Freie Universität Berlin. Currently, 128 DES-Nodes are available with future upgrade plans to a total of 150. It is hybrid in a way, that all DES-Nodes consist of a wireless mesh router equipped with multiple IEEE 802.11a/b/g radios and a MSB-A2 sensor node [16] as shown in 4d. Thus, a WMN based on IEEE 802.11 technology, called DES-Mesh, and a WSN, called the DES-WSN, are operated in parallel. In this manner it is possible to constitute all the possible network configurations for *wireless multi-hop networks* (WMHNs).

The DES-Nodes are scattered in an irregular topology across several buildings on the campus. Most of the nodes are deployed inside the offices, while some outdoor nodes are added to improve the connectivity and increase the approximation to real world scenarios. A testbed server DES-Portal functions as the central control instance in the DES-Testbed. It is connected to all DES-Nodes via an Ethernet backbone. A detailed technical description of the used hardware and testbed architecture is available in our technical reports [17] and [18].

For the purpose of comparison and easy implementation of routing protocols we developed the *Distributed Embedded Systems - Simple and Extensible Routing-Framework for Testbeds* (DES-SERT) [19]. The daemon forwards Ethernet frames or raw IP datagrams in an underlay (layer 2.5 routing, like in MPLS) so that the routing is transparent to the upper layer protocols. As mobility is an important aspect for the research on WMNs and WSNs, DES-SERT has also been ported to the Android smartphone platform. An Android-based smartphone mounted on a Lego NXT robot serves as a mobile client to the testbed.

3   Geo Information Systems

To interpret sensor data correctly the context of where and when data was acquired is important. Thermometer readings taken in the shade have different meaning than readings taken in direct sunlight. Therefore, we need a system that can provide context data as further input for sensor data analysis.

A geo(graphic) information system (GIS) is a system designed to capture, store, manipulate, analyze, manage, and present all types of geographical data. GIS data represents real objects (such as roads, land use, elevation, trees, waterways, etc.) with digital data. Real objects can be divided into two abstractions:

discrete objects (e.g. a house) and continuous fields (such as rainfall amount or elevations). There are two methods used to store data in a GIS for both kinds of abstractions: vectors and raster images.

In our work and in this paper, we concentrate on vector data. There is a series of OGC (Open Geo-Spatial Consortium) standards to represent geographic vector data for different applications. Two of them are the Geographic Markup Language (GML) [20] and City GML [21]. Both standards are based on XML and XML-Schema. While GML defines a basic set of XML-types to describe arbitrary geographic objects by means of their location, shape, and composition, City GML is specialized to model cities. City GML defines specific types to define buildings, structure, furniture, and their parts. One of City GML's key features is that it is not limited to modeling the 3D properties of objects, but that it also allows its users to define semantic extensions. These semantic extensions can be used to add all kinds of related information to objects such as materials, usage, legal, or census data.

Therefore, City GML can be used to answer questions like: from which windows of which rooms in which buildings can I have free views on certain places, streets or monuments? To what floor the building were affected by a flood in each case? Which buildings of a special district have roofs, which are oriented to the south with a special angle of inclination. There are three approaches to technically serve City GML data. Relational databases (with geo-spatial extensions) with proprietary interfaces [22], managed sets of XML-files [23], or as fragmented EMF-models [24].

Since we already manage sensor data based on fragmented EMF-models and the goal is to relate City GML data with this sensor data, it makes sense to use the last approach. City GML's XML-schemata can be used to automatically derive corresponding EMF-meta-models. Therefore, City GML data can be represented as EMF-models, it can be managed with EMF-Fragments (refer to the next section), and it can be created, modified, accessed, and deleted with EMF's generated and reflection interfaces. The combination of EMF, EMF-fragments, City GML schemata therefore forms a GIS for City GML data that we can use within the same data analysis framework that we use to store, manage, and analyze sensor data. Refer to the next section for more details.

4   Data Analysis Frameworks

There are three goals of a data analysis framework. First, heterogeneous sets of data from different sources (e.g. WSNs and GISs) can be persisted and organized automatically on a cluster. Secondly, complex computations can be described with data-type specific concepts and independent from the details of their distributed execution. Thirdly, the logical connections between input and output of each computation step are recorded to allow for later interpretation of the potentially vast amounts of individual results. To achieve these goals, we apply meta-modeling and model transformation based on EMF to distributed data processing based on Apache's HBase and Hadoop. Fig. 5a depicts the architecture overview. In the following subsections, we describe three necessary

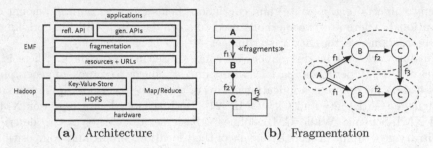

(a) Architecture   (b) Fragmentation

Fig. 5. Overview of our architecture and the idea of model fragmentation

steps: collecting data from WSNs, organizing data in a distributed data store, and finally running computations on this data.

4.1 Collecting Sensor Data

Both testbeds provide means to design and control experiments, to collect corresponding data and organize it in a central data store.

DES-Testbed Management System (DES-TBMS): The *DES-TBMS* comprises all steps of an experiment, namely the definition, automatized execution, and evaluation of experiments. *DES-Cript* is a domain specific language (DSL) based on XML, which defines and describes network experiments in a holistic way. *DES-Exp* provides an experiment manager which is responsible for the scheduling and execution of experiments. *DES-Web* provides a web interface to *DES-Exp*, which allows to create, modify, and schedule experiments using *DES-Cript*. The network monitoring tool *DES-Mon* is based on SNMP and retrieves the network state from the *DES-Nodes*. *DES-Mon* collects data from the wireless interfaces, the kernel routing table, ETX neighborhood information, and data from the sensor nodes. *DES-Vis* is a 3D-visualization software based on the JavaView framework. The evaluation tool *DES-Eval* enables the post-processing of the experiment results supporting work flows for an automatic evaluation process.

HWL-ClickWatch: ClickWatch [25] is an experiment control and analysis framework. ClickWatch connects to the Click runtime installed on all HWL-Testbed nodes and constantly collects data provided by all software components on the node (e.g. sensor, network protocol, and system components). This data comprises sensor data, network and system statistics, and configuration parameters. ClickWatch allows to visualize and change the nodes internal state and configuration at runtime. Furthermore, ClickWatch transforms incoming heterogeneous data into a homogeneous strongly typed representation. ClickWatch stores data in an HBase database and allows to access this data through statically typed APIs. This allows to write safe, reusable analysis scripts. ClickWatch represents all data within the Eclipse Modeling Framework (EMF). EMF based parser tools allows to transform the log-file style data provided by the DES-testbed or other

3rd-party networks into the same structured ClickWatch representation. This allows an integrated analysis of data provided by both the Smart Berlin networks: DES and HWL.

4.2 Homogenisation and Distributed Organisation of Data

Our sensor networks and the used GISs provide complex sets of interconnected data based on a large amount of different types and based on different data modeling methodologies (EMF, XML, log-files, CSV-files, etc.). Dealing with complex, interconnected, well typed data-structures is the core trait of model driven software engineering. Meta-models allow to define fine grained object oriented types and references; constraints can elaborate meta-models, and semantics can be assigned to data structures. There is a large zoo of model transformation languages, programming frameworks, and other techniques. Software modeling (especially model driven architecture) provides the tools to integrate different typed structures (typically called languages). Furthermore, software modeling (especially EMF-based) integrates well with other core technologies like XML, ontologies, or even databases (e.g. via ORMs like CDO). But, software models are usually small enough to fit into main memory and scaleablity is less of an issue. Therefore, there are two challenges. First, we need to determine how meta-modeling can be used to integrate the different data sets. Secondly, we need to extend existing meta-modeling frameworks to handle large amounts of data.

Meta-Modeling as Integrator for Different Kinds of Data: If we look at our three data sources, we have EMF-based data, text/log-file based data, and XML-data. EMF- and XML-based are covered through modern meta-modeling frameworks like EMF. EMF-data explains itself, and XML-data can be intgrated since EMF use XML as native persistence format. Text- and log-file-based needs some efforts to describe its formal structure. We can use text-to-model transformation techniques to create parsers that extract data from text-based files and create an EMF-based representation of this data.

Distributed Storage of Large Meta-Model-based Data Sets: We build a model persistence framework for EMF [26] called *EMF-fragments* [24,27]. EMF-Fragments is different from frameworks based on object relational mappings (ORM) like Connected Data Objects (CDO) [28]. While ORM mappings map single objects, attributes, and references to database entries, EMF fragments map larger chunks of a model (fragments) to URIs. This allows to store models on a wide range of distributed data-stores including distributed file-systems and key-value stores (e.g. Hadoop's HBase).

EMF-Fragments use and extend the regular EMF resource API. Clients designate references that shall fragment the model in the meta-model. Fig. 5b exemplifies fragmentation on meta and model level. EMF-Fragments then automatically and transparently create and manage resources and their content. This allows to control fragmentation without the need to trigger it programatically. Fragments/resource are continuously managed in the background, i.e. resources are loaded and also unloaded as necessary. Each fragment is backed by an EMF resource and identified by its URI. Resources and URIs are canonically mapped to keys and values in a key-value store (e.g. Hadoop's HBase). From the client perspective one just uses the regular reflective (refl.) or generated (gen.) EMF-APIs.

There are two general ways to describe fragmentation in the meta-model. The first one is to mark containment references in the Ecore meta-model with annotations. This tells EMF-fragments to create a new resource for each value in those references. This works well when the number of anticipated values per feature is relatively low. This is usually the case in software models. In a large Java code base for example, we have a large number compilation units (i.e. Java class files), but a single package only contains a small set of sub-packages and compilation units (example in Fig. 6a).

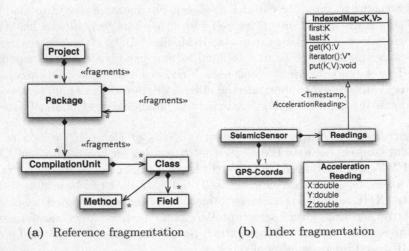

(a) Reference fragmentation   (b) Index fragmentation

Fig. 6. Examples for the different methods for describing model fragmentation

With the described method the container has to keep references to all its contents. If we have millions of values the references alone require too large resources even though the values are stored in different resources. Therefore, we also need a second approach: clients can use predefined index classes to define relationships with large value sets. This happens for example, if we want to store sensor readings in EMF: each sensor might have million of readings depending on the period of time and sample rate (example in Fig. 6b).

An index is simply a sorted list of key-value pairs. Indices are mapped to the underlying key-value store. Therefore, the used key-value store has to be sorted (e.g. like Hadoop's HBase). The index managing class stores the first and the last key of the index. Elements can be accessed directly using keys or they can be iterated.

4.3   Distributed Computation of Data

The Hadoop web site describes it's Map/Reduce capabilities like this: "Map-Reduce is a software framework for easily writing applications which process vast amounts of data (multi-terabyte data-sets) in-parallel on large clusters (thousands of nodes) of commodity hardware in a reliable, fault-tolerant manner." Map/Reduce has proven itself as a successful programming model. But, Map/Reduce has two known disadvantages. First, Map/Reduce is only suited for so called *embarrassingly parallel problems*. Engineers struggle to implement algorithms for problems that do not canonically fall into independent parts. Secondly, Map/Reduce deliberately ignores the structure of the data that it is used to analyze. This issue is delegated to users. The consequences are many; examples are hardly reusable algorithms based on proprietary data-structures or slow, defective, and proprietary parsers.

We use EMF to help with the second problem: the EMF-Fragments framework introduced in the prior section stores data as fragmented EMF models in a key-value-store, and Map/Reduce implementations are designed to work with these stores. We are using Hadoop as an implementation of Map/Reduce, and we use Hadoop's HBase key-value-store as our datastore. In the Hadoop/HBase framework, clients have to extend abstract Map and Reduce classes to define their own Map/Reduce function pairs. Abstractions for input and output of these functions are arbitrary text files (stored with Hadoop's distributed file system HDFS), or key-value entries (stored in HBase tables). We extend these Hadoop/HBase's abstractions to use EMF objects as input and output. Instead of raw values, clients are given the EMF contents of the corresponding resources, and instead of writing raw values, clients can create new EMF-objects.

Despite all this convenience, users still have to put a lot of thought into their problems. First, clients have to design their meta-models intelligently (i.e. create reasonably fragments). The goal is to create fragments that allow each map task to only work with a single fragment. This allows Hadoop to preserve locality and execute map tasks on nodes that already store their input data. Secondly of course, only a small set of problems maps to the Map/Reduce paradigm trivially.

5   Application I: Earthquake Early Warning

Disasters caused by natural phenomena are considered as one of the most threatening events of today's modern world. Even though most of them cannot be predicted, efforts can be made for mitigating human and economic losses. This can be achieved by means of early warning, which allows individuals exposed to hazard to take action to avoid or reduce their risk and prepare for effective response. In this context, the main challenge is to minimize the delay between the detection of an occurred event and the delivery of alarm messages in order to maximize the time available for preventing possible damages. Nevertheless, the development of reliable infrastructures for supporting early warning is not trivial because of the diversity of the natural phenomena and cost related issues.

Earthquake Early Warning (EEW), as a special case of early warning, is characterized by a very short delay between the actual earthquake event and its destructive impact. Current EEW Systems (EEWS) are composed of few expensive and highly sensitive sensor stations, installed outside of urban areas, and connected to a single data center. These centralized infrastructures have a number of problems related to single point of failure, insufficient node density, and an increased delay between event and warning propagation caused by the missing integration into the target area.

In contrast to existing EEWS, our approach, the Self-Organizing Seismic Early Warning Information Network (SOSEWIN) [29], is technically a decentralized, self-organizing wireless mesh network (WMN), equipped with seismological sensors, made up of low-cost components. With a relatively low price, a very dense network (hundreds or thousands of nodes) can be established directly in the threatened regions. A new question connected with a self-organized warning system concerns the potential end user of the warnings. An alarm could be more than the information of a centralized disaster management facility; it can be used for a direct information of the private owners and their neighborhoods, a decentralized control (power-downs, gas pressure reduction) of technical devices, plants and more.

SOSEWIN realizes EEW by means of a distributed application with hard real-time constraints, raising the early warning inside the network itself. We follow a generally approved model-driven development paradigm using standardized languages to generate code for the target platform (sensor nodes) and for different kinds of simulators. These simulators are combined with environment models in order to evaluate the early warning performance of the network. The environmental model consists of synthesized timed data series as imitations of the ground shaking for each chosen geographical sensor node position in dependence to the distance of the epicenter and the magnitude of that imaginary event.

Earthquakes produce different types of seismic waves, which travel from the hypocenter in every direction. Their analysis is the foundation for different activities in disaster management (i.e. earthquake classification, early warning, and first response). There are four types of seismic waves divided into two groups:

- P-waves and S-waves (called body waves). They travel through the interior of the Earth. P-waves (primary waves) travel faster than S-waves (secondary waves)[1]. They are less destructive than the S-waves and surface waves that follow them.
- Rayleigh waves and Love waves (called surface waves). They remain below the Earth's surface and can be much larger in amplitude than body waves.

Even though it is not possible to predict an earthquake event, preparations can be made for the incoming disaster. This can be achieved by using the time delay between the arrival times of the P-wave and S-wave (Figure 7). This delay varies from a few seconds to some minutes depending on the distance between the epicenter of the earthquake and the critical area locations.

---

[1] Dependent upon the geology of the specific region and the hypocenter depth, P-waves travel at 5-8 km/s, and S-waves at 3-7 km/s.

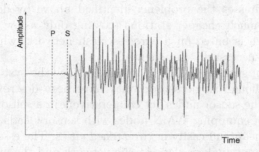

Fig. 7. Time delay between P-wave and S-wave

Nowadays Earthquake Early Warning Systems (EEWS) are based on the detection of the harmless P-waves that precede the slower and destructive S-waves and surface waves. Therefore, the primary goal of an EEWS is to maximize the early warning time under a minimal number of false alarms (false positives and false negatives).

An important secondary goal is the fast generation of the so-called shake maps [30] for affected regions, which show the maximal ground shaking in a dense grid. The combination of such maps with information about building structures and population densities in the affected area is important for fast and proper disaster management.

Almost all current EEWS use a centralized approach (e.g. Taiwan: [31]; Japan: [32]; Istanbul: [33]; Bucharest: [34]). Each station delivers its measured data over a direct connection to a central data center. These EEWS often consist of only a few, but expensive stations (several thousands of Euro), resulting in a number of problems:

- Malfunction: If one station breaks down, then the area it would normally observe can only be monitored from afar, resulting in time delays that could seriously compromise the network's early warning capacity.

- Density: This problem is related to the generation of precise information about an earthquake's intensity for city square cells, generally in size of 500 m. By comparison, EEWS usually have a station spacing of several kilometers.

- Cost: However, increasing the density of seismic stations is limited by their expense.

- Communication: The reliable transmission of all station information to central data center or civil protection headquarters is very important, especially following an earthquake, where usually centralized communication infrastructures may have collapsed.

Our approach addresses the problems identified above by deploying a much higher number of much cheaper stations (costing only a few hundreds of Euros). This approach is based on a wireless mesh network, where each node is equipped with the necessary components.

The reliability of such an EEWS is improved since the system can detect an earthquake even though single sensors may have been destroyed. This can be achieved because the sensor nodes act cooperatively in a self-organizing way.

The approach of equipping WMN nodes with sensors leads to a EEWS that can be deployed cheap and easily in threatened cities. The essential principle is the cooperative signal analysis done in the network and the availability of several services for self-organizing management, enabling the distinction between medium earthquakes and other events in urban environment like construction sites or trains. Centralized disaster management facilities as well as the possessors of our nodes can be directly informed by such a system. This creates a new culture of early warning where everyone can participate. Cooperative signal analysis and alarming can be used for other early warning use cases which require a sensing acquisition of environmental phenomena under real-time constraints.

Additionally to our HWL testbeds in Berlin, we deployed a test-bed of 20 nodes in Istanbul. The testbed in Istanbul with its difficult conditions and the missing direct access to the nodes led to the development of a collection of remote administration and experiment management tools. The HWL testbed with its reliable network topology allowed a repetitive analysis and performance evaluation of the alarming protocol for EEW. Still, the sensitivity for false-alarms in a noisy environment has to be studied.

While we have realized and shown that earthquake early warning is possible with such a system we are still lacking robustness to achieve the real-time constraints in changing network conditions. In this context, the improvement of transport and routing protocols, link metrics and topology optimization is still an open research issue.

6   Application II: Traffic Surveillance

6.1   Motivation

Traffic infrastructure isn't build in abundance and temporal overload due to regular and periodical spikes in traffic volume or due to extra ordinary causes (e.g. accidents) is normal. To understand this behavior, many traffic models differentiate between classes of vehicles. Different travel purposes are assigned to different classes and consequently different classes of vehicles show different behavioral patterns [35].

Stationary detection systems (e.g. induction loops, traffic-Eyes) and Floating Car Data (FCD) are today's preferred tools to collect the data that is fed into respective traffic models. For economic and data privacy reasons these techniques cannot be extended arbitrarily and not all techniques excel at vehicle classification. As a result coverage and quality of traffic data is unsatisfactory. To

implement innovative traffic management and control methods, a precise knowledge of the current traffic situation and a reliable prediction of future traffic
situations is required.

The use of commodity measurement instruments based on meshed sensor
networks can be a viable new method, provided we can improve the quality
of vehicle identification and classification while securing anonymity. Therefore,
we currently apply our acceleration sensor based WSN to the detection of road
fright traffic.

6.2   Experiments

In this section, we report on our first experimental results using HWL sensor
nodes for traffic surveillance.

Methodology: The basic approach is to validate acceleration sensor data and the
results of corresponding analysis algorithms against reference data to determine
statistical quality criteria (false-positive rate, sensitivity, specificity, etc.). The
input of each experiment is a specific road, a sensor network, and a set of analysis
algorithms; the output is a set of quality criteria for the given algorithm.

We choose actual roads or empty test roads of different difficulty: varying
number of lanes, varying traffic patters, controlled (test roads) or actual traffic.
We deploy four sensor nodes at each side of the road (if applicable also on
the median strip) at an equal distance of several vehicle lengths. Each sensor
node is equipped with a 3-axis accelerometer and GPS (for time and position).
Additionally a video camera is deployed. The camera has a global view on all
sensors and the corresponding parts of the road.

Sensor data and video feed are recorded for a period of time. Video data is
manually analyzed and a formal (computer-understandable) transcript of the
traffic is produced. This transcript determines what vehicles (based on a prior
classification) have passed which sensor at what time. All algorithms are applied
to the recorded sensor data. The algorithms are designed to produce output of
similar structure to the video transcripts. Analysis output and transcripts are
used to compute the statistical quality criteria. Fig. 8 shows our experiment
setup at a four-lane road.

Algorithms: We developed and analyzed several algorithms with different complexity. There are algorithms that only compute the input of a single node,
algorithms that use data from a neighborhood of nodes, or even all nodes. Algorithms can analyze in time and frequency domains. Typical operators used
in our algorithms includes Fast Fourier Transformations (FFTs), binning, sliding windows, band filters, calculating statistical moments, etc. It is generally
favorable to express these algorithms in a language that allows for mathematical
expressions and libraries that supports the identified operations. Fig. 9 shows
the different steps of an FFT-based algorithm.

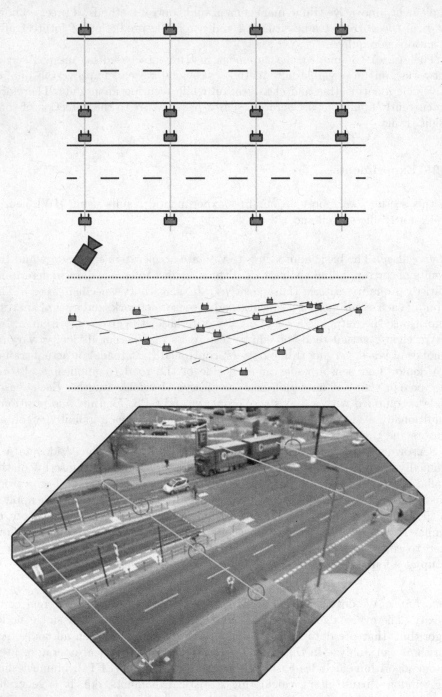

Fig. 8. Experiments on traffic surveillance: Setup

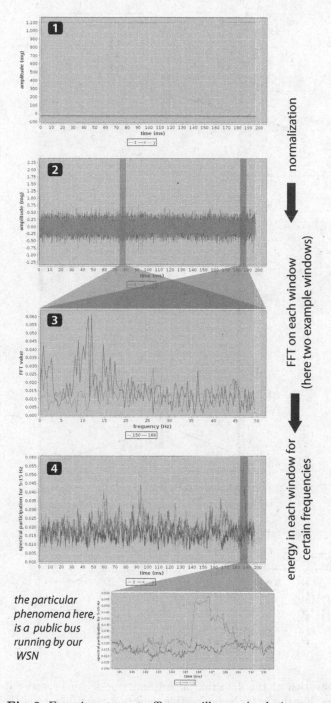

Fig. 9. Experiments on traffic surveillance: Analysis steps

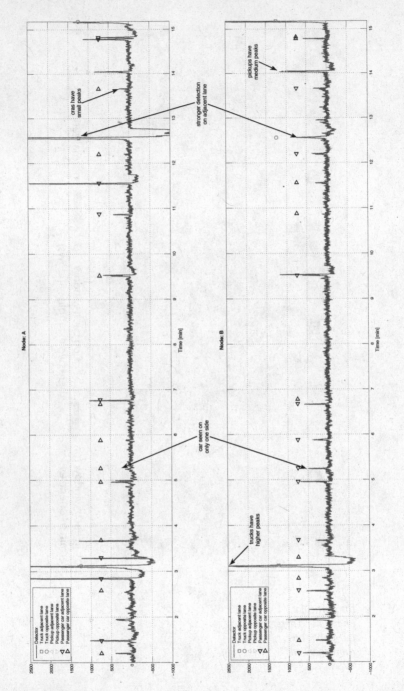

Fig. 10. Illustration of the detection algorithm: trucks can be easier detected than passenger cars. For the latter a cooperative detection algorithm using the sensor data from multiple sensors is required (sensor fusion).

Evaluation: Fig. 10 shows algorithm results from two of our nodes, placed on different road sides. The used algorithms normalizes the measured accelerations and creates compared moving averages of a short and long sliding window, similar to the algorithm used in earth quake early warning. The figure also shows the potential for cooperative vehicle detection: trucks can be detected on both sides of the road, while smaller vehicles are only visible on one side.

6.3 Future Work

The described experiments can only be a first step. In the future, we have to extend experiments to different traffic situations, employ larger amounts of sensors, and combine different types of sensors (sensor-fusion). Similar to earth quake early warning, we expect that the cooperative use of many sensors allows us to increase the quality of our technique. Furthermore, we have to improve our research methodology. A test-road for new vehicle detection methods operated by the *Deutsches Zentrum für Luft und Raumfahrt* (DLR) will allow us to experiment in a more efficient environment and automatically acquired controll data enables us to work with data sets of more statistically relevant sizes.

7   Conclusions

We identified different technologies for smart city applications: wireless sensor networks, geo-information systems, and frameworks for data analysis. While all these technologies exists, it is still a challenge to provide a concise smart city platform that allows developers to use all these technologies together. We successfully used our sensor network HWL to concept proof the applications early earthquake warning and traffic surveillance; we are also able to represent sensor and geo-spatial data within the same infrastructure; and there are a myriad studies on processing large amounts of geo-spatial data. But a large case study that combines all necessary technologies and proofs the practical development of smart city applications is still an open subject, not only for us, but for the research community at large.

References

1. Vojdani, A.: Smart Integration. Power and Energy Magazine 6(6), 71–79 (2008)
2. Samadi, P., Mohsenian-Rad, A., Schober, R., Wong, V.W.S., Jatskevich, J.: Optimal Real-Time Pricing Algorithm Based on Utility Maximization for Smart Grid. In: First IEEE International Conference on Smart Grid Communications, pp. 415–420. IEEE Press (2010), http://dx.doi.org/10.1109/SMARTGRID.2010.5622077
3. Fischer, J., Redlich, J.P., Zschau, J., Milkereit, C., Picozzi, M., Fleming, K., Brumbulli, M., Lichtblau, B., Eveslage, I.: A wireless mesh sensing network for early warning. Journal of Network and Computer Applications 35(2), 538–547 (2012)

4. Hernández-Muñoz, J.M., Vercher, J.B., Muñoz, L., Galache, J.A., Presser, M., Gómez, L.A.H., Pettersson, J.: Smart Cities at the Forefront of the Future Internet. In: Domingue, J., Galis, A., Gavras, A., Zahariadis, T., Lambert, D., Cleary, F., Daras, P., Krco, S., Müller, H., Li, M.-S., Schaffers, H., Lotz, V., Alvarez, F., Stiller, B., Karnouskos, S., Avessta, S., Nilsson, M. (eds.) Future Internet Assembly. LNCS, vol. 6656, pp. 447–462. Springer, Heidelberg (2011)
5. Murty, R., Mainland, G., Rose, I., Chowdhury, A.R., Gosain, A., Bers, J., Welsh, M.: Citysense–An urban-scale wireless sensor network and testbed. In: 2008 IEEE Conference on Technologies for Homeland Security. IEEE Press (2008), http://www.eecs.harvard.edu/~mdw/papers/citysense-ieeehst08.pdf
6. Chatzigiannakis, I., Fischer, S., Koninis, C., Mylonas, G., Pfisterer, D.: WISEBED: An Open Large-Scale Wireless Sensor Network Testbed. In: Komninos, N. (ed.) SENSAPPEAL 2009. LNICST, vol. 29, pp. 68–87. Springer, Heidelberg (2010)
7. Estrin, D., Girod, L., Pottie, G., Srivastava, M.: Instrumenting the world with wireless sensor networks. In: IEEE International Conference on Acoustics, Speech, and Signal Processing (ICASSP 2001), vol. 4, pp. 2033–2036. IEEE Press (2001)
8. Lynch, J.P.: A summary review of wireless sensors and sensor networks for structural health monitoring. The Shock and Vibration Digest 38(2), 91–128 (2006)
9. Akyildiz, I.F., Su, W., Sankarasubramaniam, Y., Cayirci, E.: Wireless sensor networks – a survey. Computer Networks 38(4), 393–422 (2002)
10. Akyildiz, I.F., Melodia, T., Chowdhury, K.R.: A survey on wireless multimedia sensor networks. Computer Networks 51(4), 921–960 (2007)
11. Günes, M., Juraschek, F., Blywis, B., Mushtaq, Q., Schiller, J.: A testbed for next generation wireless network research. Praxis der Informationsverarbeitung und Kommunikation - Special Issue on Mobile Ad-hoc Networks 34(5) (2009)
12. Scheidgen, M., Zubow, A., Sombrutzki, R.: HWL – A High Performance Wireless Research Network. In: Ninth International Conference on Networked Sensing Systems (INSS). IEEE Press (2012)
13. Kohler, E., Morris, R., Chen, B., Jannotti, J., Kaashoek, M.F.: The click modular router. ACM Transactions on Computer Systems 18(3), 263–297 (2000)
14. Zubow, A., Sombrutzki, R., Scheidgen, M.: A low-cost mimo mesh testbed based on 802.11n. In: IEEE Wireless Communications and Networking Conference. IEEE Press (2012)
15. Scheidgen, M., Zubow, A., Sombrutzki, R.: ClickWatch – An Experimentation Framework for Communication Network Test-beds. In: Proceedings of the IEEE Wireless Communications and Networking Conference, Paris, France, April 1-4, pp. 3296–3301. IEEE (2012)
16. Baar, M., Will, H., Blywis, B., Liers, A., Wittenburg, G., Schiller, J.: The ScatterWeb MSB-A2 Platform for Wireless Sensor Networks. Technical report, Freie Universität Berlin (2008)
17. Günes, M., Blywis, B., Juraschek, F.: Concept and design of the hybrid distributed embedded systems testbed. Technical Report TR-B-08-10, Freie Universität Berlin (2008), ftp://ftp.inf.fu-berlin.de/pub/reports/tr-b-08-10.pdf
18. Günes, M., Blywis, B., Juraschek, F., Schmidt, P.: Practical issues of implementing a hybrid multi-nic wireless mesh-network. Technical Report TR-B-08-11, Freie Universität Berlin (2008), ftp://ftp.inf.fu-berlin.de/pub/reports/tr-b-08-11.pdf
19. Blywis, B., Günes, M., Juraschek, F., Schmidt, P., Kumar, P.: DES-SERT – A framework for structured routing protocol implementation. In: Proceedings of the 2nd IFIP Conference on Wireless Days (WD 2009). IEEE Press (2009)

20. Portele, C.: OGC Geography Markup Language (GML) 3.3. Technical report, Open Geospatial Consortium (OGC) (2012)
21. Gröger, G., Kolbe, T.H., Czerwinski, A., Nagel, C.: OpenGIS City Geography Markup Language (CityGML) 2.0. Open Geospatial Consortium, http://portal.opengeospatial.org/files/?artifact_id=47842
22. Stadler, A.: Making interoperability persistent: A 3D geo database based on CityGML. In: Proceedings of the 3rd International Workshop on 3D Geo-Information, pp. 175–192. Springer (2008)
23. Kolovos, D.S., Rose, L.M., Williams, J., Matragkas, N., Paige, R.F.: A Lightweight Approach for Managing XML Documents with MDE Languages. In: Vallecillo, A., Tolvanen, J.-P., Kindler, E., Störrle, H., Kolovos, D. (eds.) ECMFA 2012. LNCS, vol. 7349, pp. 118–132. Springer, Heidelberg (2012)
24. Scheidgen, M., Zubow, A., Fischer, J., Kolbe, T.H.: Automated and Transparent Model Fragmentation for Persisting Large Models. In: France, R.B., Kazmeier, J., Breu, R., Atkinson, C. (eds.) MODELS 2012. LNCS, vol. 7590, pp. 102–118. Springer, Heidelberg (2012)
25. Scheidgen, M., Zubow, A., Sombrutzki, R.: Clickwatch – an experimentation framework for communication network test-beds. In: IEEE Wireless Communications and Networking Conference. IEEE Press (2012)
26. Steinberg, D., Budinsky, F., Paternostro, M., Merks, E.: EMF – Eclipse Modeling Framework 2.0, 2nd edn. Addison-Wesley Professional (2009)
27. Scheidgen, M.: EMFFrag – Meta-Model-based Model Fragmentation and Persistence Framework, http://code.google.com/p/emf-fragments
28. Stepper, E.: Connected Data Objects (CDO), http://www.eclipse.org/cdo/
29. Fleming, K., Picozzi, M., Milkereit, C., Kühnlenz, F., Lichtblau, B., Fischer, J., Zulfikar, C., Ozel, O., et al.: The Self-organizing Seismic Early Warning Information Network (SOSEWIN). Seismological Research Letters 80(5), 755–771 (2009)
30. Wald, D.J., Worden, B.C., Quitoriano, V., Pankow, K.L.: ShakeMap Manual - Technical Manual, Users Guide and Software Guide. U.S. Geological Survey (2006)
31. Wu, Y.M., Teng, T.I.: A Virtual Subnetwork Approach to Earthquake Early Warning. Bulletin of the Seismological Society of America 92(5), 2008–2018 (2002)
32. Horiuchi, S., Negishi, H., Abe, K., Kamimura, A., Fujinawa, Y.: An Automatic Processing System for Broadcasting Earthquake Alarms. Bulletin of the Seismological Society of America 95(2), 708–718 (2005)
33. Erdik, M., Fahjan, Y., Ozel, O., Alcik, H., Mert, A., Gul, M.: Istanbul Earthquake Rapid Response and the Early Warning System. Bulletin of Earthquake Engineering 1, 157–163 (2003)
34. Ionescu, C., Böse, M., Wenzel, F., Marmureanu, A., Grigore, A., Marmureanu, G.: An Early Warning System for Deep Vrancea (Romania) Earthquakes. In: Earthquake Early Warning Systems, pp. 343–349. Springer (2007)
35. Schröder, S., Zilske, M., Liedtke, G., Nagel, K.: A computational framework for a multi-agent simulation of freight transport activities. In: Annual Meeting Preprint 12-4152, Transportation Research Board (2012), https://svn.vsp.tu-berlin.de/repos/public-svn/publications/vspwp/2011/11-19/

On Deriving Detailed Component Design from High-Level Service Specification

Urooj Fatima and Rolv Bræk

Department of Telematics, Norwegian University of Science and Technology (NTNU),
Trondheim, Norway
{urooj,rolv.braek}@item.ntnu.no

Abstract. The development of distributed reactive systems is quite complex. They provide services where two or more active components collaborate that may take independent initiatives, operate concurrently and interact with each other and their environment in order to provide services. We need precise and complete global behaviour definitions in the domain of these distributed reactive systems that will enable us to derive component designs automatically in a systematic way. In this paper, we continue the previous research where an approach is proposed to map flow-global choreographies to flow-localized choreographies and further to distributed component designs. The proposed approach has the potential to become highly automated, however, some issues still need to be addressed manually while deriving the components. These issues are identified in this paper and solutions are proposed by defining precise rules to support component derivation by taking into account the problems that need to be solved in a distributed realization. The derived component types will be available to compose larger components and systems. The challenge for the designer is to ensure correct behaviour of the resulting composite reactive system.

Keywords: Component design, model-driven development, service choreography, service composition.

1   Introduction

The concept of "service" is widely used and many informal definitions pertaining to different domains can be found. The service engineering approach [1] we use considers services in general as collaborative, partial and possibly distributed functionalities Generally, the behaviour of services is composed from partial component behaviours, while component behaviour is composed from partial service behaviours as already recognized in [2]. The behaviour of each component is designed as a composition of the roles played by that component in different services.

The component behaviour can be synthesized from service specification. The services of a distributed reactive system can be specified by the use of UML collaboration and activity diagrams. We use the term *choreography* to define

Ø. Haugen, R. Reed, and R. Gotzhein (Eds.): SAM 2012, LNCS 7744, pp. 142–159, 2013.

global collaborative behaviour that may involve participation of two or more components, whereas the term *orchestration* is used to denote the local behaviour of each component.

Ideally, the component behaviour should be automatically synthesized if the choreography is precise and complete. This enables the service engineer to concentrate on choreographies only, instead of going into the detailed component behaviour level. For this we need mechanisms to define the global behaviour completely so that a systematic way can be defined to derive local component behaviour from global behaviour. Related work has been published in previous SDL proceedings. An approach has been proposed in [3] to derive component type behaviours with well-defined interfaces from which implementation code can be generated using existing techniques. The envisaged overall service engineering approach is outlined in Fig. 1. It is illustrated with the help of a *TaxiSystem* example which is explained in detail in the next section. As illustrated in Fig. 1, in the service engineering approach, individual services are first specified that are derived directly from the problem domain. A service structure is modelled as a UML collaboration which can be decomposed into elementary collaborations i.e. collaborations that are not further decomposed into collaboration uses. The UML collaboration defines the roles and collaboration uses which represents sub-services and interfaces. The complete (global) behaviour of the service is specified with choreographies, using UML activity diagrams, that describes the execution ordering of elementary collaborations referenced by collaboration uses in the main service collaboration structure.

In [3], the term choreography is further divided and explained on two levels i.e. *flow-global choreography* and *flow-local choreography*. *Flow-global choreography* is used for abstract definition of the global behaviour avoiding details of localization and resolution of coordination problems that may occur at orchestration level. *Flow-local choreography* is used to describe more detailed and complete behaviour represented by flows that are localized to the roles. This enhances the analytical power which in turn supports the automatic synthesis of component type behaviours.

The process of component derivation from high-level service specification has the potential to become highly automated. However, some issues still remain to be resolved:

- Flow-localization issues
- Multiparty decomposition
- Multi-sessions i.e. instance multiplicity
- Realizability issues
- Platform dependency and protocol layering
- Variability

At which level of a service engineering approach these issues should be addressed, is still an un-answered question. Most of the flow-localization issues are addressed in [3,4], however some of them need further exploration. In this paper, we do not address all of the above mentioned issues. Some localization issues and some

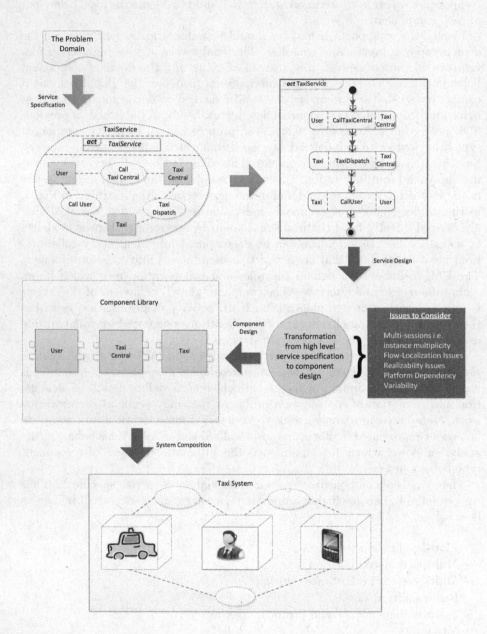

Fig. 1. Overall context of proposed approach

problems related to multiparty decomposition and multi-sessions are addressed by defining rules.

In Section 2, we present a case study to exemplify our proposed approach throughout the paper. Sections 3 and 4 describe our proposed approach for flow-localization and component derivation respectively. Multi-sessions are discussed in Section 5. Finally, we conclude in Section 6.

2 From Problem Domain to Service Specification

In this section, we introduce a *TaxiSystem* service that will be used as a running example throughout the paper. This section explains how to specify a service from the problem domain using the techniques already implemented in [1].

2.1 Service Structure of a Taxi System: A Case Study

In a *TaxiSystem*, customers can book taxis by placing taxi-booking requests to the *TaxiCentral*. A *TaxiDispatcher* receives taxi-bookings, finds a free nearby *Taxi* and sends tour orders with the pickup location to the *Taxi*. The *TaxiDispatcher* keeps an overview of available taxis and assigns taxis to customers as fairly as possible. Once a *Taxi* is assigned to a customer, it can contact the customer via phone call.

The structure of this service can be modeled as a UML collaboration . In order to model it, we have to identify the roles needed to provide the service. Each role should specify the properties and behaviour that a component should have in order to participate in one single occurrence of the service. Filled circles and filled squares have been used to identify the initiating and terminating roles of each collaboration use, respectively. That is, the roles performing the first and last actions of each collaboration use. Fig. 2 describes the structure of the *TaxiCentral* service. Three roles are identified for this service: *User*, *TaxiDispatcher* and *Taxi*. A component playing the *User* role can initiate a taxi-booking request. A component playing the *TaxiDispatcher* role can handle bookings request, keeps an overview of the available taxis, sends the tour orders with the pickup location and assigns taxis to *User*. Busy handling is one of the responsibilities of the *TaxiDispatcher*. The *TaxiDispatcher* is playing the role of a *Controller* as identified in [5]. A component playing the role of *Taxi* updates its status (busy/free) to the *TaxiDispatcher*. It can accept or reject the tour orders sent by the *TaxiDispatcher*. The *Taxi* once being assigned, can initiate voice call to the *User*.

The service behaviour is decomposed into more manageable collaboration uses, which normally correspond to phases of the service as mentioned below:

- *TaxiReq:* The *User* initiates the taxi-booking request.
- *TaxiOrder:* If a *Taxi* is available, the *TaxiDispatcher* sends the tour order to the *Taxi*.
- *UserWait:* If a *Taxi* is not available, the *User* will receive notifications from the *TaxiDispatcher*.

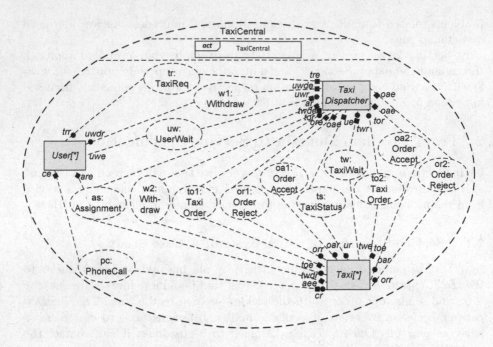

Fig. 2. Roles and collaboration uses in a *TaxiCentral* service

- *TaxiWait:* If no user request is present in the queue, the *TaxiDispatcher* will put the *Taxi* in a taxi queue.
- *TaxiStatus:* The *Taxi* updates its status (busy/free) to the *TaxiDispatcher*.
- *OrderAccept:* The *Taxi* accepts the tour order if it is free.
- *OrderReject:* The *Taxi* rejects the tour order if it is busy. In this case, the *TaxiDispatcher* will forward the taxi order to the next available *Taxi* in the taxi queue.
- *Assignment:* If the *Taxi* accepts the tour order, the *TaxiDispatcher* seizes the *Taxi* and assigns it to the *User* via *Assignment* collaboration use. This is a composite collaboration use which consists of two collaboration uses as shown in Fig. 3.

These collaboration uses are referenced by the action nodes in the choreography model, described in Section 2.2.

2.2   Service Behaviour: Flow-Global Choreography

We know from the service structure described in Section 2.1 about the collaboration uses in which the service roles participate in order to provide the service. Assuming that their behaviour has been described separately (not shown here), we need to specify the order in which these collaboration uses should be executed, so that their global joint behaviour matches the intended behaviour for

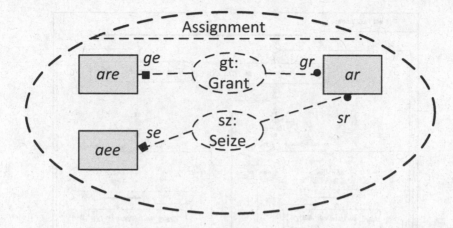

Fig. 3. UML Collaboration of *Assignment*

the *TaxiCentral* service collaboration. This global behaviour can be defined as a choreography of the collaboration uses [1], also called 'flow-global choreography' in [3]. For this, UML 2 activity diagrams can be used, as shown in Fig. 4 for the *TaxiCentral* service. Choreography is normally quite straight forward and easy to follow for sequential behaviour. Fig. 4 seems complex because the *TaxiCentral* coordinates events from many concurrent and partly independent taxis and users. In addition to handle interactions the service needs to maintain queues of waiting users and available taxis, and perform queue operations to match users with suitable taxis.

The activity nodes are *CallBehaviourActions* that invoke the behaviour associated with the collaboration uses. The UML concept of partition is utilized to represent the role participation in collaboration actions. The notation for collaboration action is illustrated in Fig. 4. It can have all types of pins that UML allows.

3   Flow-Localization

In the flow-global choreography shown in Fig. 4, the flows are not assigned to any particular role in the collaboration as is also the case when we use Interaction Overview Diagrams (IODs) or high-level MSC diagrams. The transformation from flow-global to flow-localized level means to localize the flows and ensure global ordering by means of local flows. For this purpose, all flows, pins and control nodes must be localized to roles participating in the choreography. To do this, we first determine the causality relationship between two collaboration actions C1 and C2 according to [2,3,6]. Then, we define the localization policy using the causal properties.

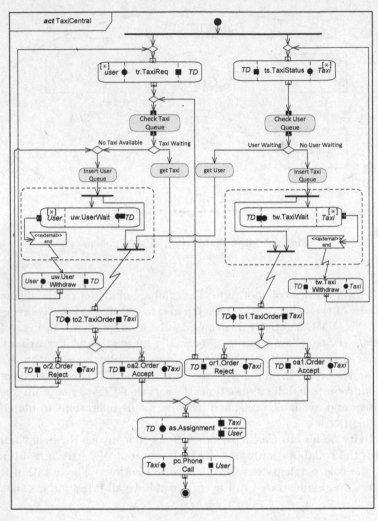

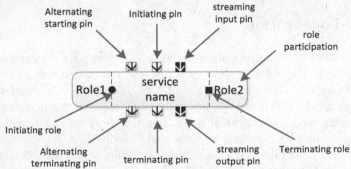

Fig. 4. Flow-global choreography model of *TaxiCentral* and notation for collaboration action

The causality relationship between two connected collaboration actions C1 and C2 can be:

- **Strong:** The terminating role of C1 and initiating role of C2 belong to the same component. In this case the flow between C1 and C2 is termed as a strong flow, and can be localized to the shared component and executed locally by that component.
- **Weak:** The initiating role of C2 is a non-terminating role in C1 and both of these roles belong to the same component. This means that the shared component may initiate C2 as soon as it is finished with its roles in C1, and that both collaborations may run in parallel for a little while.
- **Non-Causal:** The component playing the initiating role of C2 does not participate in C1. This means that the ordering between C1 and C2 cannot be achieved by means of a local flow within one component.

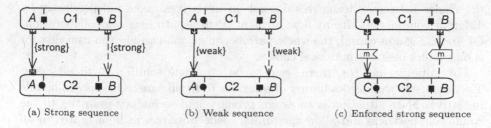

(a) Strong sequence   (b) Weak sequence   (c) Enforced strong sequence

Fig. 5. Strong and weak sequence localization [3]

3.1 Localization Policy/Rules

We explain some terminologies before describing the localization policy. The flows connected to the initiating role of the next collaboration are defined as *initiating flows*. The non-initiating roles of the next collaboration must be ready to participate in the collaboration when it is started. For this purpose, there must be local flows to enable the non-initiating roles. These are termed as *responding flows* (indicated by dashed lines). They determine when the component must be ready to respond in collaborations initiated by other components. The flows initiating from and/or ending on streaming pins are called *streaming flows*[1].

If there is any composite collaboration use in the flow-global choreography, it must be decomposed into elementary collaboration actions in the flow-local choreography before proceeding further. A global flow from collaboration action C1 to C2 is localized by following the rules stated in [3,7]. If the causality relationship is *strong* then the initiating flow is localized to the role that terminates C1 and initiates C2 as shown in Fig. 5(a). If the causality relationship is *weak* then a streaming pin is added to the role in C1 that initiates C2 as illustrated in

---

[1] For the details on streaming flows, the reader is referred to [3].

Fig. 5(b). If the relationship is *non-causal*, then the flows can only be maintained by using so called enforced strong or weak sequencing i.e. by adding interactions as shown in Fig. 5(c) or by amending the choreography.

The rules for localizing control nodes and paths are illustrated in [3,7]. In the presence of control nodes like choices, joins, forks and merge, rules may be given for each flow segment calculated upstream in the opposite direction of the token flow. In general, a flow segment links two nodes (n, n) where n = collaboration (c), choice, merge, fork, join. The localization rules are given in Table 1. In Fig. 7, it is indicated in curly brackets to which component a control node is localized. If the paths cannot be localized according to the rules stated in [3,7] and Table 1, then there is a realizability problem to resolve. There may also be realizability problems in some cases of weak sequencing. These can be easily found by analyzing the weak responding flows as explained in [8]. Finally, so-called non-local choices, where the decision to choose the next collaboration action is not localized to one single component, imply realizability problems that must be resolved. A special case of non-local choice is initiative choices where the choice between alternatives depend on initiatives taken independently by different components. If any flow segment 'f' in a path between collaborations C1 and C2 is non-causal, the whole path becomes non-causal. Non-causality for choice nodes means a non-local choice.

For initiative choices, there seem to be no single solution to fit all cases. Therefore, one will need a library of solutions to fit all cases. One way to handle initiative choice situation is to assign primary and secondary priorities to the conflicting partners and allow the primary side initiative to be accepted in all cases as described in [3].

Interruptible Region Localization. An interruptible activity region is an activity group that supports termination of tokens flowing in the part of an activity that is within the interruptible region. The region is interrupted when a token traverses an interrupting edge terminating all the flows and activity nodes in the region. There can be multiple interrupting edges. To deal with the localization policy of the interruptible regions, we use the following guidelines:

(a) The dashed-rectangle representing the interruptible region in the flow global choreography is removed.
(b) Each interrupting flow is localized to the same component as the target node of the flow.
(c) If there is only one interrupting flow from the interruptible region then the interrupting flow is replaced by a normal initiating flow followed by a fork with one branch connecting to the node following the interrupting flow and other branch(es) stopping the interrupted collaboration(s).
(d) If there are several interrupting flows all local to the same component, introduce a shared local initiative choice resolution block, Local-ICR. This block shall have an input-output pair corresponding to each interrupting flow. Each interrupting flow is replaced by a normal flow to the corresponding input with the corresponding output connected to a fork with one branch

Table 1. Localization rules for paths and control nodes

Path or control node	Cases	Localization Rule
(diagram: node 'n' with flow 'f' to collaboration 'c')	f = flow segment(n, c) from any node 'n' to a collaboration 'c'	location(f) = initiating(c); location(n) = location(f);
(diagram: input 'fi' to node 'n', output 'fo')	Non-branching node 'n' with input flow segment 'fi' and output flow segment 'fo' (local action, receive event action)	location(n) = location(fo) ; location(fi) = location(n);
(diagram: input 'fi' to node 'n', outputs fo1, fo2 ... fon)	Branching node 'n' with input flow segment 'fi' and output flow segments {fo1, fo2,...,fon} (choice or fork)	if location(fo1) = location (fo2) =...= location(fon) then location(n) = location(fo1); location(fi) = location(n); else location(n) = location(fi) = *non-causal*
(diagram: inputs fi1, fi2 ... fin to node 'n', output 'fo')	Merging node n with output flow segment 'fo' and input flow segments {fi1, fi2,...,fin} (merge or join)	location(n) = location(fo); location(fi1) =...= location(fin) = location(n);
(diagram: collaboration 'c' with flow 'f' to node 'n')	f = flowSegment(c, n) from collaboration 'c' to any node 'n'	if location(n) ∈ participants(c) then location(c) = location(n) else location(c) = *non-causal*

connecting to the node following the interrupting flow and other branch(es) stopping the interrupted collaboration(s).

(e) If there are several interrupting flows local to different components, introduce a shared global initiative choice resolution block, Global-ICR as shown in Fig. 6. For each component it will have local input output pairs as explained above.

(f) Each interruptible collaboration gets a streaming stop pin added in all its components.

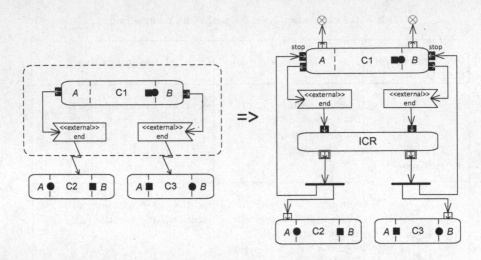

Fig. 6. Interruptible region localization - Global-(ICR) block

The ICR block handles the initiative choices and emits tokens according to the outcome of the choice. Such blocks may be designed in several different ways not to be elaborated here. The best solution will depend on the application. A priority scheme is one possible solution as described in [4].

The flow-localized choreography we achieve as a result of application of the rules explained in this section is shown in Fig. 7. We assume one token flowing per role instance through the activity flow. Only one instance is interrupted when a token is emitted from the interrupting edge. The multiplicity of the instances is described in Section 5.

As recognized by [5], the use of interrupting flows and interruptible regions helps to describe the intended behaviour without dealing with the detailed coordination needed in a distributed realization, for instance to handle mixed/colliding events. The use of sequence diagrams and Interaction Overview Diagrams (which do not support interruption) to describe such kind of behaviour will lead to a more complex diagram if at all possible.

4   Component Derivation

Precise and complete flow-local choreography enables the synthesis of component behaviour. In order to derive the local behaviour of a component, which we termed as orchestration, some guidelines are proposed in [3,7]. We will illustrate this by projecting the flow-localized choreography shown in Fig. 7 into the *User*, *Taxi* and *TD* components for our *TaxiCentral* service example. For each component:

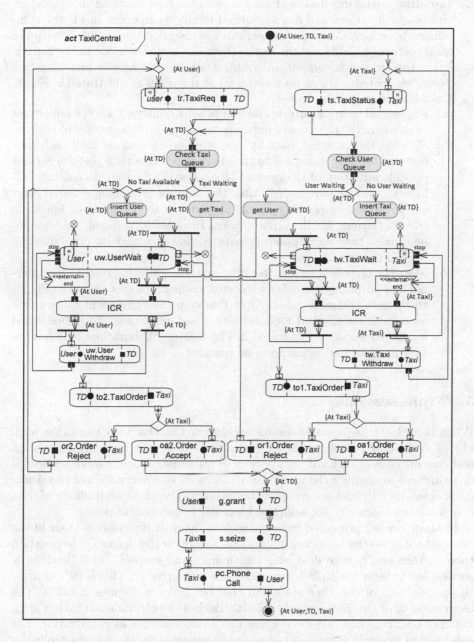

Fig. 7. Flow-localized choreography model of *TaxiCentral*

1. **Introduce component boundary**.
2. **Localize initiating flows:** Make a copy of the flow-localized choreography, and place all actions and flows localized to that component inside the component boundary. Collaboration actions are placed at the boundary with the local role action inside and the rest of the collaboration outside the boundary. After this step each component contains all its local actions and initiating flows, with collaborations (as interfaces) at the edges as illustrated in Fig. 8.
3. **Localize responding flows:**
   (a) Replace all actions outside the component boundary, except collaborations where the component participates, by no-op (no-operation) actions.
   (b) Simplify the external flows by removing no-op actions until each flow between collaborations define the shortest possible path, i.e. the earliest possible initiation of the next collaboration. Paths that do not link collaborations can be removed. After this step the remaining external flows are termed as *responding flows*. They define the ordering of initiating roles performed by the environment. In order to respond, the component must have corresponding internal flows to start its non-initiating roles in time.
   (c) Move the responding flows from the external initiating roles to the internal non-initiating roles. Attach corresponding pins (not shown in Fig. 9) to the non-initiating roles. After this step the component is complete with local actions and local initiating and *responding flows* (indicated by dashed lines), as illustrated in Fig. 9. The collaborations may now be kept for information purposes or removed.

5   Multi-sessions

When using UML Sequence Diagrams and Interaction Overview Diagrams, resp. ITU-T MSC and HMSC, to define global behaviour one normally focuses on just one instance of each role in a service. This helps to focus on the sequential ordering and to simplify the models. Furthermore, one normally seeks to define some scenarios only and not complete behaviours. Therefore, multiplicity of roles and sessions is normally not addressed but left to component design.

In the approach presented here, we seek to define complete behaviour in the choreographies so that components may be automatically derived. The question then is when and how to deal with multiplicity and sessions? The *TaxiCentral* service has to serve multiple Users and Taxis concurrently. This is indicated by the multiplicity of the *User* roles and the *Taxi* roles in Figures 2 and 4. The choreography of the *TaxiCentral* explicitly defines the coordination taking place between one *Taxi* and one *User* using the *TaxiDispatcher* as coordinator. The existence of multiple users and taxis is only indicated by the role multiplicities and the use of queues to hold waiting users and taxis. Session initiation in general, of which the taxi system is a special case, typically deals with coordination among multiple role instances. To fully define such behaviour one therefore has to consider multiplicities.

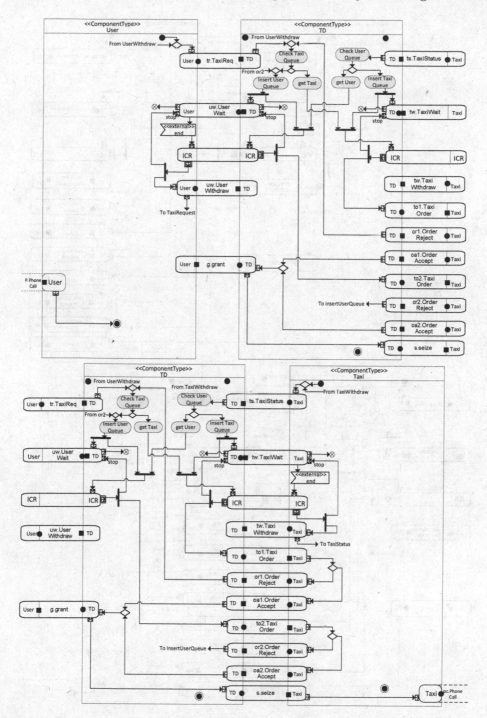

Fig. 8. Component types with local actions and initiating flows with collaborations (as interfaces) at the edges

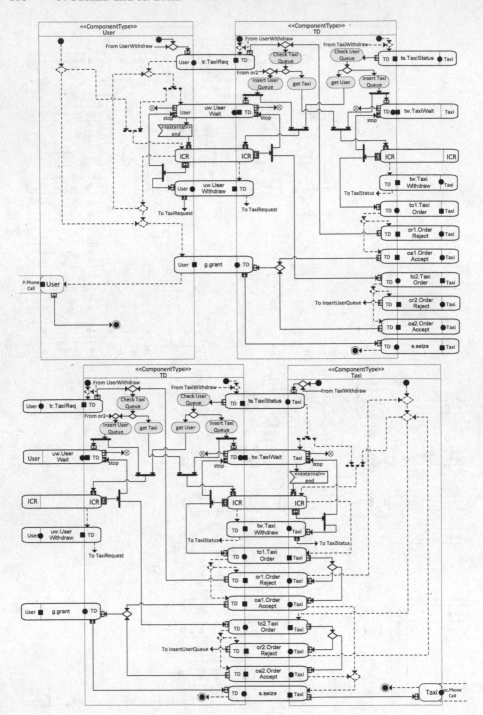

Fig. 9. Component types derived

There seems to be two options:

1. To postpone dealing with multiplicity until component design. This would be in line with the Sequence diagram tradition, and means that issues related to multiplicity such as addressing and routing be delegated to component design time. However this would conflict with our goal to derive designs as automatically as possible from global choreographies.
2. To include multiplicities in the choreography semantics. That is to allow multiple occurrences of each collaboration use running in parallel corresponding to the multiple users and taxis working in parallel, for instance many occurrences of the *UserWait* collaboration, one for each waiting *User*. Semantically that would mean to allow multiple tokens flowing through the choreography at the same time. These tokens would be generated by individual taxis and users taking initiatives. This would mean that all *Users* and *Taxis* are allowed to start in parallel, which may be inferred from the role multiplicities. Moreover, interruptible regions and termination must be understood on the basis of role instances/collaboration use occurrences. Also one would need mechanisms for role instance identification and token routing.

We propose going for alternative 2 above; modeling multiplicity in the choreography. We understand the various roles indicated in collaboration actions (*User, Taxi, TD*) as the same (anonymous) instance throughout the choreography, so that the choreography defines the local ordering performed by one instance of each role. At the same time it clearly identifies the presence of multiple instances and the need to provide addressing and token routing at the design level.

Details of communication protocols and APIs as well as addressing and routing are platform dependent. At the choreography level this is generalized to hide platform specificities. In order to generate executable systems from global choreographies user input is needed to select and integrate platform dependent details. This can be done by means of libraries of reusable activities that provide access to and encapsulate such platform dependency as has been demonstrated using the Arctis tool [9].

6   Discussion and Related Work

In this paper, we applied the approach proposed in [3,7] on a comprehensive and non-trivial system example. This application of the process of component derivation revealed some problems that were not addressed before. We propose solutions to these problems that include multi-party decomposition, transforming interruptible regions from flow-global to component level and instance multiplicity. The component derivation process helped us in identifying realizability problems. These can be easily found by analyzing the weak responding flows as explained in [8]. The so-called non-local choices and initiative choices also imply realizability problem as explained in section 3.1. These problems will be addressed in future work.

In the literature, one can find many proposals to represent high-level service specification such as sequence diagrams and Use Case Maps (UCM) [10,11]. Various mathematical approaches have been proposed to define choreography and orchestration semantics for example Labelled Transition System (LTS) is used for choreography semantics and LOTOS process to define orchestration semantics in [12]. Activity traces are used by [13] to represent choreography and orchestration. Likewise, set of conversation to represent choreography and process traces to define orchestration semantics, is proposed by [14]. Most of the proposals are based on manual derivation of the components. Moreover, these proposals do not take into account the problem of mixed initiatives that we address.

We use activity diagrams to define the choreography semantics which help us to specify service behaviour precisely and completely on the global level. The token flow semantics and the use of interrupting flows in activity diagrams enhances the flexibility to specify global service behaviour without dealing with the detailed coordination needed in a distributed realization, for instance, to deal with colliding events. Moreover, the graphical form of the activity diagrams simplifies the incorporation of the alternative solutions. Activity Diagrams are also used by [15] to represent the global specification and to derive component behaviours with emphasis on the coordination messages needed. The approach we follow is more detailed and includes the concept of flow-localized choreography while deriving the component designs from flow-global choreography. We do not provide tool support for the component derivation as yet, however, once the components have been derived, they can be further processed using the Arctis tool [9]. The resulting components are Arctis compatible. Interruptible regions are not explicitly supported by Arctis, but we provide the rules for translating the interruptible regions from flow-global and flow-localized choreography to component designs which are Arctis compatible. The Arctis tool can further analyze the component and system models, and synthesize state machines from which executable (Java) code is generated.

References

1. Castejón, H.N.: Collaborations in Service Engineering: Modeling, Analysis and Execution. PhD thesis, Department of Telematics, Norwegian University of Science and Technology (2008)
2. Castejón, H.N., Bochmann, G.V., Bræk, R.: Realizability of Collaboration-based Service Specifications. In: 14th Asia-Pacific Software Engineering Conference (APSEC 2007), pp. 73–80. IEEE Computer Society (2007)
3. Kathayat, S.B., Bræk, R.: From Flow-Global Choreography to Component Types. In: Kraemer, F.A., Herrmann, P. (eds.) SAM 2010. LNCS, vol. 6598, pp. 36–55. Springer, Heidelberg (2011)
4. Sarstedt, S., Guttmann, W.: An ASM Semantics of Token Flow in UML 2 Activity Diagrams. In: Virbitskaite, I., Voronkov, A. (eds.) PSI 2006. LNCS, vol. 4378, pp. 349–362. Springer, Heidelberg (2007)
5. Fatima, U., Bræk, R., Castejón, H.N.: Session Initiation as a Service. In: Ober, I., Ober, I. (eds.) SDL 2011. LNCS, vol. 7083, pp. 122–137. Springer, Heidelberg (2011)

6. Han, F., Kathayat, S.B., Le, H.N., Bræk, R., Herrmann, P.: Towards Choreography Model Transformation via Graph Transformation. In: IEEE 2nd International Conference on Software Engineering and Service Science (ICSESS 2011), pp. 508–515. IEEE Press (2011)
7. Kathayat, S.B.: On the Development of Situated Collaborative Services. PhD thesis, Department of Telematics, Norwegian University of Science and Technology (2012), http://ntnu.diva-portal.org/smash/get/diva2:566435/FULLTEXT01
8. Kathayat, S.B., Bræk, R.: Analyzing Realizability of Choreographies Using Initiating and Responding Flows. In: 8th International Workshop on Model-Driven Engineering, Verification and Validation (MoDeVVa 2011), Article 6. ACM Press (2011)
9. Kraemer, F.A., Slåtten, V., Herrmann, P.: Tool Support for the Rapid Composition, Analysis and Implementation of Reactive Services. Journal of Systems and Software 82(12), 2068–2080 (2009)
10. Buhr, R.J.A.: Use Case Maps as Architectural Entities for Complex Systems. IEEE Transactions on Software Engineering 24(12), 1131–1155 (1998)
11. Martínez, H.N.C.: Synthesizing State-Machine Behaviour from UML Collaborations and Use Case Maps. In: Prinz, A., Reed, R., Reed, J. (eds.) SDL 2005. LNCS, vol. 3530, pp. 339–359. Springer, Heidelberg (2005)
12. Salaün, G., Bultan, T.: Realizability of Choreographies Using Process Algebra Encodings. In: Leuschel, M., Wehrheim, H. (eds.) IFM 2009. LNCS, vol. 5423, pp. 167–182. Springer, Heidelberg (2009)
13. Qiu, Z., Zhao, X., Cai, C., Yang, H.: Towards the Theoretical Foundation of Choreography. In: Proceedings of the 16th International Conference on World Wide Web, pp. 973–982. ACM Press (2007)
14. Busi, N., Gorrieri, R., Guidi, C., Lucchi, R., Zavattaro, G.: Choreography and Orchestration Conformance for System Design. In: Ciancarini, P., Wiklicky, H. (eds.) COORDINATION 2006. LNCS, vol. 4038, pp. 63–81. Springer, Heidelberg (2006)
15. Laamarti, F.: Derivation of Component Designs from Global Specifications. Master thesis, Ottawa-Carleton Institute for Computer Science, School of Information Technology and Engineering, University of Ottawa (2010)

Type-Safe Symmetric Composition
of Metamodels Using Templates

Henning Berg and Birger Møller-Pedersen

Department of Informatics,
Faculty of Mathematics and Natural Sciences, University of Oslo
{hennb,birger}@ifi.uio.no

Abstract. Composition of models is a key operation in model-driven engineering where it is used for, e.g., elaborating models with additional concepts, acquiring a holistic system view, or making model variants. However, there are few state-of-the-art composition mechanisms that support type-safe symmetric composition of metamodels and their behavioural semantics. This hampers the flexible customisation and reuse of metamodels in model-driven engineering approaches. This paper presents a new mechanism for composing metamodels by defining metamodels as reusable templates. Composition of metamodels is achieved using template instantiations that allow customising the metamodel classes as part of the composition process. The work includes a prototypical metamodel composition tool that supports the ideas presented. The result is an approach for composing metamodels in a type-safe manner, where name conflict resolution, composition of behavioural semantics and reuse of tools are supported.

Keywords: Metamodelling, composition, reuse, behavioural semantics, metamodel templates, domain-specific languages.

1 Introduction

Metamodelling is a central aspect of *Model-Driven Engineering (MDE)* [1] where it is used to formalise languages, transformations and domain knowledge. Metamodels can be created in two different ways: directly from scratch or by some kind of model transformation where existing metamodel definitions are used. A model transformation is a process where a set of source models is used as basis for creating a target model. Metamodel composition can be seen as a specific kind of model transformation, with the purpose of elaborating a metamodel with additional concepts or semantics, or weave in variability as part of software product line development.

There exist many different kinds of model composition mechanisms/languages/tools, e.g., *Kompose* [2], *XWeave* [3], *Atlas Model Weaver (AMW)* [4], *Epsilon Merging Language (EML)* [5], *SmartAdapters* [6], *GeKo* [7,8], and *RAM* [9]. Unfortunately, most of these mechanisms are constrained to particular usage scenarios and/or they require a considerable initial effort to facilitate composition of a given set of models. For example, using AMW requires constructing

Ø. Haugen, R. Reed, and R. Gotzhein (Eds.): SAM 2012, LNCS 7744, pp. 160–178, 2013.
© Springer-Verlag Berlin Heidelberg 2013

a weaving model, composition in EML is described using a set of rules whose definition is demanding, SmartAdapters require creating a ConcreteAdapter that describes bindings between the constituent models of a composition. In addition, many composition mechanisms are designed explicitly for composing models rather than metamodels. Hence, composition of behavioural semantics is not addressed. Other limitations of current composition mechanisms are: no resolution of name conflicts, no support for composition of more than two models at the same time, and no support for symmetric composition - models typically take a base or aspect role. While there are a few composition mechanisms available that address these limitations, the work of this paper additionally discusses how existing tools can be reused. This is the main contribution of the paper.

Models are primary artefacts in MDE, whereas model transformations, including model compositions, are important operations on the models. Metamodels are models, yet their composition using state-of-the-art composition mechanisms, as we discuss in the related work, is not flexible enough to support the MDE philosophy. Specifically, composition of metamodels can not be performed in a simple, efficient, and context-free manner. The work of this paper addresses these issues. We will discuss how metamodel templates facilitate composition of metamodels' abstract syntax *and* behavioural semantics in a type-safe manner. Type safety is a requirement to be able to compose behavioural semantics. Our approach builds on the package template mechanism [10,11,12]. Specifically, we extend the package template mechanism with additional features that are particularly useful for metamodel composition, yielding metamodel templates. The ideas and examples have been validated by the construction of a metamodel composition tool[1].

The work is presented as follows. Section 2 gives an overview of our approach and introduces the metamodel template mechanism. In Sect. 3, we illustrate application of the composition tool by constructing a *Domain-Specific Language (DSL)*, while Sect. 4 delves into details on how metamodel templates work and how type safety is preserved with reference to the example application. Section 5 describes a set of new template features specifically designed for composition of metamodels; including the possibility of retyping class attributes. Section 6 presents and reviews several state-of-the-art composition mechanisms and discusses related work. Finally, Sect. 7 concludes the paper.

2   Metamodel Templates and Our Approach

The metamodel composition approach described in this paper is based on metamodel templates. Metamodel templates have taken some of the basic features from the package template mechanism [10,11,12]. A metamodel template (or template for short) comprises a class model that defines a metamodel or metamodel fragment. The class model is compatible with *Ecore/Essential MetaObject Facility (EMOF)* [13,14]. A template has to be instantiated in order to use the

---

[1] The metamodel composition tool can be found at this URL:
http://swat.project.ifi.uio.no/software

classes defined within the template. An instantiation of a template within a given scope (a package or another template) will make the template classes available in this scope, as if they were defined there (unique class copies). The same template can be instantiated several times, both in the same scope and in different scopes. Template classes may be adapted for a specific purpose as part of the template instantiation. This is achieved by renaming classes and class properties (which also affects the types of operations and their parameters' types), by adding new properties to classes, and by merging of classes from different templates (in case more than one template is instantiated in the same scope). Overriding of operations and thereby dynamic binding are also supported. The resulting classes of one template instantiation are not type-compatible with those of other instantiations of that template. Templates can be type checked independently at development time. Type safety is also preserved after template instantiation, and this still holds when classes are customised and merged.

Type checking of classes is required for composing the behavioural semantics of metamodels. There are several environments that support defining behavioural semantics for metamodels, including *Eclipse Modeling Framework (EMF)* [13] and *Kermeta* [15]. In EMF, the behavioural semantics is known as model code and is separated from the abstract syntax of the metamodel. The model code is expressed using Java. In Kermeta, both the abstract syntax and behavioural semantics are defined in the class model, i.e., the class operations contain definitions of the behavioural semantics of the metamodel. The metamodel composition tool discussed in this paper is constructed as a Kermeta pre-processor. It accepts a mixture of Kermeta code and template instantiation code/directives. However, the ideas also apply to EMF and modelling environments like *MetaEdit+* [16] and *Generic Modeling Environment (GME)* [17].

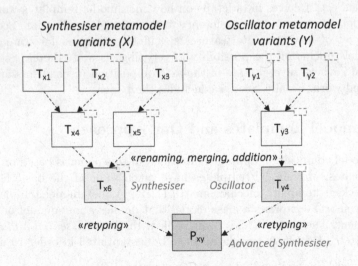

Fig. 1. Building template hierarchies

An overview of how templates can be organised in hierarchies is given in Fig. 1. The figure shows how an advanced synthesiser (P_{xy}) is made by utilising a template for modelling of synthesisers (T_{x6}) and a template for modelling of oscillators (T_{y4}). Each of these templates is created by instantiating other templates that contain metamodels with more basic concepts.

A major difference between our approach and other state-of-the-art composition mechanisms is that instantiation code can be expressed in the same modelling space as the templates are defined; the details of a composition is not defined in separate resources or models. In particular, templates themselves may contain instantiation code which supports complex hierarchical metamodel compositions.

Metamodel composition may result in tools that are no longer compatible with the resulting metamodel. This is unfortunate since the tools have to be manually refactored. The approach of this paper addresses how class attributes and references can be retyped as part of template instantiations according to predefined metamodel integration points (using superclasses), and thereby takes a first step towards tool reuse.

3   Application of the Metamodel Composition Tool

We will use audio processing as the example domain for illustrating the metamodel composition tool and the ideas presented in this paper. Today, there exist a vast number of virtual synthesisers. These synthesisers are realised in the form of software applications and are able to utilise the hardware of a standard computer. Virtual synthesisers replace traditional hardware synthesisers in many contexts. A synthesiser is usually implemented using a software development kit, with an appropriate API defined in a general purpose language such as C++. Programming a synthesiser requires knowledge in signal processing and is considered a challenging task. However, several companies have seen the potential in releasing modelling software that allows building synthesisers using a set of pre-defined building blocks. This allows users to build custom synthesisers without being an expert in signal processing.

Here, we will see how to define and utilise a set of (experimental) metamodels for building a DSL for modelling of synthesisers. There are three metamodels that will be used in the examples. These are named: *Synthesiser*, *Oscillator*, and *Filter*, and are given in Fig. 2. As supported by Kermeta, the behavioural semantics of the metamodels can be captured directly in the class operations. The metamodels are somewhat simplified, e.g., we do not consider all aspects of static semantics like model constraints (OCL).

The Synthesiser metamodel (language) in Fig. 2 can be used to model simple synthesisers. It comprises 11 classes[2]. A synthesiser is built using one or more layers each of which is composed of a sound source and processors. At this point, the sound source is a very simple oscillator. Different types of sound processing are performed by filters and amplifiers. Envelopes and *Low Frequency Oscillators*

---

[2] The MidiEvent class used in the definition of SoundSource is not included in the figure.

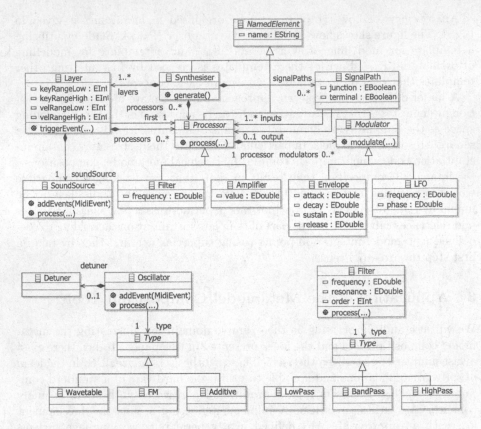

Fig. 2. Metamodels (languages) for modelling of synthesisers, oscillators, and filters

(LFOs) can be used to modulate parameters, for instance the cutoff frequency of a filter. The sound is generated by invoking the generate() operation of the Synthesiser class. We assume that this class contains logic for communicating with a USB musical keyboard. The behavioural semantics is not of interest for explaining the approach of this paper, and is thus excluded.

A synthesiser's sound depends heavily on the sound processing algorithms it uses. There are many different algorithms and methods for both generating sound (synthesis) and processing sound (filtering, effects, etc.). The ability to add/weave in variability to the Synthesiser metamodel is therefore desirable. Two metamodels for modelling of oscillators and filters, respectively, are found in Fig. 2. Only extracts of the metamodels are shown, due to size constraints.

We will now see how the described metamodels can be defined as metamodel templates and then combined to create an elaborated Synthesiser metamodel/DSL. A metamodel is converted to a metamodel template simply by defining it within a template scope, as designated by the keyword template. No other changes have to be done to the metamodel definition. The top of Fig. 3 shows an excerpt of the Synthesiser metamodel template.

```
template SynthesiserTemplate {
  abstract class NamedElement {
    attribute name : String
  }
  class Synthesiser inherits NamedElement {
    attribute layers : Layer[1..*]
    operation generate() is do ... end
    ...
  }
  class Layer inherits NamedElement {
    attribute processors : Processor[0..*]
    ...
  }
  ...
}


package advancedSynthesiser;
require "SynthesiserTemplate.kpt"
require "OscillatorTemplate.kpt"
require "FilterTemplate.kpt"
require "MidiEvent.kmt"

inst SynthesiserTemplate with
  SoundSource => Oscillator
    (addEvents() -> addEventsNative, process() -> processNative),
  Layer
    (soundSource -> oscillator),
  Filter
    (process() -> processNative, frequency -> frq)
inst OscillatorTemplate with Type => OscillatorType
inst FilterTemplate with Type => FilterType

class Oscillator adds {
  operation addEventsNative( events : Bag<MidiEvent> ) is do
    addEvents( events )
  end

  operation processNative( left : Bag<Real>, right : Bag<Real> ) is do
    process( left, right )
  end
}

class Filter adds {
  operation processNative( left : Bag<Real>, right : Bag<Real> ) is do
    process( left, right )
  end
}
```

Fig. 3. Definition of the Synthesiser template and metamodel variant

In order to create the new Synthesiser metamodel variant, we want to refine the SoundSource and Filter classes of the Synthesiser metamodel. We do this by instantiating the metamodel templates in a package. Instantiation of a template is organised in three parts: the main instantiation statement, a renaming statement, and adds clauses in which additional properties and code can be added to the derived metamodel classes. The two latter parts are optional.

As can be seen in Fig. 3, the Synthesiser, Oscillator, and Filter metamodels are instantiated in the advancedSynthesiser package by the use of the keyword inst. (Alternatively, the instantiations could have been performed within a new template to define the new Synthesiser metamodel as a reusable module.) Arrows indicate atomic transformations, e.g., renaming. There are two types of renaming performed: renaming of classes (=>) and renaming of class properties (->). The SoundSource class is renamed to Oscillator. The Oscillator template contains a class Oscillator as well. Refer to the Oscillator metamodel of Fig. 2. The semantics of the metamodel template mechanism yields a merge when two classes have the same name. Consequently, the SoundSource class of the Synthesiser template, now renamed to Oscillator, is merged with the Oscillator class of the Oscillator template. However, both the Oscillator classes in question contain equally named operations addEvents(...) and process(...), which introduces name conflicts. These are resolved by renaming the operations of the SoundSource class from the Synthesiser template. Similar considerations are made for the Filter classes originating from the Synthesiser template and the Filter template. The soundSource attribute (containment reference) of the Layer class is renamed to the more appropriate oscillator. The Type classes in the Oscillator and Filter templates are renamed to OscillatorType and FilterType, respectively.

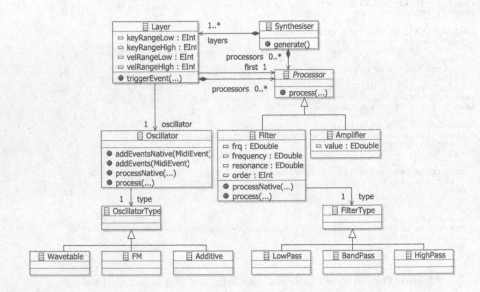

Fig. 4. Excerpt of the resulting metamodel after composition

The behavioural semantics of the Oscillator and Filter metamodels need to be integrated with the semantics of the Synthesiser metamodel. This is achieved using adds clauses, which allow adding new properties to classes and overriding operations. Operations named: addEvents(...) and process(...) are used repeatedly in the Synthesiser classes. These operations capture the behavioural semantics of synthesisers. To compose the semantics, the addEventsNative(...) operation of Oscillator (earlier the addEvents(...) operation of SoundSource) is overridden to invoke the addEvents(...) operation of the class (added from the Oscillator class of the Oscillator template as a consequence of merging). The same overriding is performed for the processNative(...) operation, whose new definition invokes the process(...) operation of the Filter class. As a result, the behavioural semantics of the Oscillator metamodel is used for sound synthesis, while the semantics of the

Filter metamodel replaces the native filter semantics. Fig. 4 shows an excerpt of the resulting metamodel for the Synthesiser variant. At this point tools have to be manually fitted for the new metamodel. We will later see how retyping addresses this.

4   How Metamodel Template Instantiation Works

4.1   Full Static Type Checking

Renaming of classes and class properties, class merging, and addition of class properties and code are performed during processing of the instantiation directives. The resulting classes from a template instantiation do not contain any template-specific code (like inst, adds and so forth).

Full static type checking is an important property of metamodel templates that differentiates this approach from, e.g., package extension [18]. There are two steps in ensuring type safety:

1. Type checking at template development time
2. Type checking of the resulting metamodel during template instantiations

Each template can be type checked at development time independently of other templates. Type safety is also checked when templates are instantiated and their classes customised and combined. Here, we will illustrate the mechanics of how type safety is preserved after processing of renaming transformations.

We have seen how classes and class properties can be renamed as part of a template instantiation. Giving a new name to a class or property is reflected in the derived class definitions resulting from the template instantiations including every place where the class or property is referred. The renaming transformations preserve type safety. We will explain this by using a subset of the Synthesiser metamodel template.

Let us see how renaming of the SoundSource class, its operations, and the sound-Source attribute of the Layer class are reflected in the template classes (copies) that are made available in the advancedSynthesiser package. Figure 5 visualises this. First, the class SoundSource is renamed to Oscillator (1). This affects every piece of code that refers to this class (2). Renaming addEvents(...) to addEventsNative(...) (3) also affects the code within the triggerEvent(...) operation (4). Finally, renaming the soundSource attribute of the Layer class (5) is reflected by the code within triggerEvent(...) as well (6). Similar actions are taken for the other renaming statements in the production of the Synthesiser metamodel variant. For clarity, these are not illustrated in the figure. The classes of the package advancedSynthesiser have the definitions found in the lower part of Fig. 5 after template instantiation (and renaming).

Renaming works at more than one level. For example, the Synthesiser template could have been constructed by instantiating other templates within this template. As a consequence, renaming a property as part of instantiating the Synthesiser template could potentially lead to renaming across several levels of templates. This "deep" kind of renaming is performed by the composition tool and ensures that all attributes, references, variables, operations, and parameters have the correct type when renaming of classes occur. The ability to rename classes and class properties supports reusing the same template multiple times (the classes within the template definitions are not changed; derived class copies are used). That is, the Filter template could have been instantiated twice or more in the package advancedSynthesiser if needed. This allows defining common metamodel patterns in the form of templates, which can then be used multiple times to construct a metamodel [19].

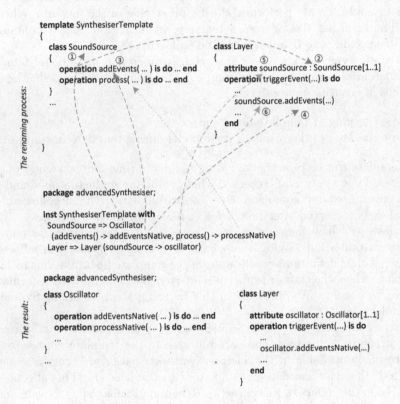

Fig. 5. Renaming of classes and class properties

4.2   Why Symmetry and Type Safety

Model composition comes in two variants: symmetric and asymmetric. In a symmetric model composition process, all constituent models are regarded equal with respect to roles (from the perspective of the composition mechanism). An asymmetric composition process identifies a base model and one or more aspect models. The approach discussed in this paper is symmetric; metamodel template instantiations are not differentiated in the composition process. Note that the concepts of the Oscillator and Filter metamodels in the example represent two distinct aspects of a synthesiser. However, the composition process does not assign contrasting roles to these metamodels with respect to the Synthesiser metamodel. Thus, the composition process is still symmetric.

Symmetric composition is important to ensure flexibility and support agility. When composing an arbitrary number of models, it is not unlikely that these are required to be composed according to different schemes. Let us consider three metamodels: $\mathcal{MM}_b$, $\mathcal{MM}_{a1}$, and $\mathcal{MM}_{a2}$, and assume that $\mathcal{MM}_b$ takes the role as a base model while the other two metamodels are aspect models, as is the case when using an asymmetric composition mechanism. In such a case, both $\mathcal{MM}_{a1}$ and $\mathcal{MM}_{a2}$ have to be composed directly with $\mathcal{MM}_b$. However, this may not be possible if the aspects overlap, or at best difficult to achieve using an asymmetric composition mechanism. For example, let us assume that $\mathcal{MM}_{a1}$ and $\mathcal{MM}_{a2}$ have classes reflecting the same domain concepts. Instead, by using symmetric composition, $\mathcal{MM}_b$, $\mathcal{MM}_{a1}$, and $\mathcal{MM}_{a2}$ can be composed arbitrarily. Specifically, the metamodels can be composed where overlapping concepts are addressed explicitly in one single composition process.

Renaming and merging of template classes result in new classes that are unknown to other classes of the instantiated templates. As we have seen, the metamodel composition tool addresses this by updating references automatically as part of template instantiations and ensures that type safety is preserved. It also verifies that overriding of operations and addition of classes and behavioural semantics are type-safe[3]. Type checking is particularly important if the metamodel classes have an associated behavioural semantics, as type errors will completely break the integrity of the metamodel. In that case type checking ensures that composition of metamodels, and in particular composition of behavioural semantics, gives an expected result. Additional details on the consistency of the package template features can be found in [20].

5   Tailoring the Metamodel Template Mechanism for Metamodelling

So far we have only used features of metamodel templates that resemble those of package templates. That is: class merging, renaming of classes and class properties, and addition of properties/overriding of operations. These features work well if the required manual rewriting of tools is not an issue. We will here discuss a slightly different approach where we utilise a new set of features. These features may be used together with the basic metamodel template features discussed so far. We will mainly illustrate *retyping* and *namespaces*.

In Fig. 3, we merged the SoundSource class of the Synthesiser template with the Oscillator class from the Oscillator template and composed the behavioural semantics by renaming and overriding the native addEvents(...) and process(...) operations. In the following, we do not want to merge the SoundSource and Oscillator

---

[3] A simplified type checking is used by the prototype tool.

classes to compose the metamodels. Instead, we give the soundSource attribute of the Layer class a new type specified as an abstract class. This type represents an "interface" between the Layer class and different kinds of sound sources.

Figure 6 gives the definition of an abstract class that declares operations that need to be implemented by a sound source: addEvents(...) and process(...). Note how SoundSourceDef is specified in a separate resource (file) and can thus be acquired in several metamodel templates.

```
// SoundSourceDef.kmt
package ssd;
require "MidiEvent.kmt"

abstract class SoundSourceDef {
  operation addEvents( events : Bag<MidiEvent> ) is abstract
  operation process( left : Bag<Real>, right : Bag<Real> ) is abstract
}
```

Fig. 6. Defining the essential properties of sound sources

```
// SynthesiserTemplate.kpt
require "SoundSourceDef.kmt"

template SynthesiserTemplate {
  class Synthesiser inherits NamedElement { ... }
  class SoundSource inherits ssd :: SoundSourceDef {
    ...
  }

  class Layer inherits NamedElement {
    attribute soundSource : ssd :: SoundSourceDef[1..1]
    ...
  }
  ...
}

// OscillatorTemplate.kpt
require "SoundSourceDef.kmt"

template OscillatorTemplate {
  class Oscillator inherits ssd :: SoundSourceDef {
    method addEvents( events : Bag<MidiEvent> ) is do ... end
    method process( left : Bag<Real>, right : Bag<Real> ) is do ... end
  }
  ...
}
```

Fig. 7. Using SoundSourceDef in the Synthesiser and Oscillator metamodels

Figure 7 shows how the Synthesiser and Oscillator metamodels are refactored to use SoundSourceDef. This is a design-time decision. For example, the Synthesiser metamodel is designed in a manner that later allows retyping the soundSource attribute. Thus, the soundSource attribute acts as an integration point. Several abstract superclasses could have been used to define additional integration points. These classes define/guide how the Synthesiser metamodel can be integrated with other metamodels using retyping. Notice how the Oscillator class inherits SoundSourceDef[4]. Hence, the Oscillator metamodel is refactored to be compatible with the Synthesiser metamodel (from the perspective of Sound-SourceDef). An important observation is that the Layer class can not utilise class properties in SoundSource that are not defined in SoundSourceDef. Otherwise there may potentially be references to properties that are no longer present in the target type of a retyping transformation.

Integration of the two metamodels can be achieved by giving a new type to the soundSource attribute of the Layer class as part of the template instantiation process. The only requirement for this retyping operation is that the new type is a subtype of SoundSourceDef. See Fig. 8.

```
package advancedSynthesiser;
require "SynthesiserTemplate.kpt"
require "OscillatorTemplate.kpt"

inst t1 : SynthesiserTemplate with
  Layer (soundSource :-> t2 :: Oscillator)
inst t2 : OscillatorTemplate
```

Fig. 8. Retyping the soundSource attribute to Oscillator

In Fig. 8, the soundSource attribute is retyped to the Oscillator class resulting from the instantiation of the Oscillator template. The Oscillator class is referenced using the namespace identifer t2. That is, all the resulting classes of a given template instantiation can be referenced using an identifier. Note the different kind of arrow used, which identifies retyping (:->) instead of renaming.

So what do we achieve by using retyping instead of class merging. First, integration of metamodels' behavioural semantics is achieved by implementing (or overriding) a set of operations as specified by the common supertype. The new operation definitions replace the previous definitions. In Fig. 3, we used adds clauses to combine the semantics. This is thus not required anymore. The inherited operations from the supertype represent an interface between two classes in the different metamodels being integrated, hence, simplifying the integration of the semantics. Second, retyping causes metamodels to be merged according to integration points defined by supertypes. This ensures that existing tools can still be used with minimal required configuration. By using basic metamodel template features and retyping in unison we achieve a powerful mechanism for composing metamodels. Retyping is resolved at template instantiation time. An overview of the integration of two metamodels using retyping is given in Fig. 9.

MM_1 and MM_2 are metamodel templates that are defined independently. Both templates contain classes that inherit from the X and Y classes. Let us focus on the x_1 reference of the M_1 class. The type of x_1 is specified to be of type X. Thus, when using MM_1 without retyping (e.g., when MM_1 is used

---

[4] Kermeta uses method as keyword for overridden operations.

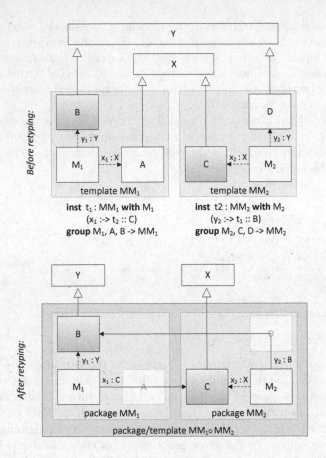

Fig. 9. The retyping process

standalone), the x_1 reference may relate objects of classes that are subtypes of X. There is only one such class in $\mathcal{MM}_1$, namely the A class (indicated with a dashed relationship symbol). Both templates are instantiated within a package (or template) named $\mathcal{MM}_1 \circ \mathcal{MM}_2$. The x_1 reference is retyped to the C class of $\mathcal{MM}_2$ as part of the template instantiations to make an explicit relationship between the M_1 class of $\mathcal{MM}_1$ and the C class of $\mathcal{MM}_2$. As a result, only objects of the C class can be related using the x_1 reference. The main point is that a class can still be utilised by a tool as long as it implements properties of a specified supertype (which the tool supports).

Notice how bi-directional integration is possible, as illustrated by retyping of y_2. Instantiating several templates causes all classes from the different templates to be mixed together in the same package. This is not desirable, and we use a *grouping* feature to maintain the existing separation of the different classes; the arguments of a group directive are added to a subpackage. One particular application of retyping is to allow using different concrete syntaxes for a DSL. Figure 10 illustrates how reuse of concrete syntaxes (modelling tools) is achieved.

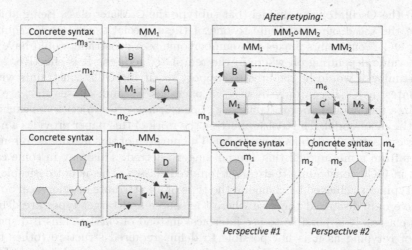

Fig. 10. Remapping of concrete syntax

Each of the two metamodels $\mathcal{MM}_1$ and $\mathcal{MM}_2$ has a unique concrete syntax. The concepts of the concrete syntaxes are mapped to the classes of the metamodels. For example, the square (m_1) is mapped to the M_1 class of $\mathcal{MM}_1$, denoted by the arrow m_1. The right part of the figure shows how the triangle (m_2) and pentagon (m_6) are remapped to the C and B classes, respectively. This is possible, since these types are subtypes of X and Y. Put differently, the triangle and pentagon concrete syntax concepts only relate to the properties declared in X and Y. Hence, it is possible to use several concrete syntaxes to describe different aspects of a composite language's problem domain. For example, $\mathcal{MM}_1$ and $\mathcal{MM}_2$ could have been two metamodel design patterns for describing typed relationships and state machines. Each of these design patterns ought to be represented with a distinct known concrete syntax. A model of the resulting metamodel will consist of two submodels expressed in the respective concrete syntaxes. Still, model objects can be shared between the submodels. For example, in the right part of Fig. 10, the circle (m_3) and the pentagon (m_6) both map to the same object of B. The triangle (m_2) and the hexagon (m_5) relate to the same C object. The objects of the B and C classes are contained by an M_1 object.

An alternative to retyping is using *Object Constraint Language (OCL)* constraints on the resulting metamodel. In the synthesiser example, it would be possible to add a constraint that restricts the type of objects contained by the soundSource attribute: the constraint would restrict objects to be instances of the Oscillator class. There are two reasons why retyping is the preferred approach. First, templates may be instantiated within other templates. In Fig. 1 we saw how this allows building template hierarchies. In particular, an attribute that has been retyped once may later be retyped again to a subtype of the current attribute type. For example, there could have been several kinds of oscillators within the Oscillator metamodel that subtype the Oscillator class. Being able to retype the soundSource attribute to one of these special oscillators is required. Using OCL constraints makes this cumbersome as a constraint would have different value depending on where in the template hierarchy it is effective. More importantly, it would be required to support specifying OCL constraints within templates, as OCL can only be used in packages. Second, classes that are not used in a metamodel after retyping, e.g., SoundSource, are subject to be excluded from the metamodel. The tool supporting the work of this paper provides a naive exclusion feature known as *suppression*. The purpose of this feature is to remove classes from a metamodel that are no longer referred. This may in some cases result in OCL constraints that target removed classes. This is not desirable.

Retyping is achieved by changing the type of an attribute or reference. So far, we have only discussed the case where the source and target types are defined using classes. It is possible to use interfaces instead of classes. This is a special case of retyping as it is not possible to define required structure (other than operations) of a target type. For example, a transformation model may refer to attributes and references defined explicitly in a superclass, and thereby improve genericity of the transformation model.

In Fig. 6, SoundSourceDef was defined as a standalone resource. Instead, it would be possible to include this class in the Synthesiser metamodel. The Oscillator metamodel could then be composed with the Synthesiser metamodel by adding the Oscillator class as a subtype to SoundSourceDef and subsequently retyping the soundSource attribute to the Oscillator class as before. The difference following such approach is minimal, but it may make more sense from an organisational point of view.

6   Related Work

Atlas Model Weaver (AMW). The *AMW* [4] builds on the concept of using weaving models for expressing links between model elements. Weaving models can be used for several applications, e.g., model composition, where link types like *merge*, *override*, and *union* are relevant. A weaving model for a specific composition scenario is made by instantiating a core weaving metamodel. That is, a composition process is described as a model with specific links detailing the model composition (used by a merging tool). The primary subject for the AMW Model Weaver is composition of models and not metamodel composition as discussed in this paper. Creating a weaving model is only reasonable when this weaving model can be reused to compose several models that are instances of a common metamodel. Composing metamodels using weaving models is a cumbersome process. Neither is the initial cost of defining a weaving model for the composition of metamodels justified, since the weaving model is likely to be used only once.

The Epsilon Merging Language (EML). *EML* is a language for merging of models [5]. A model in the EML language comprises a set of rules that dictate how model elements from source models are combined into a merged model. A central feature of EML is the ability to compare and match elements from the source models. This is achieved using match rules. Additional strategies can be applied to ensure that merging of models is carried out in the correct manner. EML is primarily intended for merging of terminal models. Creating an EML model with all required rules is not trivial. Creating rules for merging of metamodels that will only be used once is not a good approach. EML does not handle merging of models with conflicting elements well.

Weaving Metamodels using SmartAdapters. Weaving variability into metamodels can be seen as an asymmetric extension of a metamodel. An approach based on *SmartAdapters* is discussed in [6]. A SmartAdapter appears as a composition protocol that covers how an aspect model should be combined with a base model. The purpose of a SmartAdapter is to describe weaving of the aspect model separately from the base model definition, which supports reusing aspect models. Weaving is achieved by creating a ConcreteAdapter that specifies bindings between an aspect model and base model. SmartAdapters can be used to add new model elements to a base model, modify attributes and references and merge model elements. The approach is designed for defining software product lines and does not address metamodel composition in general. There are similarities between using SmartAdapters and the approach we discuss in this paper. Though, SmartAdapters do not support symmetric metamodel composition.

The GeKo Generic Aspect Model Weaver. *GeKo* is a weaver that supports weaving advice models into a base model [7,8]. The advice models and base model have to be instances of the same EMOF compatible metamodel. Compositions are described using pointcut models. A pointcut model consists of a set of objects that bridge elements in the base and advice models using morphisms (mappings). Elements from an advice model can either be added to or replace elements of the base model. The approach does not address adaption of behavioural semantics (as defined at the metamodel level), or how adding and replacing elements are reflected by a behavioural semantics.

Reusable Aspect Models (RAM). *RAM* is an aspect-oriented approach for integrating class, sequence, and state diagrams [9]. An aspect in RAM is a model of three constituent UML diagrams: a structural view, state view, and message view. Aspects are woven together as specified by instantiations. Instantiation directives describe how one aspect instantiates another and map incomplete entities in one aspect to entities of another aspect, regardless of view. The essence of RAM is support for model reuse, multi-view modelling, and view consistency checking. RAM resembles the work of this paper. One evident difference is that requirements for using an aspect are explicitly expressed in the aspect's definition; aspects may depend on each other as specified by instantiation parameters. In contrast, metamodel templates do not have parameters, though dependencies between templates are expressed using instantiation directives. RAM supports defining aspect dependency chains, where simpler aspects are combined to create more complex aspects. In a similar manner, metamodel templates allow building template hierarchies. While RAM's focus is on reusable models, RAM does not explicitly address how tools can be reused on composed models. Metamodel templates take the latter into consideration.

Model Integration Using Mega Operations. An approach for weaving and sewing of metamodels and models is discussed in [21]. Weaving is based on using weaving operators, e.g., *overrides*, *references*, *prune*, and *rename*. These operators act as directives that govern a composition process. Specifically, weaving operators can be used to compose both metamodels and conformant models. There are several similarities between this work and the approach of this paper. For example, the operators resemble the template instantiation code (*with*, *adds*, etc.). However, the approach does not address integration of behavioural semantics. It is described how one of the operators, named *prune*, can be used to remove unnecessary elements from a metamodel. Such operation can only be performed safely if metamodels are considered purely as static structures; e.g., Kermeta and EMF both associate behavioural semantics to a metamodel's structure (abstract syntax). The composition tool backing the approach of this paper supports a naive operation of removing classes from metamodels - known as suppression. However, a thorough static analysis of the metamodel is required for such operation to be carried out safely. Several requirements for removal of a given class must be fulfilled. For example, objects of the class must be optional (multiplicities of the form [0..n]), the behavioural semantics of the metamodel can not contain code that instantiates the class, the class can not be a superclass with subclasses that should still be included in the resulting metamodel, the class can not participate in a bi-directional relationship that is not optional (from both sides), etc. The topic of excluding classes from metamodels is currently being studied.

Sewing is discussed as a way of integrating models loosely. The discussed advantages are autonomous models without entangled concepts, that can utilise, e.g., existing GUI. Two sewing operators are identified: *synchronizes* and *depends*. Synchronisation is used when model elements need to be synchronised, e.g., two attributes of two distinct models may be synchronised ensuring that the attributes always have the same value. Dependency indicates that existence of one model element is required for existence of another. The actual integration of models is realised using mediating entities, e.g., *Java Metadata Interface (JMI)*. In the approach discussed in this paper, we use object links for both synchronisation and dependency (using retyping). Thus, no mediators are required to integrate the models.

7   Conclusion and Future Work

Metamodels play an essential role in MDE, yet their efficient composition and reuse are hindered by limitations of many state-of-the-art model composition mechanisms. In this paper, we have discussed a template-based approach to metamodel composition, which tackles some of the limitations of these mechanisms. We have introduced the concept of metamodel templates which promotes composition of both the structure and semantics of metamodels. A metamodel template comprises a class model whose classes can be customised for a specific usage by instantiating the template; including support for merging of classes, resolution of name conflicts, addition of semantics, overriding of operations and retyping of class properties. Specifically, retyping is not supported by any of the related approaches discussed. Hence, metamodels can be composed by utilising a set of powerful features, all of which can be fully type checked. The applicability of the approach has been demonstrated using a metamodel composition tool. Future work includes formalising how type checking is performed and elaborating the retyping and suppression concepts.

We argue that metamodel templates leverage how metamodels can be composed and address the increasing complexity and required agility in metamodel and language design.

References

1. Kent, S.: Model Driven Engineering. In: Butler, M., Petre, L., Sere, K. (eds.) IFM 2002. LNCS, vol. 2335, pp. 286–298. Springer, Heidelberg (2002)
2. Fleurey, F., Baudry, B., France, R., Ghosh, S.: A Generic Approach for Automatic Model Composition. In: Giese, H. (ed.) MODELS 2008. LNCS, vol. 5002, pp. 7–15. Springer, Heidelberg (2008)
3. Groher, I., Voelter, M.: XWeave – Models and Aspects in Concert. In: 10th International Workshop on Aspect-Oriented Modeling (AOM 2007), pp. 35–40. ACM Press (2007)
4. Didonet Del Fabro, M., Bézivin, J., Valduriez, P.: Weaving Models with the Eclipse AMW plugin. In: Eclipse Modeling Symposium, Eclipse Summit Europe 2006 (2006), http://ssei.pbworks.com/f/Del+Fabro.Weaving+Models+with+the+Eclipse+AMW+plugin.pdf
5. Kolovos, D.S., Paige, R.F., Polack, F.A.C.: Merging Models with the Epsilon Merging Language (EML). In: Wang, J., Whittle, J., Harel, D., Reggio, G. (eds.) MoDELS 2006. LNCS, vol. 4199, pp. 215–229. Springer, Heidelberg (2006)
6. Morin, B., Perrouin, G., Lahire, P., Barais, O., Vanwormhoudt, G., Jézéquel, J.-M.: Weaving Variability into Domain Metamodels. In: Schürr, A., Selic, B. (eds.) MODELS 2009. LNCS, vol. 5795, pp. 690–705. Springer, Heidelberg (2009)
7. Morin, B., Klein, J., Barais, O.: A Generic Weaver for Supporting Product Lines. In: 13th International Workshop on Early Aspects (EA 2008), pp. 11–18. ACM Press (2008)
8. Kramer, M.E., Klein, J., Steel, J.R.H., Morin, B., Kienzle, J., Barais, O., Jézéquel, J.-M.: On the Formalisation of GeKo: a Generic Aspect Models Weaver. Technical Report, University of Luxembourg (2012) ISBN: 978-2-87971-110-2
9. Kienzle, J., Al Abed, W., Klein, J.: Aspect-Oriented Multi-View Modeling. In: 8th ACM International Conference on Aspect-Oriented Software Development (AOSD 2009), pp. 87–98. ACM Press (2009)
10. Krogdahl, S., Møller-Pedersen, B., Sørensen, F.: Exploring the use of Package Templates for flexible re-use of Collections of related Classes. Journal of Object Technology 8(7) (2005), http://www.jot.fm/issues/issue_2009_11/article1/

11. Sørensen, F., Axelsen, E.W., Krogdahl, S.: Reuse and Combination with Package Templates. In: 4th Workshop on MechAnisms for SPEcialization, Generalization and InHeritance (MASPEGHI 2010), Article 3. ACM Press (2010)
12. Axelsen, E.W., Sørensen, F., Krogdahl, S., Møller-Pedersen, B.: Challenges in the Design of the Package Template Mechanism. In: Leavens, G.T., Chiba, S., Haupt, M., Ostermann, K., Wohlstadter, E. (eds.) Transactions on AOSD IX. LNCS, vol. 7271, pp. 268–305. Springer, Heidelberg (2012)
13. The Eclipse Foundation: Eclipse Modeling Framework, http://www.eclipse.org/modeling/emf
14. Object Management Group: Meta Object Facility (MOF) Core Specification, http://www.omg.org/mof
15. Muller, P.-A., Fleurey, F., Jézéquel, J.-M.: Weaving Executability into Object-Oriented Meta-languages. In: Briand, L.C., Williams, C. (eds.) MoDELS 2005. LNCS, vol. 3713, pp. 264–278. Springer, Heidelberg (2005)
16. Tolvanen, J.-P., Kelly, S.: MetaEdit+ – Defining and Using Integrated Domain-Specific Modeling Languages. In: 18th Annual ACM SIGPLAN Conference on Object-Oriented Programming, Systems, Languages, & Applications (OOPSLA 2003), pp. 92–93. ACM Press (2003)
17. Institute for Software Integrated Systems: GME – Generic Modeling Environment, http://www.isis.vanderbilt.edu/projects/gme
18. Clark, T., Evans, A., Kent, S.: Aspect-Oriented Metamodelling. The Computer Journal 46(5), 566–577 (2003)
19. Cho, H., Gray, J.: Design Patterns for Metamodels. In: SPLASH 2011 Workshops Proceedings, pp. 25–32. ACM Press (2011)
20. Axelsen, E.W., Krogdahl, S.: Package Templates: A Definition by Semantics-Preserving Source-to-Source Transformations to Efficient Java Code. In: 11th International Conference on Generative Programming and Component Engineering (GPCE 2012), pp. 50–59. ACM Press (2012)
21. Reiter, T., Kapsammer, E., Retschitzegger, W., Schwinger, W.: Model Integration through Mega Operations. In: Proceedings of the Workshop on Model-Driven Web Engineering (MDWE 2005) (2005), http://www.lcc.uma.es/~av/mdwe2005/camera-ready/3-MDWE2005_MegaOperations_CameraReady.pdf

Towards Correct Product Derivation
in Model-Driven Product Lines

Xiaorui Zhang[1,2] and Birger Møller-Pedersen[2]

[1] SINTEF, Pb. 124 Blindern, 0314 Oslo, Norway
Xiaorui.Zhang@sintef.no
[2] Department of Informatics, University of Oslo,
Pb. 1080 Blindern, 0316 Oslo, Norway
birger@ifi.uio.no

Abstract. In a product line model, the product line developer often specifies not only high-level domain features but also their low-level realization steps. We see two challenges against deriving and intended products with respect to the specification of feature realizations:

1. The developer is not provided with immediate feedback on the realization steps at design time.
2. How to ensure that the realization steps are consistent with high-level features.

The Common Variability Language (CVL) is a generic language for modeling variability and the CVL tool can be used for product line development. We propose two extensions to the CVL tool to address the aforementioned challenges:

1. A simulator that simulates the feature realizations and visualizes the resulting product model at design time.
2. A consistency checker that checks if the realizations are consistent with high-level features.

We illustrate these two added procedures by applying them to the development of a train control product line. A tool prototype is implemented and used for evaluation.

Keywords: Common Variability Language, Model-Driven Software Product Line, Product Derivation.

1 Introduction

Software Product Line Engineering (SPLE) is an efficient means to produce a family of software systems sharing a common set of features of the domain [1]. In Model-Driven Development (MDD), models are not only for documentation purpose, but also regarded as source artifacts for automated code generation [2]. As the convergence of SPLE and MDD techniques, a model-driven product line produces a family of models instead of source code compared to the traditional Software Product Lines (SPL).

Ø. Haugen, R. Reed, and R. Gotzhein (Eds.): SAM 2012, LNCS 7744, pp. 179–197, 2013.
© Springer-Verlag Berlin Heidelberg 2013

Feature/Variability modeling is widely used for model-driven SPL development, which includes four phases:

1. **Feature Identification.** Identify the variability (and sometimes commonality) of all the intended product models as features of the product line.
2. **Feature Specification.** Specify the product line model (feature model) based on the identified features.
3. **Feature Realization.** A pre-specified product model is chosen as the base model of the product line. Based on that, the developer needs to define the low-level realizations of the features, which describe how to change the base model to realize specific features.
4. **Product Derivation.** The developer configures a specific product by choosing the set of features required. The realizations of the chosen features are then applied to the base model to derive the product model.

We see two challenges against deriving products that are both correct and intended:

1. **How to provide immediate feedback on the specification of feature realizations at design time.**
   A correct specification of feature realizations is essential for the derivation of correct and intended products. In order to specify feature realizations, the developer needs to have low-level (model object level) understanding of the base product model and all the intended product models. However, specifying feature realizations is an error-prone process due to the complexity associated with the underlying domain. Moreover, with most tools for product line development, the developer does not get immediate feedback on his/her specification changes at design time. Often a wrong specification of realization steps is not discovered until incorrect or unintended products are derived during execution.
   We provide a generic simulator to address this challenge, which provides the simulation of feature realization and the visualization of the simulation result at design time.
2. **How to ensure the consistency between the high-level features and their realizations.**
   High-level domain constraints that govern the compatibility of features are often well captured in the product line model during feature specification [3], e.g. feature A implies B, indicating that these two features need to be included in the same product configuration. Nevertheless, there are also low-level realization constraints [3], e.g. the realization of feature A changes the same base model element that is also changed by the realization of feature B. Including these two features in the same product configuration will lead to conflicts during product derivation. This kind of inconsistencies between feature specification and feature realization can often go undetected until the product derivation halts or derives incorrect product models. Approaches are needed to check the product line at design time instead of getting late feedback from the derived products which are incorrect [4].

In order to address the challenges mentioned above, we propose two extensions to the current CVL tool, which is a generic tool for model-driven product line development:

1. **Feature Realization Simulator**, which provides the simulation of feature realization and the visualization of simulation result (the resulting product model) at design time.
2. **Consistency Checker**, which automatically detects any inconsistencies between feature specification and realization at design time.

Furthermore, our tool extensions have the following characteristics:

1. **Generic.** Our tool extensions are based on the Common Variability Language (CVL) [5,6]. CVL is a generic variability modeling language being considered for standardization [7] at Object Management Group (OMG). Both our extensions can be applied to product models created in any modeling language that are defined based on Meta Object Facility (MOF) [8].
2. **Incremental.** Both our extensions provide immediate and incremental analysis of the product line model, which facilitates iterative and incremental development of the product line.

2 Background

2.1 Common Variability Language

The Common Variability Language is a generic variability modeling language that can be applied to models created in any Domain Specific Language (DSL) that are defined based on Meta Object Facility (MOF) [8]. For a full description of the CVL language and how to develop a product line using CVL, we refer to [5,9,10]. When using CVL to develop a product line, the developer has three models to deal with [6]:

Base Model. A product model created in the base DSL. During the product derivation process, product models can be derived by applying the feature realizations to the base model. The "base model" can be viewed as part of the core asset in the speaking of non-model-driven product line development.

Variability Model. This model serves as the product line model. The SPL developer specifies the variability of the product line in this model. The term "variability model" is analogous to "feature model" in feature modeling.

Resolution Model. A resolution model has one-sided relation to a variability model. Thus a variability model can have several resolution models. The developer resolves the variability of the product line differently in different resolution models. Resolution models can be regarded as product configurations. The CVL generic transformation will take the base model (and the library models if applicable), the variability model and the resolution models as input to generate resolved models, which can be regarded as the product derivation process. A "resolution model" is analogous. to a "product configuration" in feature modeling.

In the variability model, the developer can specify the variability of the product line in two layers:

Feature Specification Layer. The developer specifies domain-level features in this layer. For example, the CVL language construct *CompositeVariability* can be used to model the features. Multiplicity and choices over features can be expressed using the CVL construct *Iterator*. The specification of high-level domain features in this layer can be regarded as a feature model.

Product Realization Layer. This layer is not covered by the traditional feature modeling notation. In this layer, the developer defines the CVL-specific operations that realize the high-level features in the feature specification layer. These operations apply model changes to the base model to derive new product models during product derivation, including:

1. *ValueSubstitution* changes the value of an attribute of a model element (*PlacementValue*) to another value (*ReplacementValue*);
2. *ReferenceSubstitution* redirects a reference from one model element (*PlacementObject*) to another one (*ReplacementObject*);
3. *FragmentSubstitution* substitutes an arbitrary set of model elements (*PlacementFragment*) with another set of model elements (*ReplacementFragment*) created in the same DSL. A replacement fragment can be defined either in the same base model or in separate library models.

Any arbitrary model fragment can be defined using the CVL concept *BoundaryElement*. The boundary elements record all references to and from the model fragment. As illustrated in Fig. 1, *ToP*, *FrP1* and *FrP2* define the placement fragment, whereas *ToR*, *FrR1* and *FrR2* define the replacement fragment. During the fragment substitution, the boundary elements representing the replacement fragment need to be bound to the boundary elements representing the placement fragment. The developer needs to bind the boundary elements explicitly. Two boundary elements can only be bound if their recorded references are of the same type (the references point to the same type of model elements). For example, *ToR* is allowed to bind to *ToP* since both of their recorded reference are of type *A*. Similar pairs include *FrR1* with *FrP1* and *FrR2* with *FrP2*. As illustrated in Fig. 1, these three bindings are the only legal choices; however, one boundary element can be eligible to bind to several boundary elements as long as the typing rule is followed. The CVL tool can suggest default binding candidates for each boundary element which are type-compatible. Nevertheless, with more than one eligible boundary element, it is up to the developer to decide on the final binding since only he/she knows how the resulting product model should look like.

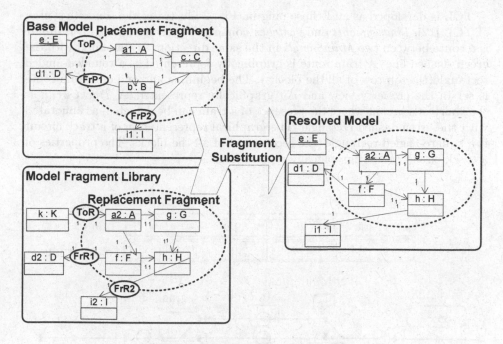

Fig. 1. Fragment substitution in CVL

Constraints. CVL constraints are defined in terms of expressions using operators NOT, AND, OR and IMPLIES. The leaf operands can be any composite variability (features) and substitutions (feature realizations).

The CVL tool support has been developed as an Eclipse plug-in. This plug-in includes a graphical editor, a tree-view editor, a fragment binding editor, a select-and-generate resolution model generator, a configuration validator and a generic CVL transformation. Furthermore, CVL provides a set of APIs to different base DSL graphical editors with the CVL editor. With a CVL-enabled base DSL editor, the developer can create placement/replacement fragment in the CVL editor automatically from the selection in the base DSL editor with automatically calculated boundary elements. The model element involved in a substitution will be highlighted in the base DSL editor when it is selected in the CVL editor.

2.2   Train Control Language

Train Control Language (TCL) [11] is a DSL developed by SINTEF in cooperation with ABB, Norway. In the TCL graphical editor, the train control experts can specify railway station models according to the structural drawings that they receive from the railway authorities. From the TCL models, the code generator can generate the interlocking source code which is loaded into Programmable Logic Circuits (PLC) to control the signaling system on train stations.

TCL is developed as an Eclipse plug-in. Fig. 2 illustrates the concrete syntax of TCL [12]. *Linesegments* and *switches* connected by *endpoints*. A *TrainRoute* is a route between two *MainSignals* in the same direction, as annotated with the green dashed line. A train route is graphically represented as a rounded-angled rectangle(the top row of all the blocks). The beginning and end of a train route is set in the property view and not graphically represented. A *TrackCircuit* is the shortest segment where the presence of a train can be detected, as annotated with the green dashed rectangle. The graphical representation of a track circuit is a square-angled rectangle (the second row of all the blocks. The properties of a track circuit are not graphically represented.

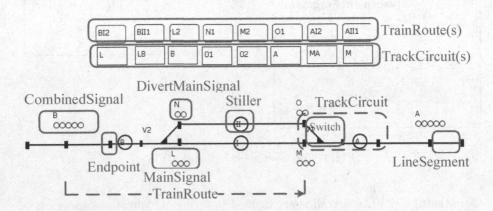

Fig. 2. Basic TCL concepts in the graphical editor illustrated with annotations

3   Motivating Example

ABB and SINTEF have developed several train control product lines together [9,10,13]. During the development, we have repeatedly experienced the aforementioned challenges, which motivate our work on the tool extensions. In this section, we present two motivating scenarios that the developer encountered during the development of one of the train control product lines, which we will also use to illustrate the application of our tool extensions in the following sections. We skip some development details for conciseness. To download the complete example, we refer to [9].

The developer starts with identifying the variability and commonality of all the intended station products. All the intended station products will have two tracks in common and differ in the existence of an additional track and/or a side track. Based on that, the developer decides on the base model and library model as illustrated in Fig. 3 (with annotations). The developer further defines the feature specification layer and the product realization layer of the CVL model.

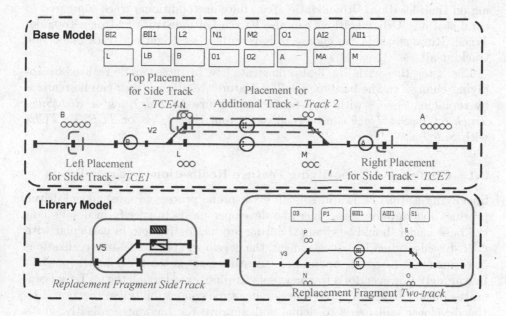

Fig. 3. Base model and model library of the station product line

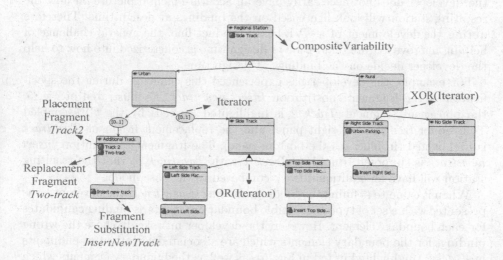

Fig. 4. The CVL model of the regional station product line

As shown in Fig. 4, stations are categorized into urban and rural ones depending on their location. Urban stations can have one additional track compared to rural stations. Urban stations can also have a LeftSideTrack and/or a TopSide-Track. Rural stations can choose to have either one RightSideTrack or no side track at all.

Fig. 4 together with Fig. 3 also illustrate how features can be realized by applying changes to the base model. The feature *AdditionalTrack* can be realized by replacing *Track2* with *Two-track*. The feature *LeftSideTrack* or *RightSide-Track* or *TopSideTrack* can be realized by replacing *TCE1* or *TCE7* or *TCE4* with *SideTrack*.

3.1   Challenge 1 - Specifying Feature Realizations is Error-Prone

Specifying feature realizations is an error-prone process in most model-driven product line development, since the developer needs to specify in details how the base model should be changed during product derivation. In particular with CVL-based product line development, the developer specifies feature realizations in terms of CVL-specific operations (substitutions) in the CVL model (product line model). However, for a fragment substitution, even though the CVL tool generates default bindings based on reference type compatibility (see Section 2.1), the developer still needs to define and approve the bindings explicitly. For a boundary element, the CVL tool may suggest several type-compatible boundary elements to be its legal binding candidates. All the legal bindings can lead to a set of products that are all syntactically correct. However, only the developer knows how the resulting model should look like in his/her intention. Moreover, the developer does not necessarily have an accurate mental picture on how the resulting station will look like based on the bindings at design time. Therefore during the development of a CVL-based product line, the general challenge of helping improve feature realization at design time is concretized into how to help the developer decide on the bindings at design time.

For example, the developer has experienced this challenge during the specification of the fragment substitution *Insert new track*. As illustrated in Fig. 5, the placement fragment *Track 2* is highlighted (in red) by the CVL-enabled TCL editor (see the top right pane) and the replacement fragment *Two-track* is highlighted (in blue, see the bottom pane). The fragment substitution *Insert new track* is supposed to replace *Track 2* with *Two-track* so that the resulting station will have an additional track compared to the base model.

When it came to defining the bindings for *Insert new track*, the developer was presented with a set of type-compatible boundary elements as binding candidates for each boundary element. However, the developer mistakenly chose the wrong bindings for the boundary elements which are associated with the two endpoints in *Track 2* (highlighted in red in Fig. 5), as well as the boundary elements which are associated with the two endpoints at the leftmost and rightmost side of *Two-track* (highlighted in blue in Fig. 5). The resulting station of this substitution did have one additional track inserted. The leftmost side of *Two-track* is connected to the right side of the base model, and its rightmost side is connected to the

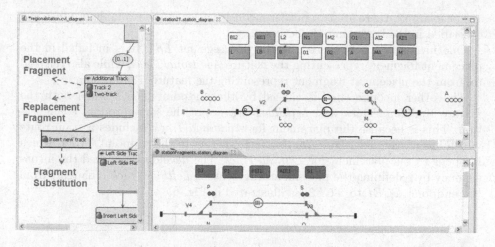

Fig. 5. Fragment substitution for inserting an additional track

left side of the base model. Such a station product is syntactically correct, since for each boundary element, the developer chose to pair it with one from the set of type-compatible boundary elements. But for this product line, such a station is not regarded as one of the intended products.

We see that specifying feature realizations for this product line is an error-prone process, since:

1. this requires manual selection which cannot be provided by the tool intelligence;
2. the developer does not get immediate feedback on his/her choices at design time.

This challenge has motivated the development of our simulator for simulating substitutions and visualizing the resulting model at design time, which we will illustrate in Section 4.

3.2   Challenge 2: Ensure Feature Realization/Specification Consistency

We have identified two types of inconsistencies that may appear between fragment substitutions [14,15]: **border inconsistency** and **element inconsistency**.

A **border inconsistency** occurs when two model elements in the base model are directly connected but included in the placement fragments of two different substitutions. If two fragment substitutions with border inconsistency coexist in the same product configuration and it is executed, either the product derivation (the CVL transformation) will halt if an exception is thrown, or the reference(s) at the "border" will be incorrectly set to *null* instead of the intended model element(s) in the generated product model.

For example, there are two border inconsistencies in the example product line described in the beginning of Section 3:

One inconsistency is caused by the line segment *LS5*. It is included in the placement fragment representing the feature *AdditionalTrack*, while also referred to/from the placement fragment representing the feature *TopSideTrack*.

The other inconsistency is caused by the Endpoint *TCE1* when both the feature *AdditionalTrack* and *LeftSideTrack* are in the same product configuration. This is because the placement for *AdditionalTrack* includes a train route which has a reference (*TrainRoute.start*) pointing to the endpoint *TCE1*, which happens to the placement for *LeftSideTrack*. The developer resolved the inconsistency by redefining the placement fragment for *LeftSideTrack* (changing from the endpoint *TCE1* to *TCE2*, as illustrated in Fig. 6).

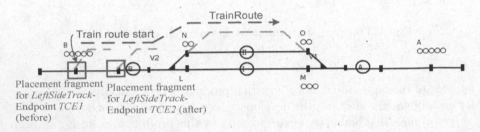

Fig. 6. Inconsistency between LeftSideTrack and AdditionalTrack (before and after redefining the placement fragment for LeftSideTrack)

An **element inconsistency** occurs when one model element in the base model is to be replaced in two fragment substitutions. It does not make sense to replace the same element twice during the same execution. Executing a product configuration containing two fragment substitutions with element inconsistency will lead to, either the termination of the product derivation, or an unintended product model. The substitution executed later will overwrite the changes applied by the substitution executed earlier.

In our example, an element inconsistency is caused by the endpoint *TCE4* (see Fig. 3) since it is contained in both placement fragments representing the feature *AdditionalTrack* and *TopSideTrack*.

The element inconsistency and the first border inconsistency were resolved by adding an *Excludes* constraint between the feature *AdditionalTrack* and *TopSideTrack*.

We notice that in this example, the element inconsistency and one of the border inconsistencies are somehow obvious and easy to observe manually without tool support. However, the border inconsistency caused by the endpoint *TCE1* shows how the developer can really benefit from tool support to detect those "well-hidden" inconsistencies automatically. This motivates us to develop the inconsistency checker to provide automated aid to the developer, which we will illustrate in Section 5.

4 Simulating Feature Realization at Design Time

We have extended the CVL editor to simulate the execution of a singular fragment substitution and visualize the abstract syntax of the resulting model excerpt (with only related model elements) at design time. The visualization is implemented using Zest [16].

The implementation of the tool is generic such that it can be applied to any MOF-based DSL. The generality of the tool is at the cost of missing certain domain-specific information. It would be ideal for the developer to inspect the resulting model excerpt if it is represented based on the concrete syntax of the DSL. With no awareness of the concrete graphical syntax beforehand, our tool provides an extended abstract syntax graph of the resulting model excerpt, with as much domain-specific information as possible that the tool is able to obtain technically.

Running the Simulation of the Substitution with the Default Bindings. As mentioned earlier, default bindings can be automatically generated for any fragment substitution. Thus the developer often starts with inspecting and possibly improving the default bindings instead of starting from scratch. It will be advantageous for the developer to run the simulation of the substitution with the default bindings at this point. We believe that the visualization of the simulation result will give valuable clues to how to improve the bindings.

With our example, the developer can start with running the simulation of the substitution *Insert new track* with the default bindings. Fig. 7 gives a visualized preview of the resulting model excerpt for this simulation. All the model elements in the preview are represented as rectangles. The rectangles representing the newly added elements (replacement fragment) are colored in blue. The dark yellow rectangles represent the elements that are directly related to the newly added elements in the resulting model excerpt.

What is displayed on each rectangle consists of three parts:

1. An icon. The preview renders the same icons as used for elements in the DSL's GMF-based graphical editor.
2. The type of the element.
3. The name of the element.

As shown in Fig. 7, the rectangle representing the line segment *FLS3* has the same icon used in the TCL editor for line segments, followed by the text *Line-Segment.FLS3* which states its type and name separated by dot.

By selecting any rectangle, the color will turn to light yellow in the preview. At the same time, the actual model element in the base model or library models will be highlighted in the CVL-enabled editor. As shown in Fig. 7, by selecting a newly added element *RemoteSwitch.V4(F)*, its color turns from blue to light yellow in the preview. In addition, the switch *V4* is highlighted in blue in the CVL-enabled TCL editor (see Fig. 7). This highlighting function can be used in situations like in motivating scenario 1 (see Section 3.1). It can help the developer

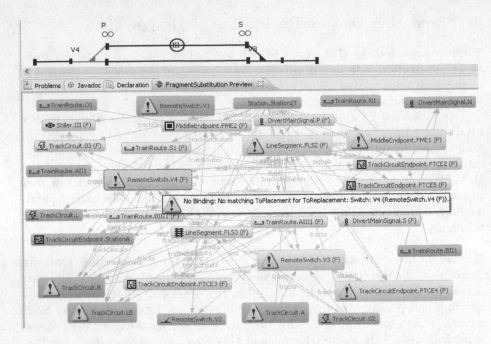

Fig. 7. Preview of the abstract syntax of the resulting model excerpt of the fragment substitution Insert new track

to get an idea at design time on whether the resulting three track station of the current bindings will be an intended one or not.

A boundary element can be bound to some other boundary element or left unbound. If a boundary element is left unbound, it will lead to the elimination of one reference which exists in the base model. Boundary elements are left unbound because:

1. The developer made a mistake during the binding definition and forgot to bind the intended boundary elements. This will introduce semantic errors into the resulting model because of the missing references.
2. The developer intentionally leaves some boundary elements unbound to reduce some references, in order to obtain the intended resulting model.

The current CVL transformations will only halt the execution when the resulting model has syntactical errors. As long as the resulting model conforms to the language definition, the CVL transformations will not react to the unbound boundary elements during execution. There is no way to tell whether they are intended or not except manual inspection.

With our preview, all the elements with missing references (due to unbound boundary elements) will be marked with a warning sign. A warning message also pops up when the element is selected in the preview. The message provides information on the type of the unbound reference. The developer should inspect the reported unbound boundary elements in the binding editor to rule out mistakes.

As shown in Fig. 7, the current bindings of the fragment substitution are warned against broken references. The warning message for the remote switch $V4$ indicates that, one boundary element which records the reference to $V4$ is left unbound. The boundary element is then inspected and found out to be left unbound by mistake. Furthermore, we find out that all the other unbound boundary elements warned in Fig. 7 are also unintentional, which leads to semantically incorrect model.

Applying the Improve-Simulate-Preview Iteratively if Necessary. The developer further improves the default bindings if the previous simulation reveals the smell of the incorrect bindings, and runs the simulation again. If there will be any warning/error in the preview, the developer can look into it to rule out mistakes. If not, the developer can still examine the correctness of the resulting model excerpt using the preview with the select-and-highlight-in-the -DSL-graphical-editor support. After applying necessary improvement to the current bindings, the simulation can be run again and this improve-simulate-preview pattern can be applied iteratively until the developer is satisfied with the bindings of this fragment substitution.

5   Detecting Specification/Realization Inconsistency

Our inconsistency checker is an extension to the current CVL tool. It aims to check before product derivation, whether any legal product configuration (resolution model) of the current product line model will allow border/element inconsistencies in the product realization layer by mistake.

The inconsistency checker supports the incremental development of the product line in the following aspects:

1. The inconsistency checker can be invoked at any point before the product derivation is executed. Therefore the inconsistencies can be detected and corrected as soon as possible during the development.
2. All the information obtained from each check of the current product line model is cached for look-up and reference during later checks. This would reduce the running time which may grow rapidly when a big product line model is checked for inconsistency.
3. The checker will always start to find border/element inconsistent fragment substitution pairs that are located near each other in the product line model hierarchy.

Suppose that the developer just performed a new change to the current product line model. The developer would like to use the inconsistency checker to see if the new change has caused any inconsistency.

If there are only changes in the feature specification layer compared to how the product line model was when the check was performed last time, the checker will skip step (1), use the cached result of step (1) from the last check and continue with step (2). If there are newly added/edited fragment substitutions compared to how it was when the check was performed last time, the checker will perform both step (1) and (2):

(1) Detecting Inconsistencies between Fragment Substitutions.

   (a) Compute the model elements changed by every newly added/edited fragment substitution. Take one newly added/edited fragment substitution at one time. Obtain the set of boundary elements representing the placement fragment of this fragment substitution. Induce which elements are contained in this placement fragment based on the information recorded by the boundary elements. Go to step (b) until every newly added/edited fragment substitution is gone through.

   (b) Search for the pairs of fragment substitutions with border/element inconsistencies. Take one newly added/edited fragment substitution at one time. Start by checking it against the fragment substitution which is placed the nearest in the hierarchy of the product line model, to see if:

   (i) two placement fragments contain the same elements (element inconsistency), or

   (ii) elements in one placement fragment are directly connected to elements in the other placement fragment (border inconsistency). The checker will continue with checking the current fragment substitution against the rest of the unchecked fragment substitutions in a nearer-to-further order. Store the pairs of fragment substitutions with inconsistencies for later use. Go to step (2) until the tool goes through all the newly added/edited fragment substitutions.

(2) Detecting Inconsistent Feature Pairs in the Product Configurations. Based on the inconsistent fragment substitution pairs and their containing features, the checker generates a list of all the inconsistent feature pairs which should not be included in the same product configuration.

Our tool utilizes Alloy [17] to detect if any of the inconsistent feature pairs will be allowed to coexist in any legal product configuration. Alloy is a structural modeling language based on first-order logic for expressing structural constraints and behaviors [17]. One of the analysis that Alloy provides is to test the validity of a specification by generating a counter-example [18]. Alloy provides a set of public accessible APIs, which we utilize in the tool implementation.

We extend the current CVL editor with an Alloy constraints generator using Java and Alloy API. The CVL language constructs which appear in the feature specification layer, such as *CompositeVariability* (feature) and *Iterator* (multiplicities and choices over features), are specified as Alloy constraints and stored in strings in the generator. They generator has a model-to-text transformation. It takes in the CVL model as input and generates a string that contains Alloy constraints specifying the feature specification layer of the CVL model.

For every inconsistent feature pair that we obtained from last step, the generator generates an Alloy assertion. It asserts that no legal CVL product configuration includes the inconsistent feature pair.

Using Alloy API, input the strings that contain the Alloy constraints describing the feature specification layer of the CVL model and the assertion into the

Alloy analyzer [19]. If the analyzer is able to find a counter-example of the assertion, it shows that the current CVL model has inconsistencies between the feature specification and realization. The result of the analyzer is interpreted back to the generator using Alloy API. An error message pops up with the necessary information if an inconsistency is detected.

The inconsistency checker is able to detect three inconsistencies in our motivating example as mentioned in Section 3.2. There are two inconsistencies regarding the feature *AdditionalTrack* and *TopSideTrack*. To show how the Alloy analysis works to detect the inconsistencies, we show the Alloy assertion generated for the feature pair *AdditionalTrack* and *TopSideTrack* in Fig. 8. The assertion asserts that feature *AdditionalTrack* and *TopSideTrack* cannot coexist in the same product configuration. Obviously the Alloy analyzer managed to find a counter-example to this assertion such that this inconsistent feature pair can appear in the same product configuration which needs to be rectified.

```
assert checkInconsistencies {
  //assert that no model with the following constraints exists
  no f1:AdditionalTrack, f2:TopSideTrack, p:ProductConfiguration{
    (f1 + f2) in p
  }
}
```

Fig. 8. The generated Alloy assertion asserts that the feature AdditionalTrack and TopSideTrack cannot coexist in any product configuration

6 Discussion

Scalability

For the preview of the resulting model of a fragment substitution, we choose to visualize only the newly added elements and the elements that are associated with them. In addition, we advise the developer to use the preview along the way of defining a fragment substitution incrementally. Therefore the approach should scale well for large base models. For the inconsistency checker, we noticed that the processing time grows rapidly with increased features in the CVL model. Therefore we specify our Alloy constraints following an optimization technique that we proposed in [20]. In addition, we will explore the possibility of improving the scalability of our simulator by applying pairwise testing of product lines. The advantage would be that only a small set of product configurations where every two (or more) pairs are covered could be checked for inconsistencies.

Generality

We have applied our tools to a steam boiler product line whose products are architecture models defined in UML. This case is provided by ABB, Norway.

The creation of fragment substitutions in this product line requires much effort due to the complexity of the UML metamodel. Our experiment shows that the developer defined feature realizations with increased efficiency and correctness, by previewing the result of the substitutions at design time incrementally and iteratively. For further evaluation of the generality of our tools, we plan to apply our tools to the development of more product lines in various domains of different size.

Soundness

Our automated analysis approach is a light-weighted solution towards the correct product derivation. A sound formalization of the approach is part of our immediate future work plan.

7   Related Work

For a product line, there are many factors that may lead to incorrect product derivation. Our approaches address two of the challenges against correct product derivation:

1. How to help improve the definition of feature realizations.
2. How to automatically detect the inconsistencies between the feature specification and the product realization.

Simulating model transformations and visualizing the result is not a new research topic in academia. However, we are not aware of many approaches that are:

1. Applicable in the context of product line development, especially in the context of CVL;
2. Generic that can be applied to any product line which base language is MOF-based.

Inconsistency checking in product lines has received increasing attention in the community of SPL development [3,4,21,22]. Thaker et al. [3] pointed out that in a product line, low-level implementation of one feature can reference elements in the implementation of another feature. They presented an approach for verifying if all the programs in a product line are type safe. Features are formalized into propositional formulas and the feature realizations (program segments) are analyzed to identify their dependencies between each other. Kästner et al. [4] presented a product-line-aware type system that statically detects type errors in annotation-based product line implementations. They have proved formally that all program variants generated from a well-typed product line are well-typed. In contrast to these two approaches:

1. Our inconsistency checker is based on the CVL approach which does not only allow "positive (additive) variability" like model composition or

"negative (subtractive) variability" like annotation-based product line implementations;

2. Our inconsistency checker deals with product models instead of source code.

Mussbacher et al. [23] propose an approach for detecting semantic interactions between aspect-oriented scenarios. This approach requires semantic annotation to the aspect models beforehand and it employs critical pair analysis to detect the semantic interaction. Our inconsistency checker focuses on the interaction caused by element/border inconsistency and does not require any semantic annotations. This approach has tool support for UML SD and GRL goal models, while our approach can be applied to any product line which base language is MOF-based.

In the context of model-driven product line development, the probably closest related work of our inconsistency checker is presented by Czarnecki et al. [21]. Their approach is about verifying feature-based model templates against well-formedness OCL constraints. A feature-based model template consists of a feature model and an annotated model that conforms to the metamodel of the base language. The purpose of their work of is to verify if both the feature model and the annotated model are well-constrained so that all possible product models will conform to the metamodel the constraints of the base language. Our approach differs in the following:

1. Our inconsistency checker applies to CVL-based product lines while their work applies to product lines developed using feature-based model templates.
2. Our approach supports both "positive (additive) variability" and "negative (subtractive) variability", while the approach in [21] only supports the latter one due to its annotation-based nature.
3. Our inconsistency checker focuses on the inconsistency between the feature specification and the product realization, while the other approach checks the model against the well-formedness OCL constraints.

8   Conclusion and Future Work

In this paper, we proposed two generic CVL-based approaches towards the correct product derivation for the model-driven product line development: (

1. Preview of the resulting model excerpt of feature realizations at design time to provide immediate feedback to the developer.
2. Automated detection of inconsistencies between feature specification and realization.

We have evaluated the feasibility of these approaches by extending the current CVL tool suite with our generic simulator and inconsistency checker, and applied to the development of product lines in various domains.

Ideas for future work include:

1. A comprehensive formalization of our automated analysis approach.
2. Extending the inconsistency checker to support verifying whether the resulting models conform to the additional rules of the base language (e.g. the rules can be formulated as OCL constraints).
3. For both the simulator and the inconsistency checker, suggesting necessary improvements to the current CVL model according to the current results.
4. Applying pairwise testing techniques to improve the scalability of the simulator.

References

1. Clements, P., Northrop, L.: Software Product Lines – Practices and Patterns. Addison-Wesley Longman Publishing (2001)
2. Czarnecki, K., Antkiewicz, M., Kim, C.H.P., Lau, S., Pietroszek, K.: Model-Driven Software Product Lines. In: Companion to the 20th Annual ACM SIGPLAN Conference on Object-Oriented Programming, Systems, Languages, and Applications, pp. 126–127. ACM Press (2005)
3. Thaker, S., Batory, D., Kitchin, D., Cook, W.: Safe Composition of Product Lines. In: Proceedings of the 6th International Conference on Generative Programming and Component Engineering (GPCE 2007). ACM Press (2007)
4. Kästner, C., Apel, S., Thum, T., Saake, G.: Type Checking Annotation-Based Product Lines. ACM Transactions on Software Engineering and Methodology 21(3), Article 14 (2012)
5. Fleurey, F., Haugen, Ø., Møller-Pedersen, B., Olsen, G.K., Svendsen, A., Zhang, X.: A Generic Language and Tool for Variability Modeling. SINTEF, Oslo (2009)
6. Haugen, Ø., Møller-Pedersen, B., Oldevik, J., Olsen, G.K., Svendsen, A.: Adding Standardized Variability to Domain Specific Languages. In: 13th International Software Product Line Conference. Limerick, Ireland (2008)
7. CVL, http://www.omgwiki.org/variability/doku.php
8. Object Management Group (OMG): Meta Object Facility (MOF) Core Specification Version 2.0 (Available Specification). OMG Document Formal/06-01-01 (2006)
9. CVL Resources (2012), http://www.omgwiki.org/variability/doku.php?id=cvl_tool_from_sintef
10. Svendsen, A., Zhang, X., Lind-Tviberg, R., Fleurey, F., Haugen, Ø., Møller-Pedersen, B., Olsen, G.K.: Developing a Software Product Line for Train Control: A Case Study of CVL. In: Bosch, J., Lee, J. (eds.) SPLC 2010. LNCS, vol. 6287, pp. 106–120. Springer, Heidelberg (2010)
11. Svendsen, A., Olsen, G.K., Endresen, J., Moen, T., Carlson, E., Alme, K.-J., Haugen, Ø.: The Future of Train Signaling. In: Czarnecki, K., Ober, I., Bruel, J.-M., Uhl, A., Völter, M. (eds.) MODELS 2008. LNCS, vol. 5301, pp. 128–142. Springer, Heidelberg (2008)
12. Ousterhout, J.K., Jones, K.: Tcl and the Tk Toolkit, 2nd edn. Addison Wesley (2006)
13. Zhang, X., Haugen, Ø., Møller-Pedersen, B.: Model Comparison to Synthesize a Model-Driven Software Product Line. In: Proceedings of the 2011 15th International Software Product Line Conference (SPLC 2011), pp. 90–99. IEEE Computer Society (2011)

14. Oldevik, J., Haugen, Ø., Møller-Pedersen, B.: Confluence in Domain-Independent Product Line Transformations. In: Chechik, M., Wirsing, M. (eds.) FASE 2009. LNCS, vol. 5503, pp. 34–48. Springer, Heidelberg (2009)
15. Svendsen, A., Zhang, X., Haugen, Ø., Møller-Pedersen, B.: Towards Evolution of Generic Variability Models. In: Kienzle, J. (ed.) MODELS 2011 Workshops. LNCS, vol. 7167, pp. 53–67. Springer, Heidelberg (2012)
16. Zest, http://www.eclipse.org/gef/zest/
17. Jackson, D.: Alloy – A Lightweight Object Modelling Notation. ACM Transactions on Transactions on Software Engineering and Methodology 11, 256–290 (2002)
18. Jing, S., Hongyu, Z., Hai, W.: Formal Semantics and Verification for Feature Modeling. In: 10th IEEE International Conference on Engineering of Complex Computer Systems. IEEE Computer Society (2005)
19. MIT: Download for Alloy Analyzer, http://alloy.mit.edu/alloy/download.html
20. Svendsen, A., Haugen, Ø., Møller-Pedersen, B.: Optimizing Alloy Models. SINTEF, Oslo (2011)
21. Czarnecki, K., Pietroszek, K.: Verifying Feature-Based Model Templates against Well-Formedness Ocl Constraints. In: Proceedings of the 5th International Conference on Generative Programming and Component Engineering. ACM Press (2006)
22. Satyananda, T.K., Lee, D., Kang, S.: Formal Verification of Consistency between Feature Model and Software Architecture in Software Product Line. In: Proceedings of the International Conference on Software Engineering Advances, p. 10. IEEE Computer Society (2007)
23. Mussbacher, G., Whittle, J., Amyot, D.: Semantic-Based Interaction Detection in Aspect-Oriented Scenarios. In: 17th IEEE International Requirements Engineering Conference (RE 2009), pp. 203–212. IEEE Computer Society (2009)

Simulation Configuration Modeling
of Distributed Communication Systems

Mihal Brumbulli and Joachim Fischer

Humboldt Universität zu Berlin, Institut für Informatik,
Unter den Linden 6, 10099 Berlin, Germany
{brumbull,fischer}@informatik.hu-berlin.de

Abstract. Simulation is the method of choice for the analysis of distributed communication systems. This is because of the complexity that often characterizes such systems. But simulation modeling is not a simple task mainly because there exists no unified approach that can provide description means for all aspects of the system. These aspects include architecture, behavior, communication, and configuration. In this paper we focus on simulation configuration as part of our unified modeling approach based on the Specification and Description Language Real Time (SDL-RT). Deployment diagrams are used to describe the simulation setup of the components and configuration values of a distributed system. We provide tool support for automatic implementation of the models for the ns-3 network simulation library.

Keywords: Simulation modeling, SDL-RT, ns-3.

1   Introduction

Simulation modeling of distributed communication systems is not a simple task. This is because of the complexity that often characterizes such systems. There are several aspects that need to be modeled, preferably using a unified and standardized approach. These include architecture, behavior, communication, and configuration. System development tools based on SDL [1] or UML [2] can model such aspects at a certain degree and independently from the target platform. Nevertheless, the lack of integration with existing simulation (and especially network simulation) libraries makes it indeed very challenging to derive the desired executable from model descriptions. This is one of the reasons that pushes the developer towards the use of general purpose languages (i.e. C/C++). It is not very difficult to obtain an executable from these models, because they are described in the same language as the simulation library. This approach is time consuming and error-prone, the models will become very soon difficult to maintain, and they cannot be used with other simulation libraries, except the one they were implemented for.

In this context, there have been several works with the aim of exploiting the advantages of both approaches. In [3] the authors show how to automatically generate an executable for the ns-2 [4] simulator from models described in

Ø. Haugen, R. Reed, and R. Gotzhein (Eds.): SAM 2012, LNCS 7744, pp. 198–211, 2013.

SDL. The idea of automatic code generation for network simulators is further described in [5], where SDL model descriptions are also used for deriving simulation models for ns-3 [6]. In [7] UML diagrams are used to construct simulation models, which in turn can be executed in an event-driven simulation framework like OMNET++ [8].

Although the approaches introduced so far do provide description means for some of the aspects of distributed systems, there is still work to be done regarding configuration modeling. A configuration model describes the setup and configuration values of the components of a distributed system. These aspects are still handled in different ways ranging from general purpose languages (like C++ in ns-3) to tools with limited (like NAM [9] in ns-2) or more complete (like OMNET++) modeling capabilities. What all these methods have in common is that, except of being dependent on the simulation framework, they do not integrate with existing approaches based on standardized languages like SDL or UML.

We use SDL-RT [10] as the main language of our unified approach for modeling all the above mentioned aspects including simulation configuration. In this paper we focus on configuration modeling and show how SDL-RT deployment diagrams can be used for this purpose. We consider automatic implementation to be very important, thus we provide code generation for the ns-3 simulator.

We start by giving a short overview of the ns-3 library, focusing on configuration modeling (Sect. 2). In Sect. 3 we briefly introduce our modeling approach based on SDL-RT by means of a simple example. The use of SDL-RT deployment diagrams for simulation configuration modeling is described in Sect. 4 and our code generator in Sect. 5. Finally, we present the conclusions of our work in Sect. 6.

2 The ns-3 Simulator

Ns-3 is a discrete-event network simulator for internet systems, targeted primarily for research and educational use. The simulation library is entirely written in C++ and implements all the components used in simulation configurations. These components include nodes, mobility models, applications, protocols, devices, and channels (Fig. 1). In ns-3 simulations, there are two main aspects to configuration:

- the simulation topology and how components are connected,
- the values used by the components in the topology.

Topology and Components The node is the core component in the model and acts as a container for applications, protocol stacks, and devices. Devices are interconnected through channels of the same type. Applications are usually traffic generators: they create and send packets to the lower layers using a socket-like API. A simulation configuration usually follows these steps:

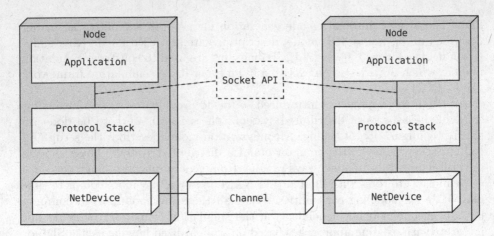

Fig. 1. Generic model for ns-3 simulation configurations

- a set of nodes is created,
- a mobility model (topology) is applied to the nodes,
- channels are created,
- devices are installed on the nodes and attached to channels,
- applications are installed on the nodes.

Configuration Values. The ns-3 library implements an attribute system that organizes the access of the configuration values of the components, thus providing a fine-grained access to internal variables in the simulation. The general C++ syntax for setting attribute values is:

```
<object-name> "->" "SetAttribute" "("
    <attribute-name> "," <attribute-value>
")" ";"
```

The `<object-name>` represents a *ns-3 Object*, which can be any of the components in Fig. 1 (i.e., Node, NetDevice, Channel, etc.). As the name suggests, the `<attribute-name>` is a string containing the attribute's name. The list of attributes for each ns-3 Object and the `<attribute-value>` they expect can be found at the ns-3 documentation.[1]

This configuration mechanism (*attribute = value*) looks quite straightforward, thus it can be used in tools for automatic implementation from model description. We use this mechanism in the context of SDL-RT deployment diagrams for providing a model-driven approach to simulation configuration and automatic code generation for the ns-3 library.

3   Simulation Modeling with SDL-RT

SDL-RT is based on the SDL standard [1] extended with real time concepts, which include [10]:

---

[1] http://www.nsnam.org/docs/release/3.10/doxygen/index.html

- use of C/C++ instead of SDL for data types,
- use of C/C++ as an action language, and
- semaphore support.

These extensions considerably facilitate integration and usage of legacy code and off the shelf libraries such as real-time operating systems, simulation frameworks, and protocol stacks [10]. The work presented in [11,12] shows how SDL-RT and simulation frameworks can be used in the development of complex distributed systems. In [13] the authors have successfully applied this approach in the development of the wireless mesh sensing network for earthquake early warning described in [14]. Further extensions to SDL-RT are provided by UML diagrams [2]:

- Class diagrams bring a graphical representation of the classes organization and relations.
- Deployment diagrams offer a graphical representation of the physical architecture and how the different nodes in a distributed system communicate with each other.

SDL-RT can be seen as a pragmatic combination of the standardized languages SDL, UML, and C/C++. We use SDL-RT for simulation modeling of distributed communication systems, including their architecture, behavior, communication, and configuration. Figure 2 illustrates these aspects by means of a simple example.

The client sends a request message (*mRequest*) to the server and waits for a reply (*mReply*). This sequence of actions is repeated every 1000 ms (tWait timer). The server waits for a request from the client. Upon receiving a request, it immediately sends a reply to the client.

By definition, the SDL-RT channels can only model local communication (i.e. between processes running on the same node). However, it is possible to describe distributed communication directly in the model, because SDL-RT uses C/C++ as an action language. We use the flexibility provided by C/C++ to define description means for distributed communication without changing the language. Figure 2 shows how this can be achieved via the *TCP_CONNECT* and *TCP_SEND* macros.[2] The *SENDER_ADDR* is used to access the sender's address of the last received message.

It is also possible to define patterns [15] for other types of communication. These patterns can be described in SDL-RT and implementation is handled automatically by the code generator (Sect. 5). We define the *NODE* macro to facilitate access on communication layers or other components. This allows us to reference the ns-3 node (from within behavior descriptions) and subsequently all the other components associated to it (see Fig. 1).

---

[2] UDP communication is also possible by using the corresponding macros.

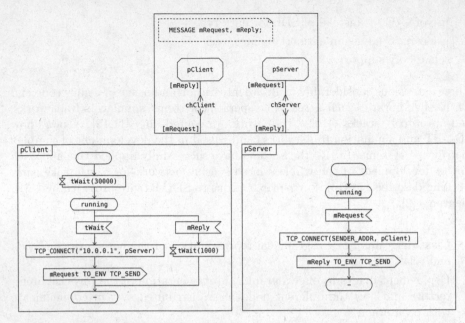

Fig. 2. SDL-RT model of a client-server application

4   Configuration Modeling

The SDL-RT deployment diagram describes the physical configuration of run-time processing elements of a distributed system and may contain [10]:

- *Nodes* are physical objects that represent processing resources.
- *Components* represent distributable pieces of implementation of a system.
- *Connections* are physical links between nodes or components.
- *Dependencies* from nodes to components mean the components are running on the nodes.

There exist many similarities between a SDL-RT deployment diagram and the ns-3 model in Fig. 1. We use this type of diagram for describing simulation configurations for the ns-3 library. For this purpose we define a set of rules to be applied as shown in Fig. 3.

4.1   Nodes

The **<<node>>** represents a *ns-3 NodeContainer*. It has no attributes and only one property, which is the set of nodes in the container. This set is represented as a comma separated list of node identifiers. Each ns-3 node in a simulation configuration model has a unique identifier, which is assigned to it incrementally (starting at 0) by the simulation library. The total number of nodes to be created is calculated automatically by our code generator based on the highest identifier

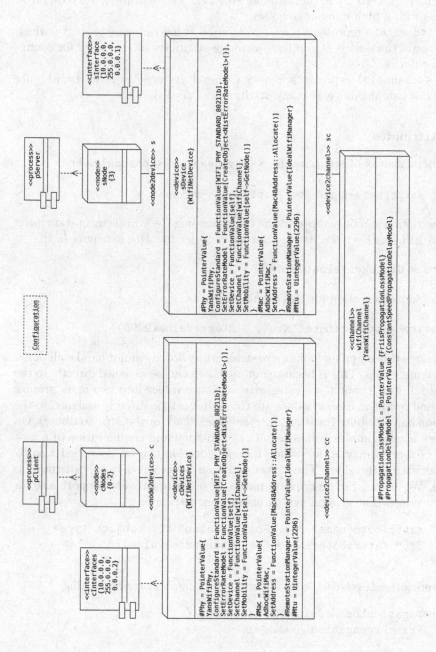

Fig. 3. A simulation configuration for the client-server example

present in the configuration model. In Fig. 3 the highest identifier is 3, thus the total number of nodes would be 4. It is also possible to express a range of identifiers (i.e. {0–2} is the same as {0,1,2}). This feature is very useful in scenarios with a high number of nodes.

The <<device>> represents a *ns-3 NetDevice*. It has only one property, which is the type of the device. It can have as many attributes as necessary for configuring the device.

The <<channel>> represents a *ns-3 Channel*. Its type is given by its only property. It can also have as many attributes as needed.

4.2   Attributes

The general syntax of attributes for <<device>> and <<channel>> is:

```
"#" <attribute-name> "=" <attribute-value>
```

This description can be mapped to the corresponding C++ implementation using the ns-3 API (see Sect. 2). As an example consider the *Mtu* attribute in Fig. 3:

```
#Mtu = UintegerValue(2296)
```

The ns-3 implementation for this attribute will be:

```
sDevice->SetAttribute("Mtu", UintegerValue(2296));
```

Even though this mapping looks quite straightforward, it cannot handle all possible attribute values. This is because not all values can be assigned directly to the attribute. In this context, we categorize attribute values into two main groups: simple and complex. Simple values are those that can be directly assigned to the corresponding attribute (i.e. the *UintegerValue(2296)* for the *Mtu* attribute). On the other hand, complex values require the creation and configuration of a *ns-3 Object* of a certain type, for which its configuration can be described also by means of attribute values. The object can then be assigned to the attribute as a value. We extend the description means in order to provide support also for complex values. The general syntax of complex attributes is:

```
"#" <attribute-name> "=" "PointerValue" "{" <object-type>
    {"," <attribute-name> "=" <attribute-value>}
"}"
```

The *PropagationLossModel* is an example of a complex attribute value:

```
#PropagationLossModel = PointerValue {
    FriisPropagationLossModel
}
```

In this case an object of type *FriisPropagationLossModel* needs to be created before it can be assigned as an attribute value:

```
Ptr<FriisPropagationLossModel> obj =
    CreateObject<FriisPropagationLossModel>();
wifiChannel->SetAttribute(
    "PropagationLossModel", PointerValue(obj)
);
```

The descriptions introduced so far can cover all possible ns-3 attribute values. Nevertheless, they are not sufficient for ensuring the minimal required configuration for normal operation of devices and/or channels. This is because the ns-3 attribute system itself is incomplete. In order to address this issue, we define a new group of attribute values named *function values*. As the name suggests, these allow us to express function calls in an attribute-value fashion, where the name of the attribute is actually the name of the function and the value represents the list of parameter values. The syntax of function attributes is:

```
"#" <attribute-name> "=" "FunctionValue" "["
    [<parameter-value> {"," <parameter-value>}]
"]"
```

As an example consider the *Mac* attribute:

```
#Mac = PointerValue {AdhocWifiMac,
    SetAddress = FunctionValue[Mac48Address::Allocate()]
}
```

This is a mix of complex and function values and is mapped to C++ as:

```
Ptr<AdhocWifiMac> obj = CreateObject<AdhocWifiMac>();
obj->SetAddress(Mac48Address::Allocate());
sDevice->SetAttribute("Mac", PointerValue(obj));
```

We also define *self*,[3] which can be used to reference the channel or device inside their configuration values (see Fig. 3).

4.3   Components

The <<process>> represents an instance of a SDL-RT process defined in the architecture (see Fig. 2). It must be linked with a <<node>> using a dependency relation. The dependency means that there is a running instance of the process for each of the ns-3 nodes in the container defined by the <<node>>.

The <<interface>> represents a range of ip addresses to be assigned to the devices. It has neither parameters nor attributes and must be linked with a <<device>> using a dependency relation.

4.4   Connections

As the name suggests, the <<node2device>> links nodes to devices. In terms of simulation configuration this means that, for each node in the container defined by <<node>>, a <<device>> of the specified type is added to it.

The <<device2channel>> attaches the devices to the specified channel.

---

[3] Not to be confused with SDL-RT's *SELF* that is used in behavior descriptions.

4.5   Topologies

The only aspect that cannot be modeled with SDL-RT deployment diagrams is the topology of the nodes. By topology here we mean the actual position of the nodes in the coordinate system used by the network simulator. This is very important especially for configuration models involving wireless and sensor networks.

In fact the topology can be modeled using attributes for the <<node>> or C++ code inside SDL-RT comments.[4] A major drawback of these solutions is that they hide the position of the nodes relative to each other. This can be addressed by using topology generators with graphical user interfaces like NAM or NPART [16], which can generate topologies for the ns-2 simulator. Our code generator (Sect. 5) can transform these into ns-3 topologies and apply them to the nodes as specified in the configuration model.

Fig. 4 shows a simple grid topology, which can be applied to the model in Fig. 3.

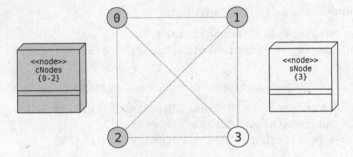

Fig. 4. Sample topology for the client-server example

Nodes with identifiers 0, 1, and 2 are client nodes (nodes represented by *cNodes*); the node with identifier 3 is a server node (*sNode*).

It is important to note that the node identifiers used in the configuration model must exist also in the topology description. If this is not the case, an error containing information on missing nodes is reported and the code generation will fail. Nevertheless, the existence of redundant nodes[5] in the topology description is treated as a warning. In this case the code generation will succeed and the redundant nodes will be ignored by default.

5   Code Generation

SDL-RT descriptions are used as a basis for the generation of an executable for the ns-3 simulator. This implies C++ code generation from SDL-RT

---

[4] C++ code can be included in the model by using SDL-RT comments (the *Configuration* rectangle in Fig. 3).

[5] These are node identifiers that appear in the topology description but not in the configuration model (SDL-RT deployment diagram).

architecture, behavior, and deployment models. Our tool for code generation is integrated with PragmaDev's RTDS.[6]

5.1   Architecture and Behavior

We have already covered SDL code generation for network simulators in [5]. In this paper we introduce further improvements to our approach by providing a generic model as shown in Fig. 5.

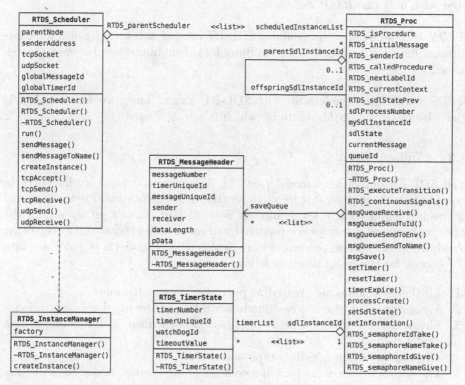

Fig. 5. Generic model for code generation

RTDS_Scheduler keeps track of all process instances running on a node and handles communication between these instances. The creation of process instances is managed by *RTDS_InstanceManager*. Communication can be local or distributed. Local communication is implemented via shared memory [10]. In this case the sender and receiver process instances are running on the same node, which means that they can be accessed by the same *RTDS_Scheduler*.

---

[6] http://www.pragmadev.com/product/index.html

On the other hand, distributed communication is handled via ns-3 sockets (TCP or UDP) and is implemented by *tcpAccept*, *tcpSend*, *tcpReceive*, *udpSend*, and *udpReceive*. There exists a one-to-one relationship between the *RTDS_Scheduler* and the ns-3 node (the <<node>> in Fig. 3). This concept is implicitly included in the <<node>> definition.

RTDS_Proc provides basic functionality for the SDL-RT processes. All SDL-RT processes (i.e. pClient and pServer in Fig. 2) extend this class by implementing the *RTDS_executeTransition* member function. Each process instance is associated with only one *RTDS_Scheduler*.

RTDS_MessageHeader encapsulates SDL-RT messages. It includes also some additional information required for handling local communication between process instances.

RTDS_TimerState implements the SDL-RT timer. The core functionality is given by the *watchDogId* attribute, which is a *ns-3 Timer*.

5.2   Configuration

The SDL-RT deployment model (see Fig. 3) and a ns-2 topology file serve as inputs to the code generator for configuration implementation. First, the model is checked against the rules defined in Sect. 4. If it doesn't satisfy any of the rules, corresponding errors are reported and no code is generated. On the other hand, in case of success (no errors were detected), the model is transformed into C++ code for the ns-3 library as follows:

1. All the ns-3 nodes are created as part of a global container.
2. A position is assigned to each node according to the topology description.
3. The nodes are grouped into containers as described in the configuration model.
4. The channel of the specified type is created.
5. The network devices (as part of a container) are created, added to the nodes, and attached to the channel.
6. The protocol stack is installed on the nodes. This step is handled automatically by the generator, therefore it doesn't need to be specified in the model.
7. The interfaces are created and attached to the devices.
8. An instance of *RTDS_Scheduler* is created for each node. Process instances are created and associated to the nodes via the *RTDS_Scheduler*.

All these steps are illustrated in Fig. 6, which shows the code generated from the model in Fig. 3 (only the server part).

```
int main(int argc, char **argv)
{
    // 1. Create nodes.
    NodeContainer globalContainer;
    globalContainer.Create(4);

    // 2. Assign positions to nodes.
    Ptr<ConstantPositionMobilityModel> pos_3 = CreateObject<ConstantPositionMobilityModel>();
    pos_3->SetPosition(Vector(0.0, 0.0, 0));
    NodeList::GetNode(3)->AggregateObject(pos_3);

    // 3. Group nodes into containers.
    NodeContainer sNode;
    sNode.Add(NodeList::GetNode(3));

    // 4. Create channels.
    Ptr<YansWifiChannel> wifiChannel = CreateObject<YansWifiChannel>();
    Ptr<FriisPropagationLossModel> p_0_0 = CreateObject<FriisPropagationLossModel>();
    wifiChannel->SetAttribute("PropagationLossModel", PointerValue(p_0_0));
    Ptr<ConstantSpeedPropagationDelayModel> p_1_0 =
        CreateObject<ConstantSpeedPropagationDelayModel>();
    wifiChannel->SetAttribute("PropagationDelayModel", PointerValue(p_1_0));

    // 5. Create devices, add them to the nodes, and attach them to the channel.
    NetDeviceContainer sDevice;
    for(uint32_t i=0; i<sNode.GetN(); i++)    {
        Ptr<WifiNetDevice> device = CreateObject<WifiNetDevice>();
        sNode.Get(i)->AddDevice(device);
        device->Attach(wifiChannel);
        sDevice.Add(device);
        Ptr<YansWifiPhy> p_0_0 = CreateObject<YansWifiPhy>();
        p_0_0->ConfigureStandard(WIFI_PHY_STANDARD_80211b);
        p_0_0->SetErrorRateModel(CreateObject<NistErrorRateModel>());
        p_0_0->SetDevice(device);
        p_0_0->SetChannel(wifiChannel);
        p_0_0->SetMobility(device->GetNode());
        device->SetAttribute("Phy", PointerValue(p_0_0));
        Ptr<AdhocWifiMac> p_1_0 = CreateObject<AdhocWifiMac>();
        p_1_0->SetAddress(Mac48Address::Allocate());
        device->SetAttribute("Mac", PointerValue(p_1_0));
        Ptr<IdealWifiManager> p_2_0 = CreateObject<IdealWifiManager>();
        device->SetAttribute("RemoteStationManager", PointerValue(p_2_0));
    }

    // 6. Install the protocol stack on all nodes.
    InternetStackHelper protocol_stack;
    protocol_stack.InstallAll();

    // 7. Attach interfaces to the devices.
    Ipv4AddressHelper sInterface_address("10.0.0.0", "255.0.0.0", "0.0.0.1");
    Ipv4InterfaceContainer sInterface = sInterface_address.Assign(sDevice);

    // 8. Create a RTDS_Scheduler and process instances for each node.
    RTDS_Scheduler *sNode_scheduler[1];
    for(uint32_t i=0; i<1; i++)    {
        sNode_scheduler[i] = new RTDS_Scheduler(sNode.Get(i));
        RTDS_Env(sNode_scheduler[i]);
    }
    for(uint32_t i=0; i<1; i++)    {
        pServer(sNode_scheduler[i]);
    }

    // Run simulation.
    Simulator::Run();
    Simulator::Destroy();
    return 0;
}
```

Fig. 6. Code generated from the configuration model in Fig. 3

6   Conclusions

Simulation modeling is not a simple task. This is especially true for distributed communication systems due to their complexity. The lack of a unified approach covering all the aspects of such systems makes modeling even more challenging. The existing methodologies and tools, which are based on standardized languages like SDL or UML, do provide modeling means but they are not complete.

In this paper we introduced simulation configuration modeling as part of our unified approach based on SDL-RT for modeling all aspects of distributed communication systems. We showed how SDL-RT deployment diagrams serve this purpose quite well, despite some limitations regarding the attribute values and topology description. To overcome these limitations we extended the description capabilities for attributes in order to provide support for more complex configuration values. Also, we defined a mapping between the configuration model in SDL-RT and topology generator tools.

We have already implemented our approach, thus providing code generation for the ns-3 network simulator. We believe that our tool can be adapted (without much effort) to support also other simulation libraries. The only limitation is the programming language. It has to be C/C++ because this is the language used by SDL-RT.

References

1. International Telecommunication Union (ITU): Z.100 series, Specification and Description Language, http://www.itu.int/rec/T-REC-Z.100/en
2. OMG: OMG Unified Modeling Language (OMG UML), Superstructure. Version 2.4.1. Tech. rep., Object Management Group (2011)
3. Kuhn, T., Geraldy, A., Gotzhein, R., Rothländer, F.: ns+SDL – The Network Simulator for SDL Systems. In: Prinz, A., Reed, R., Reed, J. (eds.) SDL 2005. LNCS, vol. 3530, pp. 103–116. Springer, Heidelberg (2005)
4. Breslau, L., Estrin, D., Fall, K.R., Floyd, S., Heidemann, J.S., Helmy, A., Huang, P., McCanne, S., Varadhan, K., Xu, Y., Yu, H.: Advances in Network Simulation. IEEE Computer 33(5), 59–67 (2000)
5. Brumbulli, M., Fischer, J.: SDL Code Generation for Network Simulators. In: Kraemer, F.A., Herrmann, P. (eds.) SAM 2010. LNCS, vol. 6598, pp. 144–155. Springer, Heidelberg (2011)
6. Henderson, T.R., Roy, S., Floyd, S., Riley, G.F.: ns-3 Project Goals. In: Proceeding from the 2006 Workshop on ns-2 – the IP Network Simulator (WNS2 2006), article 13. ACM Press (2006)
7. Dietrich, I., Dressler, F., Schmitt, V., German, R.: SYNTONY: Network Protocol Simulation Based on Standard-Conform UML 2 Models. In: 2nd International Conference on Performance Evaluation Methodologies and Tools (ValueTools 2007), ICST, article 21 (2007)
8. Varga, A., Hornig, R.: An Overview of the OMNeT++ Simulation Environment. In: Proceedings of the 1st International Conference on Simulation Tools and Techniques (Simutools 2008), ICST, article 60 (2008)

9. Estrin, D., Handley, M., Heidemann, J.S., McCanne, S., Xu, Y., Yu, H.: Network Visualization with Nam, the VINT Network Animator. IEEE Computer 33(11), 63–68 (2000)
10. SDL-RT Consortium: Specification and Description Language - Real Time. Version 2.2, http://www.sdl-rt.org/standard/V2.2/html/SDL-RT.htm
11. Ahrens, K., Eveslage, I., Fischer, J., Kühnlenz, F., Weber, D.: The Challenges of Using SDL for the Development of Wireless Sensor Networks. In: Reed, R., Bilgic, A., Gotzhein, R. (eds.) SDL 2009. LNCS, vol. 5719, pp. 200–221. Springer, Heidelberg (2009)
12. Blunk, A., Brumbulli, M., Eveslage, I., Fischer, J.: Modeling Real-time Applications for Wireless Sensor Networks using Standardized Techniques. In: SIMULTECH 2011 - Proceedings of 1st International Conference on Simulation and Modeling Methodologies, Technologies and Applications, pp. 161–167. SciTePress (2011)
13. Fischer, J., Redlich, J.P., Zschau, J., Milkereit, C., Picozzi, M., Fleming, K., Brumbulli, M., Lichtblau, B., Eveslage, I.: A Wireless Mesh Sensing Network for Early Warning. Journal of Network and Computer Applications 35(2), 538–547 (2012)
14. Fleming, K., Picozzi, M., Milkereit, C., Kühnlenz, F., Lichtblau, B., Fischer, J., Zulfikar, C., Ozel, O., et al.: The Self-organizing Seismic Early Warning Information Network (SOSEWIN). Seismological Research Letters 80(5), 755–771 (2009)
15. Schaible, P., Gotzhein, R.: Development of Distributed Systems with SDL by Means of Formalized APIs. In: Reed, R., Reed, J. (eds.) SDL 2003. LNCS, vol. 2708, pp. 158–158. Springer, Heidelberg (2003)
16. Milic, B., Malek, M.: NPART - Node Placement Algorithm for Realistic Topologies in Wireless Multihop Network Simulation. In: Proceedings of the 2nd International Conference on Simulation Tools and Techniques (SimuTools 2009), ICST, arricle 9 (2009)

GRL Model Validation: A Statistical Approach

Jameleddine Hassine[1] and Daniel Amyot[2]

[1] College of Computer Science and Engineering, KFUPM, Dhahran, Saudi Arabia
jhassine@kfupm.edu.sa
[2] EECS, University of Ottawa, Ontario, Canada
damyot@eecs.uottawa.ca

Abstract. Goal models represent interests, intentions, and strategies of different stakeholders. Reasoning about the goals of a system unavoidably involves the transformation of unclear stakeholder requirements into goal-oriented models. The ability to validate goal models would support the early detection of unclear requirements, ambiguities and conflicts. In this paper, we propose a novel GRL-based validation approach to check the correctness of goal models. Our approach is based on a statistical analysis that helps justify the modeling choices during the construction of the goal model as well as detecting conflicts among the stakeholders of the system. We illustrate our approach using a GRL model for the introduction of a new elective security course in a university.

1   Introduction

There is a general consensus on the importance of good Requirements Engineering (RE) approaches for achieving high quality software. Requirements elicitation, modeling, analysis and validation are amongst the main challenges during the development of complex systems. A common starting point in requirements engineering approaches is the elicitation of goals that the targeted system will need to achieve once developed and deployed. Goal modeling can be defined as the activity of representing and reasoning about stakeholder goals using models, in which goals are related through relationships with other goals and/or other model elements, such as, e.g., tasks that system is expected to execute, resources that can be used, or roles that can be played [1]. Over the past two decades, several goal modeling languages have been developed. The most popular ones are *i** [2], the NFR Framework [3], Keep All Objects Satisfied (KAOS) [4], TROPOS [5] and the Goal-oriented Requirement Language (GRL) [6] part of the ITU-T standard User Requirement Notation (URN).

The growing popularity of goal-oriented modeling, and its adoption by a large international community, led to the development of many goal-oriented analysis methodologies [1,3,5,7,8,9]. These methodologies differ in their targeted notation and in their purpose. However, it is worth noting that most of these methodologies focus on the qualitative or/and quantitative evaluation of satisfaction levels of the goals and actors composing the model given some initial satisfaction levels [3,5,7,8,9]. Based on the *i** framework, Horkoff et al. [9] have developed

Ø. Haugen, R. Reed, and R. Gotzhein (Eds.): SAM 2012, LNCS 7744, pp. 212–228, 2013.

an interactive (semiautomated), forward propagation algorithm with qualitative values. A more recent work by Horkoff et al. [7] proposes an interactive backward propagation algorithm with quantitative values. Amyot et al. [8] have proposed three algorithms (qualitative, quantitative, and hybrid) to evaluate satisfaction levels of the intentional elements of a GRL model. Initial satisfaction levels for some of the intentional elements are provided in a strategy and then propagated, using a forward propagation mechanism, to the other intentional elements of the model through the various graph links. Giorgini et al. [5] have used an axiomatization approach to formalize goal models in TROPOS using four qualitative contribution levels (-, - -, +, ++). The authors have provided forward and backward propagation algorithms to detect three types of conflicts (weak, medium and strong). Ayala et al. [10] have presented a comparative study of $i*$ [2], TROPOS [5], and GRL [6]. The authors have identified (1) eight structural criteria that consider the characteristics of the language constructors, and are related to models, actors, intentional elements, decomposition elements, additional reasoning elements and external model elements, and (2) six non-structural criteria that analyze the definition of the languages, its use, and also the elements that complement them, as can be formalizations, methodologies and software tools. These criteria are syntactical.

As goal models gain in complexity (e.g., large systems involving many stakeholders), they become difficult to analyze and to validate. Indeed, tentative requirements provided by the stakeholders of complex systems may be, among others, ambiguous, contradictory, and vague, which may cause many issues when the requirements engineer transforms such requirements (expressed usually in natural language) into a formal syntax in a specific goal description language. As incorrect system requirements generated from goals can lead to cost, delays, and quality issues during system development, it is essential to ensure the validity of the source goal models. Jureta et al. [1] have proposed a question-based Goal Argumentation Method (GAM) to help clarify and detect any deficient argumentation within goal models. However, their approach considers neither survey administration nor statistical analysis. To the best of our knowledge, no empirical approach has been proposed to validate goal models. In this paper, we present an approach to tackle the issue of validating complex goal models using empirical data that can be analyzed using proven statistical methods such as *Cluster Analysis* and *ANOVA (Analysis of Variance)*. We have chosen GRL [6] as target language, given its status as an international standard, but our proposed methodology can likely be applied to other goal-oriented language that visually supports actors, intentional elements, and their relationships (including i* and TROPOS), thus maintaining the discussion generic.

The remainder of this paper is organized as follows. The GRL [6] features are briefly overviewed in Sect. 2. In Sect. 3, we present and discuss the proposed GRL validation approach. Section 4 discusses how to design the validation survey from goal models. Next, empirical data analysis is presented in Sect. 5 and applied to a case study in Sect. 6. Finally, conclusions and future work are presented in Sect. 7.

2   GRL in a Nutshell

The Goal-oriented Requirement Language (GRL) [6] is a visual modeling notation that is used to model intentions, business goals and non-functional requirements (NFR). GRL integrates the core concepts of:

1. The NFR Framework [3], which focuses on the modeling of NFRs and the various types of relationships between them (e.g., AND, OR decomposition, positive and negative contributions, etc.). NFR comes with goal decomposition strategies along with propagation algorithms to estimate the satisfaction of higher-level goals given the attainment or non-attainment of lower-level ones.
2. The i^* goal modeling language [2], which has as primary concern the modeling of intentions and strategic dependencies between actors. Dependencies between actors concern goals, softgoals, resources and tasks.

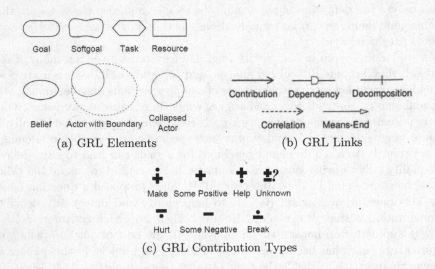

Fig. 1. Basic Elements of GRL [8]

The basic notational elements of GRL are summarized in Fig. 1. Figure 1(a) illustrates the GRL intentional elements (i.e., goal, task, softgoal, resource and belief) that optionally reside within an actor. Actors are holders of intentions; they are the active entities in the system or its environment who want goals to be achieved, tasks to be performed, resources to be available, and softgoals to be satisfied [6]. Figure 1(b) illustrates the various kinds of links in a goal model. Decomposition links allow an element to be decomposed into sub-elements (using AND, OR, or XOR). Contribution links indicate desired impacts of one element on another element. A contribution link has a qualitative contribution type (see Fig. 1(c)) and an optional quantitative contribution. Correlation links describe side effects rather than desired impacts. Finally, dependency links model relationships between actors. For a detailed description of GRL language, the reader is invited to consult [6].

3 GRL Statistical Validation Approach

Figure 2 illustrates the steps of our GRL-based goal model validation approach. It is an iterative process that starts with the construction of a GRL model. In this step, the requirement engineer plays a central role in shaping the problem and solution knowledge, provided by the system stakeholders, into a GRL model. Difficulties arise when many stakeholders with different backgrounds participate in the engineering of requirements over a long period of time, which hinders the quality of the goal model. The GRL model will be used to design a validation survey (described in Sect. 4) that would be administrated to the system stakeholders (steps 2 and 3).

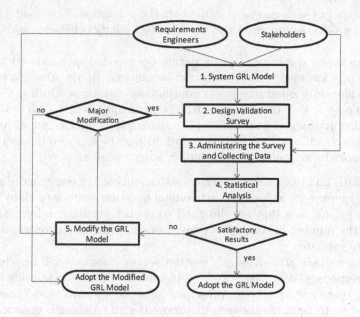

Fig. 2. GRL Validation Approach

Next, the resulting data is analyzed (step 4) and the identified conflicts, if any, are communicated to the involved parties. The requested modifications are incorporated into the GRL model in step 5. For major modifications, such as the deletion of many GRL elements/links or the modification of link decompositions types, we need an additional iteration. The process stops when satisfactory results are obtained.

4   Designing the Validation Survey

In this step, we design a survey that would be administered to the system stake-holders. Stakeholders include anyone who has an interest in the system (e.g., Customers, end users, system developers, system maintainers, etc.). The survey questions are produced based on the GRL graph intentional elements (e.g., goals, tasks, etc.), links (e.g., dependency, contribution, etc.) and constructs (e.g., AND, OR, etc.). Two types of questions may be designed:

- **Attitudinal questions** [11] typically consist of a series of statements for which stakeholders are asked to express their agreement or disagreement. A five point Likert scale [12] may be used to measure the level of agreement or disagreement. The format of a typical five-level Likert item is:
  1. Strongly agree
  2. Agree
  3. Neither agree nor disagree
  4. Disagree
  5. Strongly disagree

  The output of such questions would help the validation of the model relation-ships (or GRL sub-models) and would detect conflicts between stakeholders, if any.
- **Exploratory questions** are by nature open-ended as we are trying to re-trieve new knowledge about a particular subject. In our strategy, we either use exploratory questions as (1) contingency questions which are adminis-trated only in case the respondent has chosen options 3, 4, or 5 to the corre-sponding attitudinal question, or (2) as a simple standalone question with no prior preconditions. Exploratory questions may be completely unstructured, word association, sentence completion, story completion, etc.

For each GRL link (e.g., dependency, contribution, etc.) or construct (e.g., AND, OR, etc.), we produce at least one attitudinal question and one or many optional contingency questions that are designed to collect pertinent information. The type and the number of contingency questions depend on the relationship that we want to validate.

Creating well structured, simply written survey questions will help in collect-ing valid responses. While there are no predefined rules on the wording of survey questions, there are some basic principles such as *relevance* and *accuracy* [13] that do work to improve the overall survey design. Although generic, the in-tent of Table 1 is to provide some tips on how to derive question vocabulary from goal model constructors. The presented examples of question vocabulary are derived from the inherent definition of goal-model constructors. However, to produce relevant, accurate, and well-understood surveys, the designed questions may include technical words from the targeted domain. Therefore, this exercise is done manually.

Figure 3 illustrates an example of a contribution relationship of type **HELP** between task *Task-1* and goal *Goal-1*, and its associated set of survey questions. In the attitudinal question, specific words are used to describe the relationship

Table 1. Examples of GRL Constructors and their Corresponding Questions Vocabulary

GRL Intentional Elements	
Constructor	**Question Vocabulary**
Goal/Softgoal <id>	Realization/Fulfillment of Goal/Softgoal <id>
Task <id>	Completion/Execution of Task <id>
Resource <id>	Uses Resource <id>
Belief <text>	We believe that <text>
Actor <id>	Actor <id> participates
Actor with Boundary <id>	Actor <id> encloses
GRL Intentional Relations	
Constructor	**Question Vocabulary**
Make	Makes
Help	Helps
SomePositive	Has some positive contribution
Unknown	Has an unknown contribution
Hurt	Hurts
SomeNegative	Has some negative contribution
Break	Breaks
Decomposition AND	... AND ... constitute
Decomposition OR	... OR ... constitute
Dependency	Depends on

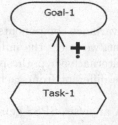

Contribution Link
of Type **HELP**

Attitudinal Question: "The <u>execution</u> of **Task-1 helps** the <u>realization</u> of **Goal-1**". Please tell us to what extent you agree with this statement?

1. Strongly agree
2. Agree
3. Neither agree nor disagree
4. Disagree
5. Strongly disagree

Contingency Question 1: In case you don't agree with the goal **Goal-1**, please complete the sentence with an appropriate goal: "the **completion** of **Task-1 helps** the **realization** of goal ......". Otherwise rewrite **Goal-1**.

Contingency Question 2: In case you don't agree with task **task-1**, please complete the following sentence with an appropriate task: "The **completion** of task ...... **helps** the **realization** of goal *Goal-1*". Otherwise rewrite **Task-1**.

Contingency Question 3: Please complete the sentence with an appropriate verb (make, helps, has some positive contribution, hurts, breaks, etc.): "The **completion** of *Task-1* ...... the **realization** of goal *Goal-1*".

Fig. 3. Contribution of Type **Help** and its Associated Questions

type (i.e., verb **helps**), the involved participants with appropriate achievement description (i.e., **completion of task Task-1, realization of goal Goal-1**). If the respondent makes a negative answer (i.e., 3, 4 or 5), he will be asked to answer three contingency questions. In this example, we have chosen a *word completion* type of questions to check whether the issue lies within the specification of the goal (i.e., *Question 1*), within the specification of the task (*Question 2*), or within the contribution type (*Question 3*).

Deriving a question from every GRL construct/link may lead to a scalability issue when validating large models (with hundreds of links). One approach to mitigate this issue is to minimize the number of generated questions. This may be achieved by deriving questions from GRL sub-models. Section 6.1 illustrates such an optimization. For instance in decomposition links, all children are included in a sub-model. In addition, beliefs are always included in sub-models and are not assessed separately.

5   Validation Survey Data Analysis

Our main goal is to check whether stakeholders (survey respondents) agree on the proposed GRL model. Conflicts arise when we have major differences in the answers of the stakeholders. Therefore, such conflicts should be addressed and resolved.

Our model analysis strategy is based on the data collected from the attitudinal questions only. Contingency questions would help understand and later fix the goal model in case of negative answers to the attitudinal questions. The collected data from the attitudinal questions may be analyzed using one-way analysis of variance (one-way ANOVA), a statistical technique that can be used to evaluate whether there are differences between the mean value across several population groups. This technique can be used only for numerical data. More specifically, one-way ANOVA tests the null hypothesis:

$$H_0 : \mu_1 = \mu_2 = \mu_3 = \cdots = \mu_k$$

where μ = group mean and k = number of groups. These variance components are then tested for statistical significance, and, if significant, we reject the null hypothesis of no differences between means and accept the alternative hypothesis (i.e., $H_1 =$ not H_0) that the means (in the population) are different from each other [14].

We use SPSS[1] software [15] to perform one-way ANOVA analysis. SPSS generates several useful tables:

- **Descriptives Table** provides useful descriptive statistics including the mean, standard deviation and 95% confidence intervals for the dependent variables for each separate group as well as when all groups are combined (see Table 2). In our context, group means relative to a question would indicate whether the groups agree (e.g., mean between 1 and 2) or disagree (e.g., mean between 4 and 5) with the corresponding GRL sub-model.

---

[1] Release 16.0.

- **Test of Homogeneity of Variances Table** shows the result of Levene's Test of Homogeneity of Variance (see Table 3), which tests for similar variances. If the significance value (σ, or *Sig.*) is greater than 0.05 (the α level of significance) then the assumption of homogeneity of variance is met and we have to look for the ANOVA Table. If the Levene's test was significant (i.e., *Sig.* is less than 0.05), then we do not have similar variances. Therefore, we need to refer to the Robust Tests of Equality of Means Table instead of the ANOVA Table.
- **ANOVA Table** shows the output of the ANOVA analysis and whether we have a statistically significant difference between our group means (see Table 4). If the significance level is less than 0.05, then there is a statistically significant difference in the group means. However, the ANOVA table does not indicate which of the specific groups differed. This information can be found in the Multiple Comparisons Table, which contains the results of post-hoc tests.
- **Robust Tests of Equality of Means Table:** Even if there was a violation of the assumption of homogeneity of variances (i.e., *Sig.* less than 0.05 in the Test of Homogeneity of Variances), we could still determine whether there were significant differences between the groups by not using the traditional ANOVA but using the *Welch* test (see Table 5). Like the ANOVA test, if the significance value is less than 0.05 then there are statistically significant differences between groups.
- **Multiple Comparisons Table** shows which groups differed from each other (*Sig.* should be less than 0.05 – see Table 6). The Tukey post-hoc test is generally the preferred test for conducting post-hoc tests on a one-way ANOVA but there are many others.

ANOVA assumes that we have a prior knowledge about the stakeholder groups and the population group to which each respondent belongs. However, when this assumption is not met, first we have to perform a cluster analysis [16], then apply ANOVA. Cluster analysis [16] is a statistical method for finding relatively homogeneous clusters of cases based on measured characteristics. Forming groups may be inferred from additional information collected in the survey (e.g., sex, role in an organization, age, etc.). When such information is missing, the actual questions (those derived from the GRL model) may be used to form our groups.

SPSS has three different procedures that can be used to cluster data: *hierarchical cluster analysis*, *k-means cluster*, and *two-step cluster*. The *two-step* procedure is recommended for large sets of cases, whereas *hierarchical clustering* is more suitable when we want to easily examine solutions with increasing numbers of clusters. *k-means* clustering is used when we know how many clusters we want and we have a moderately sized data set.

Because we usually do not know the number of clusters that will emerge in our data set and because we want an optimum solution, a two-stage sequence of analysis may occur as follows:

1. We carry out a hierarchical cluster analysis using Ward's method applying *Squared Euclidean Distance* as the distance measure. This helps determine the optimum number of clusters we should work with. The number of clusters can be derived visually using a *dendrogram* (a hierarchical tree diagram that shows the linkage points, e.g., Fig. 12).
2. The next stage is to rerun either the hierarchical cluster analysis with our selected number of clusters, or apply k-means. This would result into allocating every case in our data set to a particular cluster.

For more details on applying cluster analysis and ANOVA using SPSS, the reader is invited to consult [16].

6 Illustrative Example: Introduction of a New Security Elective Course

In this section, we apply our proposed approach to a simple GRL model (see Fig. 4) that describes the introduction of a new elective course "Ethical Hacking" into the security program at King Fahd University of Petroleum & Minerals (KFUPM).

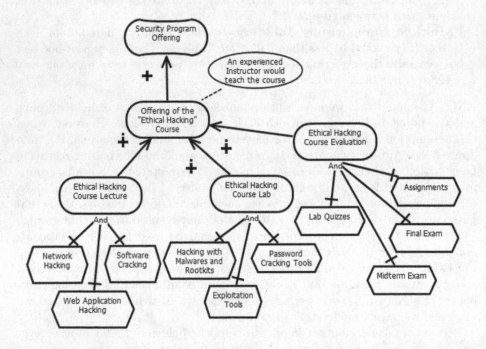

Fig. 4. GRL Model for the Introduction of a new Security Course

6.1   Designing Survey Questions

Figures 5, 6, 7, 8, 9, 10, and 11 illustrate the questions that have been derived from the GRL model artefacts. Only attitudinal questions are considered, contingency questions are out of the scope of this example. The designed survey has been administrated to the undergraduate students from the college of Computer Science and Engineering at KFUPM.

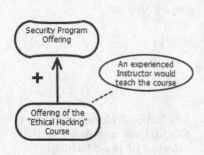

The **offering of the "Ethical Hacking" Course** has **some positive contribution** on the **realization** of the **Security Program Offering**. We believe that **An experienced Instructor would teach the course**. Please tell us to what extent you agree with this statement?

1. Strongly agree
2. Agree
3. Neither agree nor disagree
4. Disagree
5. Strongly disagree

Fig. 5. Question 1

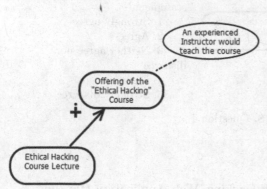

The **Ethical Hacking Course Lecture** contributes to the **offering of the "Ethical Hacking" Course**. We believe that **An experienced Instructor would teach the course**. Please tell us to what extent you agree with this statement?

1. Strongly agree
2. Agree
3. Neither agree nor disagree
4. Disagree
5. Strongly disagree

Fig. 6. Question 2

In addition to the listed questions, we have asked the students to specify their major (e.g., SWE (Software Engineering), CS (Computer Science), COE (Computer Engineering), etc.), to indicate whether they are familiar with security topics (e.g., Yes/No response), and to fill in their GPA. Since SPSS assumes that the variables are represented numerically, we have to convert the answers to (1) the major and to (2) the familiarity with security topics, to numeric values. Majors SWE, CS, and COE are converted to 1, 2, and 3 respectively while the Yes/No response is converted to 1/0.

222   J. Hassine and D. Amyot

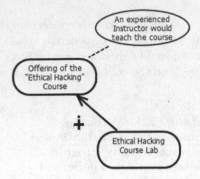

The **Ethical Hacking Course Lab** contributes to the **offering of the "Ethical Hacking" Course**. We believe that **An experienced Instructor would teach the course**. Please tell us to what extent you agree with this statement?

1. Strongly agree
2. Agree
3. Neither agree nor disagree
4. Disagree
5. Strongly disagree

Fig. 7. Question 3

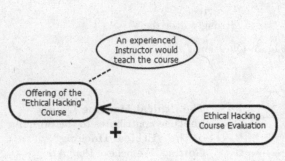

The **Ethical Hacking Course Evaluation** contributes to the **offering of the "Ethical Hacking" Course**. We believe that **An experienced Instructor would teach the course**. Please tell us to what extent you agree with this statement?

1. Strongly agree
2. Agree
3. Neither agree nor disagree
4. Disagree
5. Strongly disagree

Fig. 8. Question 4

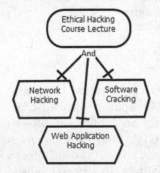

Network Hacking, Web Application Hacking, AND Software Cracking constitute the topics of the **Ethical Hacking Course Lecture**. Please tell us to what extent you agree with this statement?

1. Strongly agree
2. Agree
3. Neither agree nor disagree
4. Disagree
5. Strongly disagree

Fig. 9. Question 5

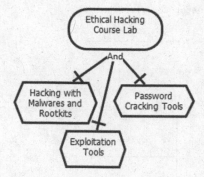

Hacking with Malware and Rootkits, Exploitation Tools, **AND** Password Cracking Tools <u>constitute</u> the topics of the **Ethical Hacking Course Lab**. Please tell us to what extent you agree with this statement?
1. Strongly agree
2. Agree
3. Neither agree nor disagree
4. Disagree
5. Strongly disagree

Fig. 10. Question 6

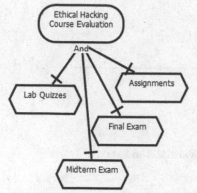

Lab Quizzes, Assignments, Midterm Exam, AND Final Exam <u>constitute</u> the **Ethical Hacking Course Evaluation**. Please tell us to what extent you agree with this statement?
1. Strongly agree
2. Agree
3. Neither agree nor disagree
4. Disagree
5. Strongly disagree

Fig. 11. Question 7

6.2   Survey Data Analysis

We aim to identify conflicts between students and later clear any ambiguity about the introduction of this new course. Because we do not know the number of groups, the first step is to carry out a hierarchical cluster analysis in order to classify the 28 collected cases into distinct groups based on students' majors, GPA, and their familiarity with security topics. The application of Ward's method produces three clusters, as shown in the dendrogram in Fig. 12 (considering a reasonable linkage distance within [8,15] interval). Next, we rerun hierarchical cluster analysis with three groups which allows for the allocation of every case to a particular cluster.

Table 2 shows the group means and the standard deviation for each group. At first glance, we notice that contrary to groups 1 and 2, group 3 had a negative response to question Q7 (Mean = 4 (i.e., Disagree)).

For each question from Q1 to Q7, the Test of Homogeneity of Variances output (see Table 3) tests H_0: $\mu_1 = \mu_2 = \mu_3$. To interpret this output, we look at the column labeled *Sig*. This is the p value. If the p value is less than or equal to

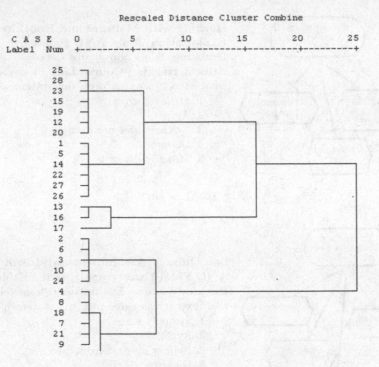

Fig. 12. Dendrogram Using Ward Method

the α level (0.05) for this test, then we can reject the null hypothesis H_0. If the p value is greater than α level for this test, then we fail to reject H_0, which increases our confidence that the variances are equal and the homogeneity of variance assumption has been met. We can see from this case study that Levene's F Statistic have significance values of 0.613, 0.419, 0.269, 0.946, and 0.110 for questions Q2, Q4, Q5, Q6, and Q7 respectively. Therefore, the assumption of homogeneity of variance is met for these questions. Questions Q1 and Q3 (having *Sig* values of 0.024 and 0.038 respectively) do not have similar variances and we need to refer to the Robust Tests of Equality of Means Table (Table 5) instead of the ANOVA Table (Table 4).

From the ANOVA table (Table 4), we can see that the significance levels for questions Q2 (0.279), Q4(0.277), Q5(0.495) and Q6(0.822) are greater than 0.05. Hence, there is no significant differences between the groups for the underlined questions. For question Q7, the significance level is 0.00, which is below 0.05 and, therefore, there is a statistically significant difference between the three groups. The Multiple Comparisons Table (Table 6) determines which of the specific groups differed.

As stated above, there was a violation of the assumption of homogeneity of variances for questions Q1 and Q3. We could still determine whether there were significant differences between the groups by not using the traditional ANOVA

Table 2. Descriptive Statistics Table

		N	Mean	Std. Deviation	Std. Error	95% Confidence Interval for Mean		Minimum	Maximum
						Lower Bound	Upper Bound		
Q1	1	13	1.46	.967	.268	.88	2.05	1	4
	2	12	1.33	.492	.142	1.02	1.65	1	2
	3	3	2.00	1.732	1.000	-2.30	6.30	1	4
	Total	28	1.46	.881	.167	1.12	1.81	1	4
Q2	1	13	1.62	.961	.266	1.03	2.20	1	4
	2	12	1.67	.985	.284	1.04	2.29	1	4
	3	3	2.67	1.528	.882	-1.13	6.46	1	4
	Total	28	1.75	1.041	.197	1.35	2.15	1	4
Q3	1	13	1.23	.439	.122	.97	1.50	1	2
	2	12	1.50	.905	.261	.93	2.07	1	4
	3	3	2.67	1.528	.882	-1.13	6.46	1	4
	Total	28	1.50	.882	.167	1.16	1.84	1	4
Q4	1	13	2.00	.913	.253	1.45	2.55	1	3
	2	12	1.67	.888	.256	1.10	2.23	1	4
	3	3	2.67	1.528	.882	-1.13	6.46	1	4
	Total	28	1.93	.979	.185	1.55	2.31	1	4
Q5	1	13	1.85	.801	.222	1.36	2.33	1	3
	2	12	2.00	1.348	.389	1.14	2.86	1	5
	3	3	2.67	.577	.333	1.23	4.10	2	3
	Total	28	2.00	1.054	.199	1.59	2.41	1	5
Q6	1	13	2.15	1.214	.337	1.42	2.89	1	5
	2	12	2.25	1.288	.372	1.43	3.07	1	5
	3	3	2.67	1.528	.882	-1.13	6.46	1	4
	Total	28	2.25	1.236	.234	1.77	2.73	1	5
Q7	1	13	1.85	.376	.104	1.62	2.07	1	2
	2	12	1.75	.866	.250	1.20	2.30	1	4
	3	3	4.00	1.000	.577	1.52	6.48	3	5
	Total	28	2.04	.962	.182	1.66	2.41	1	5

Table 3. Test of Homogeneity of Variances

	Levene Statistic	df1	df2	Sig.
Q1	4.322	2	25	.024
Q2	.500	2	25	.613
Q3	3.754	2	25	.038
Q4	.900	2	25	.419
Q5	1.383	2	25	.269
Q6	.056	2	25	.946
Q7	2.413	2	25	.110

but using the *Welch* test. Like the ANOVA test, if the significance value is less than 0.05 then there are statistically significant differences between groups. It is not the case since the *Welch* significance for Q1 is 0.784 and for Q3 is 0.320.

From the results so far, we know that there is significant difference between the groups for Q7 only. The *Multiple Comparisons* table (Table 6), shows which groups differed from each other. We can see that there is a significant difference between groups 1 and 3 (P = 0.00), and between groups 2 and 3 (P = 0.00). Hence, the GRL goal "Ethical Hacking Course Evaluation" *AND* decomposition needs to be reviewed involving all participants from the three groups. Once this conflict is resolved, the model might be updated, if need be.

Table 4. Anova Table

		Sum of Squares	df	Mean Square	F	Sig.
Q1	Between Groups	1.067	2	.533	.670	.521
	Within Groups	19.897	25	.796		
	Total	20.964	27			
Q2	Between Groups	2.840	2	1.420	1.344	.279
	Within Groups	26.410	25	1.056		
	Total	29.250	27			
Q3	Between Groups	5.026	2	2.513	3.933	.033
	Within Groups	15.974	25	.639		
	Total	21.000	27			
Q4	Between Groups	2.524	2	1.262	1.352	.277
	Within Groups	23.333	25	.933		
	Total	25.857	27			
Q5	Between Groups	1.641	2	.821	.723	.495
	Within Groups	28.359	25	1.134		
	Total	30.000	27			
Q6	Between Groups	.641	2	.321	.197	.822
	Within Groups	40.609	25	1.624		
	Total	41.250	27			
Q7	Between Groups	13.022	2	6.511	13.630	.000
	Within Groups	11.942	25	.478		
	Total	24.964	27			

Table 5. Robust Tests of Equality of Means

		Statistic[a]	df1	df2	Sig.
Q1	Welch	.255	2	4.932	.784
Q2	Welch	.582	2	5.303	.591
Q3	Welch	1.456	2	4.852	.320
Q4	Welch	.758	2	5.250	.514
Q5	Welch	1.950	2	7.471	.208
Q6	Welch	.134	2	5.560	.878
Q7	Welch	6.097	2	4.916	.047

a. Asymptotically F distributed.

Table 6. Post Hoc Multiple Comparisons

Q7
Tukey HSD

(I) Ward	(J) Ward	Mean Difference (I-J)	Std. Error	Sig.	95% Confidence Interval	
					Lower Bound	Upper Bound
1	2	.096	.277	.936	-.59	.79
	3	-2.154*	.443	.000	-3.26	-1.05
2	1	-.096	.277	.936	-.79	.59
	3	-2.250*	.446	.000	-3.36	-1.14
3	1	2.154*	.443	.000	1.05	3.26
	2	2.250*	.446	.000	1.14	3.36

*. The mean difference is significant at the 0.05 level.

7   Conclusion and Future Work

In this paper, we have proposed a novel GRL-based validation approach based on empirical data collection and analysis. We have applied cluster analysis and analysis of variance (ANOVA) methods in order to detect conflicts between stakeholders. Furthermore, our approach would guide argumentation and justification of modeling choices during the construction of goal models. As part of our future work, we plan to develop our survey further to go beyond conflict detection to conflict resolution.

Acknowledgment. The authors would like to acknowledge the support provided by the Deanship of Scientific Research at King Fahd University of Petroleum & Minerals (KFUPM) for funding this work through project No. IN111017.

References

1. Jureta, I.J., Faulkner, S., Schobbens, P.Y.: Clear justification of modeling decisions for goal-oriented requirements engineering. Requirements Engineering 13(2), 87–115 (2008)
2. Yu, E.S.K.: Towards modeling and reasoning support for early-phase requirements engineering. In: Proceedings of the 3rd IEEE International Symposium on Requirements Engineering (RE 1997), pp. 226–235. IEEE Computer Society (1997)
3. Chung, L., Nixon, B.A., Yu, E., Mylopoulos, J.: Non-Functional Requirements in Software Engineering. International Series in Software Engineering, vol. 5. Springer (2000)
4. van Lamsweerde, A.: Requirements engineering: from craft to discipline. In: Proceedings of the 16th ACM SIGSOFT International Symposium on Foundations of Software Engineering (SIGSOFT 2008/FSE-16), pp. 238–249. ACM Press (2008)
5. Giorgini, P., Mylopoulos, J., Sebastiani, R.: Goal-oriented requirements analysis and reasoning in the TROPOS methodology. Engineering Applications of Artificial Intelligence 18(2), 159–171 (2005)
6. International Telecommunication Union (ITU): Z.151 – User requirements notation (URN) - Language definition, http://www.itu.int/rec/T-REC-Z.151/en
7. Horkoff, J., Yu, E.S.K.: Qualitative, interactive, backward analysis of i* models. In: 3rd International i* Workshop (iStar 2008), CEUR-WS.org (2008), http://ceur-ws.org/Vol-322/paper11.pdf
8. Amyot, D., Ghanavati, S., Horkoff, J., Mussbacher, G., Peyton, L., Yu, E.: Evaluating goal models within the goal-oriented requirement language. International Journal of Intelligent Systems - Goal-driven Requirements Engineering 25(8), 841–877 (2008)
9. Horkoff, J., Yu, E., Liu, L.: Analyzing trust in technology strategies. In: Proceedings of the 2006 International Conference on Privacy, Security and Trust: Bridge the Gap Between PST Technologies and Business Services (PST 2006), Article 9. ACM Press (2006)

10. Ayala, C.P., Cares, C., Carvallo, J.P., Grau, G., Haya, M., Salazar, G., Franch, X., Mayol, E., Quer, C.: A comparative analysis of i*-based agent-oriented modeling languages. In: Proceedings of the 17th International Conference on Software Engineering and Knowledge Engineering (SEKE 2005), pp. 43–50. Knowledge Systems Institute Graduate School Calgary (2005)
11. Schuman, H., Presser, S.: Questions and answers in attitude surveys – Experiments on question form, wording, and context. Academic Press (1981)
12. Likert, R.: A technique for the measurement of attitudes. Archives of Psychology 140, 1–55 (1932)
13. Iarossi, G.: The power of survey design – a user's guide for managing surveys, interpreting results, and influencing respondents. World Bank (2006)
14. Hill, T., Lewicki, P.: STATISTICS – Methods and Applications. Statsoft Inc., http://www.statsoft.com/textbook/
15. IBM: SPSS software, http://www-01.ibm.com/software/analytics/spss/
16. Norusis, M., SPSS, I.: IBM SPSS Statistics 19 Statistical Procedures Companion. Pearson Education Canada (2011)

Configuration-Based Service Availability Analysis for Middleware Managed Applications

Ali Kanso[1], Maria Toeroe[1], and Ferhat Khendek[2]

[1] Ericsson Inc., Montréal, Canada
{Ali.kanso,Maria.toeroe}@ericsson.com
[2] Electrical and Computer Engineering, Concordia University, Montréal, Canada
Ferhat.Khendek@concordia.ca

Abstract. High availability is a key ingredient in the design of mission critical and revenue generating software applications. With the release of the Service Availability Forum specifications, the availability of these applications can be managed by standardized middleware. Such middleware is capable of detecting and reacting to the application's components failures. In order to manage the availability of the services provided by the applications, the middleware requires a system configuration that describes the system's hardware as well as the software application organization and the recovery policies that define the runtime behavior of the middleware. Different configurations for the same application may render different levels of service availability. Quantifying the availability of an application under a given configuration before deployment is an important issue. In this paper we present an approach to approximate from the system configuration the availability of the services provided by a middleware-managed application.

Keywords: Availability analysis, system configuration, recovery analysis, middleware-managed applications, configuration model, stochastic Petri Nets.

1 Introduction

The complexity of software applications is constantly increasing with the advancements in the information technology and the increased expectations of the users [1,2]. Component Based Software Development (CBSD) aims at reducing this complexity by building applications using software components [3]. CBSD also promotes the notion of re-use of existing Commercial-Off-The-Shelf (COTS) components for building new applications. In order for these applications to provide their services in a highly available fashion (at least 99.999% of the time), they need to incorporate several mechanisms (such as failure monitoring, recovery management, checkpointing etc.) which dramatically increases the complexity of the application development. An alternative solution is to embed all of those common mechanisms into a middleware, also seen as another component of the system, which is responsible for managing the availability of the application's services. The application components would need to interface with the

Ø. Haugen, R. Reed, and R. Gotzhein (Eds.): SAM 2012, LNCS 7744, pp. 229–248, 2013.

middleware in order to enable this management. The Service Availability Forum (SAForum) [4] has specified standards that define

- the interface between the application and the middleware;
- the features that a middleware implementation must incorporate in order to be able to maintain the service availability.

The specifications have defined a versatile middleware behavior that can perform various recoveries and support various redundancy models to protect the services against failures. The middleware requires a specific system configuration that describes

- the application organization, in terms of the component's grouping, their dependencies, and the services they provide;
- the protection policy, i.e. how many redundant component replicas will collaborate to protect a service against failure;
- the recovery policy that must be executed by the middleware in case of failure (e.g. failing over the services or restarting the component etc.).

The system configuration is designed based on a standardized Unified Modeling Language (UML) [5] class diagram that describes how the application is logically structured [6]. The system configuration constitutes an instance of this diagram. Estimating the service availability that a system can offer based on a given configuration is extremely important, especially in cases where the service supplier is bounded by a Service Level Agreement (SLA). Thus the availability analysis becomes a necessity that must be addressed when the system configuration is constructed. Performing the availability analysis based on a given system configuration requires deep knowledge of the domain (i.e. the middleware behavior) and requires modeling skills that the system integrators designing the configuration might not possess. To target this issue, we propose a configuration-based availability analysis method, which transforms the configuration model to a stochastic model that can be solved to quantify the service availability. We also present the prerequisite steps needed to enable this transformation.

This paper is organized as follows; in Section 2 we present the background to our work. Section 3 is where we present our approach for the availability analysis. In Section 4 we show our case study. Section 5 surveys the related work. In Section 6 we discuss the issues we addressed, and the lessons we learned. We conclude in Section 7.

2   Background

The SAForum middleware consists of a set of services, each of which offers a specific functionality towards the construction of a highly available distributed system. Perhaps the most important middleware service is the Availability Management Framework (AMF) [6], which is the service responsible for maintaining the availability of the services provided by the application(s) using the middleware. This is achieved by managing the redundant components of an application and dynamically shifting the workload of a faulty component to a healthy replica, and/or attempting to repair it. AMF manages the availability according to the system configuration (henceforth referred to as the AMF configuration). The AMF configuration defines a logical grouping of the application resources, according to which failures can be isolated, and the application services can be protected.

The basic building block of the AMF configuration is the component, which abstracts a deployable instance of the COTS component. The service(s) provided by such a component is represented by a component-service-instance. The components that collaborate closely and that must be collocated to provide a more integrated service are grouped into a service-unit. The workload[1] assigned to the service-unit is referred to as the service-instance, which is a grouping of component-service-instances. The service-units composed of redundant component replicas form a service-group. The service availability management takes place within the service-group. The service-instances are provided by service-units and protected against failures within the scope of the service-group. The system integrator is responsible for dimensioning the scope of those units and groups, and to define the recovery policies that are deemed most suitable for ensuring the service availability. An application is perceived as a set of service-groups. The AMF configuration also represents the nodes on which the components are deployed. We can consider the different entities increasing fault zones - scopes that can be isolated and repaired to recover from a fault. The configuration model includes attributes associated with the protection and recovery policies such as the number of components assigned active/standby on behalf of a component-service, any restrictions on standard recoveries, etc. These attributes are also configured by the system integrator designing the configuration. In addition, AMF supports the notion of a redundancy model for a service-group. The redundancy model defines the redundancy scheme according to which the service-instances are protected. For instance a 2N redundancy dictates that the service-group can have one active service-unit for all the service-instances and one standby for all the service-instances. A service-unit cannot simultaneously be active for some service-instances and standby for others. On the other hand an N-way-active redundancy model allows for multiple active (but no standby) service-units in the service-group even for the same service-instance.

AMF supports various categories of components. For instance, the components that interface with the middleware are considered Service-Availability (SA) aware components. While other components that can only interact with the AMF through a proxy (SA-aware) component that mediates the interactions between these components and AMF are considered proxied components. For example a legacy database may already support some high availability notions, such as the active and standby assignments. Such database may be managed by the middleware if there is a proxy component (e.g. a dedicated process) that

---

[1] The term workload is used interchangeably with the term service-instance or component-service-instance that respectively represents the workload of the service-unit and the component.

translates the AMF requests to the database. To clarify these concepts we present an example video streaming application using the Video LAN Client (VLC) [7] as a (SA-aware[2]) streaming server that, upon request, streams videos that are stored in a database. The database is assumed to be a proxied component that requires a proxy to be able to interact with AMF. Figure 1 illustrates a possible configuration of such an application, where we have two service-groups: The Streaming_SG has two service-units, each grouping a VLC and a database component. This service-group is protecting one service-instance (Streaming-SI) and has a 2N redundancy model. The second service-group (Proxy_SG) has a similar structure and it is protecting the proxying service-instance (Proxy-SI), where as long as this service-instance is assigned active, AMF can instantiate and assign the database its workload (the DB-CSI component-service-instance).

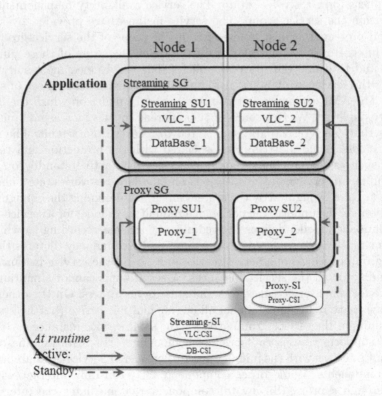

Fig. 1. An example of AMF configuration

---

[2] VLC is originally developed as non-SA-aware component. In a previous work [8] we modified this application by implementing a wrapper that allows it to support the standby assignment and communicate with OpenSAF [9] (an open-source implementation of the SAForum middleware), and thus rendering VLC an SA-aware component.

The availability of any system is mainly threatened by failures that occur in a sporadic manner. Therefore stochastic models are well suited to capture runtime system behavior and to analyze its non-functional properties. The availability analysis is based on capturing the various states where the system is considered healthy and then calculating the probability of the system being in these states within a time interval or in steady state. For this purpose, Markov models have been extensively used e.g. [10,11], due to their expressiveness, and their capability of capturing the complexity of real systems. A major drawback of using Markov models is that the state space tends to explode for complex systems [12]. An alternative would be to use Stochastic Petri Nets [13]. In our case, we are modeling the behavior of a system where deterministic and stochastic events occur. In fact the transition from one state to another occurs in one of the following ways:

- a stochastic manner, e.g. when a failure occurs causing a node to malfunction, or

- in a deterministic manner, e.g. when instantiating a component, the time needed for the instantiation is fairly deterministic or at least bounded, or

- immediately, e.g. when a node is abruptly shut-down and all the components running on that node become instantly un-instantiated.

For this reason, a more suitable formalism to model our system would be Deterministic and Stochastic Petri Nets (DSPNs) [14]. DSPNs are an extension of Petri Nets that support all the transitions we have described.

The key building blocks of a DSPN are places, tokens, arcs, guards and transitions. A place (denoted by a hollowed circle), is used to abstract a certain state. A token (denoted by a filled circle) resides in a place, and signifies that we are currently in the state represented by the place hosting the token (we refer to this as the current "marking"). Tokens can leave a state through transitions. Stochastic transitions are denoted by a hollowed rectangle. A stochastic transition is characterized by a probability distribution function (e.g. the exponential distribution) according to which it fires. Timed transitions are denoted by filled rectangles and are characterized by constant delays. Immediate transitions are denoted by a line (or a thin filled rectangle). Transitions in general and especially immediate ones can be guarded by an enabling function (which is a Boolean expression referred to as the transition guard or simply guard). A transition is only enabled when its guard evaluates to true. Finally, arcs (denoted by arrows) are used to connect places to transitions and vice versa. Arcs can have multiplicities to denote the number of tokens they can transport from one place to another when the transition fires. Under certain conditions, DSPNs can be solved analytically by transforming them into a Markov Regenerative Process [15]. However in our analysis more than one transition of any type can be simultaneously enabled and therefore the model needs to be solved by simulation.

3   Service Availability Analysis

The AMF specification makes a clear distinction between the services and the service provider entities. The service provider entities consist of the components used for building the application. These components normally originate from different software vendors. The information regarding the reliability of these components in terms of the Mean Time To Failure (MTTF) or simply the failure rates can be derived by testing, or runtime monitoring etc. Nevertheless this information is not a good indicator of the outage rates of the services provided by these components [16,17], especially when these components are deployed in a different context from the one where they were tested. Different contexts imply different component grouping and interactions which may cause various — unaccounted for — dependencies (such as deployment, lifecycle, service dependencies etc.) that can expose the services provided by these components to additional outages. This means that the analysis model must be defined in such a way that translates the service provider failure information into the real service outage. To achieve this, the analysis model, i.e. the DSPN model we defined, must capture (among others) the interdependencies between the configuration entities, the service assignment preferences, and the escalation policies enforced by AMF in case a certain recovery fails to overcome the failure.

The standardized UML class diagram used to describe the AMF configuration is defined for runtime availability management purpose and not for the availability analysis. Therefore, we needed to go through various (prerequisite) steps before defining the mapping from the UML configuration model to the stochastic model and solve the latter to quantify the service availability. Figure 2 illustrates the various steps of our approach. On the upper side we show the steps that we performed once at the model level. On the lower side, we show the application of our approach at the instance level, i.e., analyze the availability of any configuration by applying the steps.

3.1   Extending the Configuration Model

The standardized model of the AMF configuration does not capture all the needed information for availability analysis. Therefore, to enable a configuration-based availability analysis we needed to extend this model to include the failure and recovery information (including the recommended recoveries specified by the software vendor to overcome a particular failure type). In the AMF configuration the only entities susceptible to failures are the components and the nodes, therefore we extended the model by associating them with the class failure type which has the rate and the recommended recovery as attributes. The failure type is in turn associated with an actual recovery class that has the actual recovery attribute. Moreover we extended the configuration with some timing attributes (such as the node startup time) and some probability values (e.g. the probability of successful instantiation of a component). These extensions are needed to reflect a more realistic runtime behavior in our analysis model.

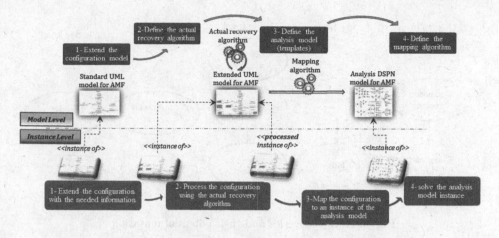

Fig. 2. Overview of the availability analysis process

3.2 Defining the Actual Recovery Algorithms

The recommended recovery is either set as a default for a component or recommended through the API, which means it is embedded in some code. As a result it may not suit all configurations and therefore can be tuned to better suit a particular configuration. For instance in the example shown in Fig. 1 the VLC server and the database originated from two different vendors/providers, and were grouped together in the same service unit by the system integrator to provide a more integrated service. The software provider may be agnostic of how the software will be used or grouped by the system integrator. Therefore the software provider cannot for instance recommend a recovery that is at the service-unit level, simply because he/she is not aware of the scope of the service-unit and how it is formed. It is the system integrator's responsibility to determine the proper scope of recovery and hence adjust the configuration accordingly. For instance, if the VLC server and the database collaborate closely, then the system integrator can force a recovery on both of them when either one fails. In other words regardless of what the recovery recommended is to either of them, it will be altered to include both of them. An AMF configuration model includes attributes that allow the mutation of certain recommended recoveries into different recoveries, namely, what we refer to as the actual recoveries. Hence, with a particular setting of the AMF attributes, a configuration designer can craft more suitable recoveries and force the AMF to execute them when needed. We refer to these attributes as recovery altering attributes. Such attributes increase the complexity of determining the actual recovery that the middleware will execute at runtime as opposed to the recommended one, to target this issue we defined the actual recovery algorithms [18] which annotates the configuration with the actual recoveries (instead of the recommended recoveries) that are used subsequently in the availability analysis.

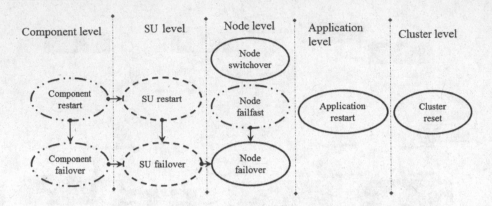

Fig. 3. AMF recoveries and their potential mutation

Not all the recommended recoveries can mutate. Figure 3 shows the AMF recoveries and the mutation path the mutable ones (denoted by dashed circles) can follow.

3.3 Defining the Analysis Model Templates

In order to enable the mapping of an extended AMF configuration to a DSPN model we decided to define the building blocks of the DSPN model in terms of templates that capture the semantics of their corresponding AMF concepts. For each qualified[3] entity in the AMF model, we defined a DSPN template, which describes all the possible behavior that this entity can exhibit. The outcome is a catalog of DSPN templates that we can use to build our DSPN model. The DSPN model must capture the runtime behavior of AMF. The main aspects affecting this behavior are:

- the dependencies among entities,
- the service assignment that AMF is expected to perform, and
- the escalation policies that AMF enforces when a recovery fails.

In order to avoid redundancies, in this subsection we present these aspects and leave the templates as such for the next subsection.

Dependency Handling in the Availability Analysis

We distinguish between two types of dependencies, the implicit one and the explicit dependency.

---

[3] A qualified entity is either a service or an entity on which one of the recoveries of Fig. 3 can be executed.

Implicit Dependency

The implicit dependency is a structural dependency that holds all the time. For instance whenever a node fails, all the components running on the node will be impacted, and thus a recovery at the node level should propagate all the way down to the components. The same applies for the cluster, application and service-unit recoveries.

Explicit Dependencies

The explicit dependency is the one that exist in a specific context, and is explicitly specified. For instance not all components depend on other components, but in certain contexts some components or services may depend on others. Without going into all the details we categorize these dependencies in the following manner:

- *Instantiation level dependency:* this dependency signifies that the dependent component cannot be instantiated if the sponsor is not instantiated. However AMF can assign the component-service-instances to the dependent component regardless of the sponsor. We model this dependency in the analysis (DSPN) model by blocking the move of the dependent into the instantiated state while any of the sponsors are still in the un-instantiated state.

- *Proxy-proxied dependency:* we have already discussed this dependency in Section 2. We model this dependency by not allowing the dependent to be instantiated or assigned any workload until the sponsor (proxy) has been assigned its proxying workload.

- *Service assignment dependency:* this is a dependency among the service-instances within the cluster and the component-service-instances within the scope of the service-instance. This dependency implies that the dependent cannot be assigned until the sponsor is assigned.

- *Container-contained dependency:* AMF supports the notion of container and contained components, where the container represents an execution environment for the contained e.g. a container can be a virtual machine where the contained can run. The dependent (container component) cannot be instantiated nor assigned any service until the sponsor (container) is instantiated and assigned the containing workload. Without the container, the contained cannot exist.

The Runtime Service-Instance Assignments

According to the redundancy model of the service-group, the service-instance can be configured to have different active/standby assignments at runtime. In the DSPN model we must make sure that the preferred assignment is always satisfied for the service-instance. Certain constraints apply, such as limited service-unit capacity in terms of serving service-instances. This capacity is inferred from the service-unit's components capacity of handling the component-service-instances. When a failure occurs and the workload of a service-unit has to be redistributed among its sibling in the service-group, we might lack the capacity of accommodating all the service-instances. In such cases the service-instance rank (a configuration attribute) will come into the picture to specify the priority of the service-instance, where the service-instances with lower ranks will be dropped first if they compete for the same resources of the service-units with the service-instances with higher priority.

The Recovery Escalation Policy

The AMF configuration allows the specification of escalation policies through the attributes of the service-group and the node. Figure 4 illustrates the potential escalation path when a recovery fails repeatedly. For example, when within a bounded period of time (referred to as probation period) a threshold of service-unit failovers on the same node is reached, we can escalate to failover the entire node since clearly the failure has manifested into the node itself. From this perspective the escalation can be viewed as a measure to contain the failure by widening the scope of the recovery. In other situations the initial recovery may not be executed in the first place due to the instantiation/termination failure of the component. The component moves to the instantiation failed state after a configurable number of attempts with and/or without delay between attempts. But the component directly moves to the termination failed state if AMF cannot terminate it. In either cases a node failfast (abrupt shut-down of the node) can be configured to be executed.

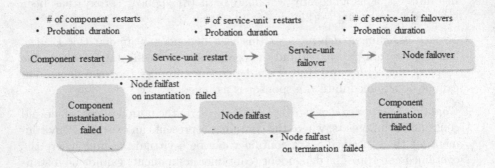

Fig. 4. The recovery escalation path and the policy attributes

The escalation policy is captured in the DSPN model by mapping the policy attributes to the template instances of the relevant entities.

Mapping from the Configuration Model to the Analysis Model

The mapping from the configuration to the template instances is achieved by:

1. Performing the structural mapping, i.e. selecting the proper template for each qualified entity and instantiating it by creating its transitions, places, etc. with the proper naming relevant to the entity.

2. Annotating the transition delays, guard conditions and arc multiplicities with the proper values based on the attribute values of the entity. This results in a more methodical mapping, where, for each qualified entity in the AMF configuration (i.e. an instance of an entity of the AMF model), the related template is selected and instantiated, and according to the attributes of the entity, the template is annotated with the appropriate values (rates, guard conditions etc.). By this, we remain at the same level of abstraction, where, the DSPN template catalog is aligned with the AMF configuration model, while the instantiated templates correspond to an instance of the AMF configuration.

We proceed by defining some of the main (3 out of the 8) templates we use in our analysis. In order to elaborate more on the mapping, we describe the template as if we are describing a potential instance of this template. It should be noted here that the guards defined in these templates play an important role that is not only limited to capturing the various dependencies and recoveries discussed earlier, but also to glue the various DSPNs together. E.g. although the component and node DSPNs are not connected through arcs, a token shift in the node DSPN might cause another token shift in the component DSPN, the latter shift is enabled through the guards. The transitions firing delays presented in the templates are based on the values specified in the configuration attributes. It is the responsibility of the configuration integrator to configure these delays. Configuring these attributes is application specific and outside the scope of this work.

The Component Template:
   The component DSPN template (Fig. 5) captures the life-cycle states of the component (instantiated, terminated etc.) as well as its recovery states.
   Initially the component is in the un-instantiated state (denoted by a token in the Comp_un-instantiated place), when all the conditions allowing the component to be instantiated are satisfied, it can move to the instantiated state after a certain delay representing the time needed to instantiate the component (captured in the time value of the timed transition $T\_t\_cu\_ci$, which is extracted from the configuration). One of the guard conditions of this transition is that the node must have started and not undergoing any recovery. Other conditions may apply according to

- the explicit dependencies specified in the configuration, e.g. if the component is a proxied component, then it cannot be instantiated until the proxying component-service-instance is assigned active to the proxy component.
- implicit dependencies, e.g. if there is a recovery ongoing such as an application restart, then the component cannot start instantiating before all the components of the application have terminated.

This is due to the semantics of the application restart recovery. From the instantiated state the component can go into a recovering state either due to a recovery intended for the component itself, in which case the transition is stochastic

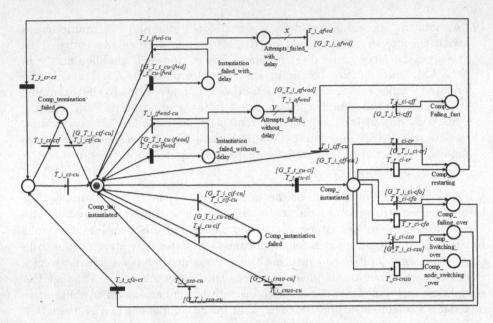

Fig. 5. The component DSPN template

with a rate equal to the failure rate for which this recovery was evaluated to be the actual recovery; or through an immediate transition which means that the recovery is intended for another entity and due to implicit/explicit dependency the recovery was enforced on the component. For example, a token in the Comp_Failing_fast place denotes that the hosting node is failing fast. Finally, a recovering component may be unresponsive to the termination or instantiation requests of AMF. In the latter case, AMF may try a number of instantiation attempts with and/or without delay with different probabilities of success. We capture this by duplicating the token with each attempt to keep track of the attempts, when the threshold is reached, a node-level recovery is enabled, and the added tokens are flushed.

The Service-Unit DSPN Template:

The service-unit DSPN template (see Fig. 6) consists of five places. The SU_healthy place denotes that none of the service-unit components are faulty. The service-unit goes to the restarting place through an immediate transition caused by a recovery escalation due to successive restarts of the components of the service unit. More specifically this transition is triggered when the number of component restarts exceeds a configured value within a configured (probation) duration. The SU_comp_restart place is defined for the purpose of keeping track of the component restarts. If the probation period expires without reaching the component restart threshold, then the tokens in this place are flushed, otherwise a token is placed in the SU_restart_prob place which will trigger an escalation to the SU restart, and start an SU probation period. The service-unit

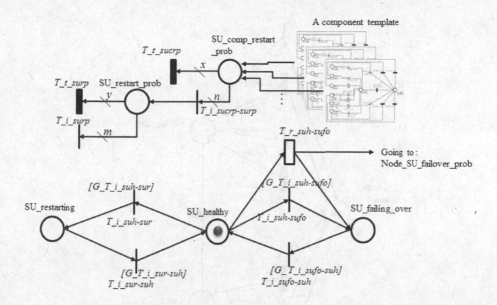

Fig. 6. The service-unit DSPN template

can go to the failing over state either through an immediate transition caused
by a recovery escalation due to successive restarts of the service unit or through
a stochastic transition, if the service-unit is configured to fail over as a single
unit whenever any of its components fail. The rate of this stochastic transition
is the sum of all the rates of the component failures that have the service-unit
failure as an actual recovery. Note that this recovery is a mutated one that has
to be determined by the actual recovery algorithm (Section 3.2).

The Component_ component-service-instance DSPN Template:

The component-service-instance is not tied down to a single component; in
fact several components can assume different roles (active, standby, unassigned)
for the same component-service-instance depending on the redundancy model
of the service group. We defined the component_component-service-instance
DSPN template (Fig. 7) to reflect the role that each candidate[4] component is
playing at runtime. For a single component-service-instance, this template will
be instantiated for each candidate component in the service group.

In this template we have three places reflecting the active, standby, and unassigned roles that a component can assume on behalf of a component-service-
instance. AMF supports the notion of non-pre-instantiable components. Such
components cannot be idle or standby, instead they start providing their service the moment they are instantiated by AMF, and the service assignment is

---

[4] A candidate component in this context is the one capable of serving the component-
service-instance within the service-group.

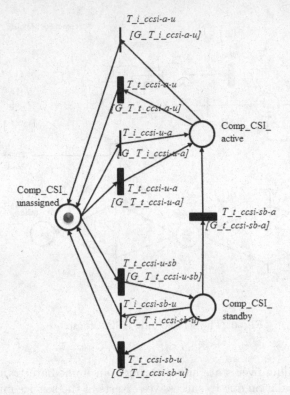

Fig. 7. The component_component-service-instance DSPN template

removed by terminating such components. For this purpose the transition from the unassigned state to the active state and vice versa can be achieved through either timed transitions (applicable for pre-instantiable components) or immediate transitions (applicable for non-pre-instantiable components). Note that when a component is abruptly terminated it immediately loses its assignment and that is why we have the immediate transitions from the Comp_CSI_standby and Comp_CSI_active places to the Comp_CSI_unassigned place.

All the transitions in this template are guarded. The guards are enabled according to different criteria that dictate whether a transition is permanently disabled or only temporarily. A transition can be permanently disabled because of

- the component capability model which defines the number of component-service-instances of a particular type that the component can be active and/or standby for, e.g. if the component can only assume the active role, then the transitions to the standby state are permanently disabled.
- the service-group redundancy model, e.g. in Nway active redundancy all the components are active and no standby assignment is allowed at any time.

A transition is temporarily disabled because of
- the service-instance assignment to the parent service-unit, if the service unit is assigned standby on behalf of the service-instance then none of the components of the service-unit are allowed to be active for any of the component-service-instances of the service-instance;
- the component reaching its maximum capacity in terms of handling the workload, i.e. when the component reaches its maximum active/standby capacity, the transition to the active/standby state is disabled for the component-service-instances that cannot be supported any more;
- the component-service-instance dependency requiring the sponsor component-service-instance to be assigned first, and therefore the transition leading to the assignment of the dependent is disabled until the sponsor is assigned.

It should be noted that another analogous template is defined to capture the service-instance and the service-unit runtime relation. This relation is similar to the one explained in this section where a service unit can be active, standby or unassigned on behalf of a service-instance.

4   Numerical Results

In this section we present a case study to illustrate our availability evaluation process. We remain with the example in Fig. 1. Due to the lack of space, Table 1 shows only the values of the attributes related to the VLC failure and recovery rates. The parameters marked in bold are the ones which are not part of the standard AMF configuration, with which we extended the configuration model as discussed in Section 3.1.

Table 1. Failure and recovery rates

Parameter Value	Description
0.542 sec	VLC instantiation duration
0.027 sec	VLC cleanup duration
0.080 sec	VLC assignment duration
0.030 sec	**VLC switching from standby to active assignment duration**
64800^{-1} sec^{-1}	**VLC failover recommended recovery rate (MTTF=18 hrs.)**
43200^{-1} sec^{-1}	**VLC restart recommended recovery rate (MTTF=12 hrs.)**
95%, 99%	**The probability of the successful instantiation of VLC respectively without and with delay**
98%	**The probability of the successful termination of VLC**

The recovery altering attributes in our configuration are set as follows: we disabled the restart of VLC, i.e. forcing a recommended recovery of restarting the VLC component to mutate to a component failover. We also specified that any component failover at the service-unit level will mutate into a service-unit failover. In short the failure of the VLC component will trigger at least a service-unit failover, including the failover of the database.

For our case study, the escalation policy attribute values are follows: we allow for a maximum of two attempts to instantiate the components, if this fails, or if the component termination fails we escalate to a node failfast. We tolerate a maximum of also two failovers/restarts within a probation period of 60 seconds; if this maximum is exceeded we escalate to the recovery action of a higher scope. E.g. within a probation period, two service-unit restarts will escalate to a service-unit failover, which will start another probation period during which two service-unit failovers will trigger a node failfast.

We proceed with the availability analysis according to Fig. 2 as follows: we first annotate the extended AMF configuration with the information specified (in bold) in Table I. Then we process the configuration using the actual recovery algorithms that will mutate certain recommended recoveries. For example the VLC restart will be mutated into an entire service-unit failover.

The next step is to map the extended AMF configuration into the DSPN instances, this mapping is performed by first selecting and instantiating the needed templates, and thereafter annotating these instances with the proper guard values and transition rates as discussed earlier.

Finally when the DSPNs are completed, they are fed to a simulation tool. We specify the measure of interest to be the probability of having all the component-service-instances of the streaming service-instance assigned active at steady state. Due to the dependency between the database and the proxy component, when the node fails and both service-instances are assigned to the same node, the proxy service-instance will lose its active assignment and hence the streaming service-instance cannot be reassigned active until the sponsor is assigned active. Therefore we analyzed the availability of two configurations, where the only difference was that in the first we specified that we prefer both service instances to be assigned to the same node while in the second we reversed the assignment preferences of the sponsor and the dependent. In both configurations we specified the preference to go back to the preferred assignment after the repair. Then we simulated the DSPNs (using TimeNet [19]) while doubling the failure rate of the node by multiplying it by the integer $2^{\lambda-1}$ (where λ is between 1 and 5). Fig. 8 clearly shows in the context of our example the availability improvement by a simple modification of a configuration attribute. We use this observation to motivate our future work in Section 7.

5   Related Work

The work presented in [20] is the only work we are aware of that partially tackled the problem of calculating the availability of the services in the context of AMF. In this work the authors define the service availability based on user behavior, and derive formulas to compute service availability starting with the user behavior model. The authors built a Stochastic Reward Net (SRN, a Petri Net extension which does not support deterministic transitions) to model a specific configuration; based on the SRN they calculate the probability that both servers are up in steady state. Accordingly they use this information in the user

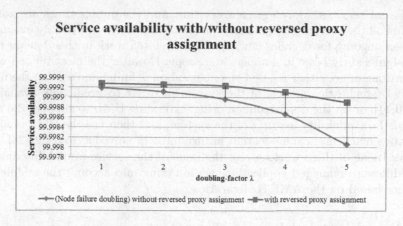

Fig. 8. Numerical results for the availability assessment

behavior model to calculate the user perceived availability. This work is not reusable in our case for the following reasons:

- it did not present a generic approach to build the analysis model; instead they built one specific model that captures one specific configuration with one specific runtime recovery behavior;
- it did not provide any dependency analysis which is a crucial part of the availability analysis in complex/real systems;
- the analysis is not configuration driven, and does not consider the recovery altering configuration attributes;
- there are no components included in the configuration, and hence there is no consideration of different component categories and their implications on the analysis.

In short the model is too simplistic and does not reflect the real system. So basically the case study, which is the only part of the work related to AMF, did not consider the specificities of the AMF configuration and its effect on the AMF behavior.

Another interesting work is presented in [21]. This work deals with the automatic dependability analysis of systems designed using UML. An automatic transformation is defined for the generation of models to capture systems dependability attributes, like reliability. The main objective aims at the creation of an integrated environment where UML-based design toolsets are augmented with modeling and analysis tools. Within this work, the authors present an automatic transformation from UML diagrams to Timed Petri Net (TPN) models for model based dependability evaluation. The drawback of this work is that it does not separate the concept of service from service provider. In other words, their work is directed towards the system availability rather than the service availability. Our analysis is quite different by nature since for instance in our analysis, the same failure on a service provider entity can have different impacts on different services. Moreover recovery time and the outage times are not the same for all the services. In summary the work on system availability evaluation has been ongoing for decades now; the list of related work in this domain tends to be significantly large in numbers and scope. However the most related works for our domain are either focused on one hand on defining and solving the mathematical (stochastic) models of the system in order to predict its availability e.g. [10,11], or on the other hand on using/extending UML to support the modeling of the availability features of the system, and then use the UML model to generate a mathematical model that in turn must be solved as in [22,23,24]. Nevertheless none of these works target the issue of the service availability analysis for middleware managed applications while taking into account the middleware behavior based on the AMF configuration.

6   Discussion and Lessons Learnt

In this paper we have presented an approach for the service availability analysis of AMF managed applications. This analysis is based on the middleware behavior. When such behavior is driven by the system configuration, then the analysis must be configuration-based. It is essential to consider the system dependencies in the analysis, since they have a tremendous impact on the service availability. Using the templates to define the analysis model proved to be an important factor in the systematic mapping of the configuration to an analysis model. In fact, this also enabled the traceability of the analysis model back to the original system configuration. In our analysis model we captured the middleware recovery at a lower level of granularity. I.e. we decomposed the recoveries to the 'atomic' actions that the middleware performs to recover the services. Although this increased the complexity of our approach (more specifically the templates), it improved the accuracy of our model, and thus, the use of this model is no longer limited to the availability analysis, in addition, it can also be used to verify the behavior of an AMF implementation. In other words our formal (DSPN) description of the middleware recovery behavior that we defined based on the specifications can be used to verify the actions that a middleware implementation performs to recover the services, and by this, verify the compliancy of this middleware implementation against the SAForum specifications.

7   Conclusion and Future Work

In this paper we tackled the issue of the service availability analysis based on the configuration. This allows the system integrator to determine beforehand the achievable runtime service availability, and as a byproduct compare two configurations based on the availability levels they offer to the services. As we have seen in the case study in this paper, a minor modification to the configuration can have significant effects on the service availability, which motivates our future work of determining the criteria that allow us to maximize service availability. Accordingly we aim at defining configuration design patterns that guide the configuration generation process we defined in [25] whereby, we would be able to generate configurations that satisfy the availability requirements by construction.

Acknowledgments. This work is partially supported by the Natural Sciences and Engineering Research Council of Canada (NSERC) and Ericsson Research.

References

1. Yanming, C., Shiyi, X.: Exploration of complexity in software reliability. Tsinghua Science and Technology 12(s1), 266–269 (2007)
2. Zuse, H.: Software Complexity: Measures and Methods. Walter de Gruyer (1990)
3. Capretz, L., Capretz, M., Li, D.: Component-based software development. In: The 27th Annual Conference of the IEEE Industrial Electronics Society, vol. 3, pp. 1834–1837. IEEE conference publications (2001)
4. Service Availability Forum: Application Interface Specification, http://www.saforum.org/Service-Availability-Forum:-Application-Interface-Specification 217404 16627.htm
5. Object Management Group (OMG), Unified Modeling Language - Superstructure Version 2.1.1 formal/2007-02-03 (2007) http://www.omg.org/spec/UML/2.1.1/
6. Service Availability Forum: AIS Availability Management Framework, http://www.saforum.org/HOA/assn16627/images/SAI-AIS-AMF-B.04.01.pdf
7. VideoLAN Client, http://www.videolan.org/
8. Kanso, A., Mishra, A., Toeroe, M., Khendek, F.: Integrating Legacy Applications for High Availability – A Case Study. In: IEEE 13th International Symposium on High-Assurance Systems Engineering (HASE), pp. 83–90. IEEE conference publications (2011)
9. OpenSAF foundation, http://www.opensaf.org/
10. Xie, W., Sun, H., Cao, Y., Trivedi, K.S.: Modeling of user perceived webserver availability. In: Proceedings of the IEEE International Conference on Communications (ICC), vol. 3, pp. 1796–1800. IEEE conference publications (2003)
11. Tokuno, K., Yamada, S.: Markovian model for user-perceived software service availability measurement with operation-oriented restoration. In: 7th International Conference on Service Systems and Service Management (ICSSSM), pp. 1–6. IEEE conference publications (2010)
12. Ambuj, G., Stephen, L.: Modeling and analysis of computer system availability. IBM Journal of Research and Development 31(6), 651–664 (1987)
13. Natkin, S.: Les Reseaux de Petri Stochastiques et leur Application a l'Evaluation des Systemes Informatiques. PhD thesis, CNAM Paris (1980)
14. Ajmone Marsan, M., Chiola, G.: On Petri Nets with Deterministic and Exponentially Distributed Firing Times. In: Rozenberg, G. (ed.) APN 1987. LNCS, vol. 266, pp. 132–145. Springer, Heidelberg (1987)
15. Choi, H., Kulkarni, V.G., Trivedi, K.S.: Transient Analysis of Deterministic and Stochastic Petri Nets. In: Ajmone Marsan, M. (ed.) ICATPN 1993. LNCS, vol. 691, pp. 166–185. Springer, Heidelberg (1993)
16. Reussner, R., Schmidt, H., Poernomo, I.: Reliability prediction for component-based software architectures. Journal of Systems and Software 66(3), 241–252 (2003)

17. Harrold, M.J., Liang, D., Sinha, S.: An approach to analyzing and testing component-based systems. In: First International ICSE Workshop on Testing Distributed Component-Based Systems, pp. 333–347. ACM Press (1999)

18. Kanso, A., Khendek, F., Toeroe, M.: Automatic Annotation of Software Configuration Models with Service Recovery Information. IEEE Ninth International Conference on Dependable, Autonomic and Secure Computing (DASC), pp.121-128. IEEE conference publications (2011)

19. Zimmermann, A., Freiheit, J., German, R., Hommel, G.: Petri Net Modelling and Performability Evaluation with TimeNET 3.0. In: Haverkort, B.R., Bohnenkamp, H.C., Smith, C.U. (eds.) TOOLS 2000. LNCS, vol. 1786, pp. 188–202. Springer, Heidelberg (2000)

20. Wang, D.-Z., Trivedi, K.S.: Modeling User-Perceived Service Availability. In: Malek, M., Nett, E., Suri, N. (eds.) ISAS 2005. LNCS, vol. 3694, pp. 107–122. Springer, Heidelberg (2005)

21. Bondavalli, A., Mura, I., Majzik, I.: Automated dependability analysis of UML designs. In: Proceedings of the 2nd IEEE International Symposium on Object-Oriented Real-Time Distributed Computing (ISORC 1999), pp. 139–144. IEEE conference publications (1999)

22. Bernardi, S., Merseguer, J., Petriu, D.C.: A dependability profile within MARTE. In: Software and Systems Modeling. LNCS, vol. 10(3), pp. 1–24. Springer (2011)

23. Bernardi, S., Merseguer, J.: A UML profile for dependability analysis of real-time embedded systems. In: A UML profile for dependability analysis of real-time embedded systems, pp. 155–124. ACM press (2007)

24. Majzik, I., Pataricza, A., Bondavalli, A.: Stochastic Dependability Analysis of System Architecture Based on UML Models. In: de Lemos, R., Gacek, C., Romanovsky, A. (eds.) Architecting Dependable Systems. LNCS, vol. 2677, pp. 219–244. Springer, Heidelberg (2003)

25. Kanso, A., Khendek, F., Toeroe, M., Hamou-Lhadj, A.: Automatic Configuration Generation for Service High Availability with Load Balancing. In: Concurrency and Computation: Practice and Experience, Wiley (2012), doi: 10.1002/cpe.2805

Author Index